FINDEN'S
PORTS AND HARBOURS
OF
GREAT BRITAIN,

Drawn by G. Balmer.

Engraved by E. Finden.

TYNEMOUTH PRIORY AND LIGHT-HOUSE.

THE LIFE-BOAT

Painted by T. Creswick.

Engraved by E. Finden.

BRIGHTON,

SUSSEX.

London, Published 1837, by Charles Tilt, 86, Fleet Street

VIEWS OF

PORTS AND HARBOURS,

WATERING PLACES, FISHING VILLAGES,

AND OTHER

PICTURESQUE OBJECTS ON THE ENGLISH COAST.

———

ENGRAVED BY WILLIAM AND EDWARD FINDEN,

FROM PAINTINGS BY J. D. HARDING, G. BALMER, E. W. COOKE, T. CRESWICK, AND OTHER EMINENT ARTISTS.

EP PUBLISHING LIMITED
1974

First published Charles Tilt, London, 1838

ISBN 0 85409 976 X

Please address all enquiries to EP Publishing Limited
(address as above)

Printed in Great Britain by
The Scolar Press Limited, Ilkley, Yorkshire

PREFACE.

———•———

THE volume of Ports and Harbours of Great Britain, now completed, comprises, in a series of fifty engravings, views of most of the principal ports, naval stations, watering-places, and fishing-towns, on the English coast, from Berwick-upon-Tweed to Plymouth. In the delineation of each place, the chief object of the artists has been to give a faithful view—to represent the place as it really is, and not to overstep the modesty of nature, for the sake of giving to their subjects the false ornaments of meretricious beauty. That the English coast abounds in picturesque scenery, which requires no aid from the imagination of the painter, many of the views in the present work will afford ample evidence; and even in views of places which are in a great measure devoid of the essentials of a beautiful picture, the sober delineation of truth is, in such a work as the present, infinitely preferable to the exaggerated representations of fancy.

Among others will be found views of the ports of Berwick, Shields, Newcastle-on-Tyne, Sunderland, Whitby, Hull, Yarmouth, and Southampton; and among the views of the principal watering-places on the coast are those of Scarborough, Burlington, Ramsgate, Dover, Hastings, Brighton, and Weymouth. Among the smaller towns and villages which are visited for the sake of sea-bathing, the following

PREFACE.

may be enumerated : Tynemouth, Cromer, Folkstone, Cowes, Sidmouth,
Exmouth, and Budleigh Salterton. The views of old castles that
"crown the wave-worn steep" are those of Holy Island, Bambrough,
Dunstanbrough, and Tintagel; of the smaller ports those of Blyth,
Hartlepool, and Harwich; and of the fishing towns and villages,
those of Cullercoats, Robin Hood's bay, and Brixham. The great
naval stations of which views are given, are Chatham, Portsmouth,
and Plymouth. In short, taking the whole line of coast illustrated,
views are given of almost every important and interesting place.

In the brief space allowed for the descriptions, the editor has endeavoured to unite the useful with the interesting. In the account of some
of the more important places, he has attempted to give an outline of the
principal events in their history, and to trace their progress, as places of
trade, from the earliest period to the present time. Could he persuade
himself that he has performed his more humble task as ably as Harding,
Balmer, Cooke, and Creswick, have executed their portion of the work, he
should congratulate himself on his success.

W. A. C.

London,
23rd November, 1837.

LIST OF PLATES,

ARRANGED ACCORDING TO THE LINE OF THE COAST, FROM NORTH TO SOUTH.

4   CONTENTS.

PORTS AND HARBOURS

OF

GREAT BRITAIN.

TYNEMOUTH LIGHT-HOUSE AND PRIORY,

WITH THE LIFE-BOAT SAVING A SHIP'S CREW.

THE first engraving of the present work is a view of Tynemouth Lighthouse and Priory, with the life-boat in the act of saving the crew of a vessel, which has struck upon the rocks at the foot of the cliff on which the lighthouse is built. This incident, so effectively and appropriately introduced by the artist, Balmer, who has frequently witnessed the scene which he has depicted, is peculiarly characteristic of the neighbourhood of Tynemouth; for, in consequence of the danger of the entrance to Shields Harbour in stormy weather, with the wind from the eastward, more vessels are there lost than at the entrance of any other harbour in Great Britain; and in no part of the kingdom has the value of the life-boat been more frequently experienced.

The view is taken from the entrance to Shields Harbour, about half a mile to the south-west of the lighthouse, which is seen rising from behind the extremity of the cliff which overlooks the entrance to Prior's Haven. Towards the centre of the land view are the ruins of Tynemouth Priory; while farther to the left, in the same distance, is seen the castle, now modernised and occupied as a garrison. The fore-ground to the left is the bank which forms the south-western boundary of Prior's Haven; and the rocks which are seen at its foot are a portion of the formidable *Black Middens*, which lie on the north side of the entrance to the harbour.

The grand feature of the engraving under observation is the view of the life-boat,

B.

which is introduced with a thorough knowledge of the subject, and with a feeling and a character of truth which mere imagination can never inspire. The downward plunge of a boat's bows among broken water, while her stern is at the same time elevated by a slanting wave, was never more happily represented. A person who has been at sea may almost fancy that he hears the resounding dash of the water against the curved bow, and the seething of the angry wave as it rises on each side. The idea of motion is admirably conveyed in the representation of the wave lashing over the floating mast, which is tossed about like a light spar by the violence of the sea; and the continued inward roll of the water, from the side and bow of the boat towards the shore, is no less naturally expressed.

Part of the life-boat's crew, with most of the oars double-manned, are seen "giving way," with strenuous effort, through the breakers, while others are endeavouring to save the shipwrecked seamen; and one of the men at the steer-oar appears encouraging the sailor who clings to the floating mast. The position of the boat, with her stem towards the harbour, and the shipwrecked men seated towards her stern, indicate that she is returning from the vessel, the top of whose masts are seen, and that she is now endeavouring to save such men as were washed overboard when the vessel sunk. The flying of the spray declares the loudness of the wind; and though a cheering glimpse of sunshine appears to illumine the land, yet the dark cloud, which seems to rest upon the waters to the right, sufficiently informs us of the gloominess of the prospect when looking towards the sea.

In consequence of a bar of sand, which stretches across the mouth of the Tyne where the outward current of the river at ebb tide is met by the inward roll of the sea; and from the Herd Sand on the south, and the Black Middens on the north, the entrance to Shields Harbour is attended with great danger when the wind is blowing hard from the eastward and a heavy sea running. In crossing the bar, at such a time, a loaden ship, with rather a heavy draught of water, will sometimes strike, and unship her rudder; and a light one, in consequence of being struck by a heavy sea, will sometimes broach to. A vessel thus rendered unmanageable, is almost certain, with the wind from the north-east and a flood tide, to be driven on the Herd Sand; and, should the wind be blowing strong from the south-east, she is extremely liable to be driven either on the Black Middens, or on the rocks at the foot of Tynemouth Castle; more especially in attempting to gain the harbour after the tide has begun to ebb. In the latter case, when vessels have been too late to save tide and are land-locked, and when it may seem less hazardous to attempt to pass the bar than to bring up, with evening approaching, on a lee shore, the danger of being wrecked on the rocks to the northward is more especially imminent.

Few ideas are more distressing than that of a vessel, on her return from a voyage, being wrecked at the entrance of her port, and of her crew perishing within sight and hearing of their relatives and friends, who behold them, one by one, as the sea sweeps over the wreck, become a prey to the devouring element, but who are unable to render them any assistance. In the morning, the seaman, when he first comes within sight of the hope-inspiring objects which distinguish his native coast, may be cheered with a delightful vision of home and joyful welcome, and may exclaim, with the Ancient Mariner of Coleridge,

> " O dream of joy ! is this indeed
> The lighthouse top I see ?
> Is this the hill ? is this the kirk ?
> Is this mine own countree ?"

and before evening he may lie a corpse, "lifeless flat," on the shore, wept over by the sorrowing eyes that he had hoped would brighten at his arrival.

Notwithstanding the many lives that were lost, from year to year, by shipwreck at the mouth of the Tyne, it does not appear that any attempts to construct a life-boat were made at Shields previous to 1789. In the month of September, in that year, a vessel called the Adventure, of Newcastle, struck upon the Herd Sand, and though she was within a quarter of a mile of the shore, no assistance could be rendered to her, in consequence of the violence of the sea; and as she continued to beat against the sand, and the waves to make a free passage over her, her crew were seen to drop from the shrouds, to which they had betaken themselves when the vessel struck, and to perish among the broken water.

This distressing event, which was witnessed by numbers of people from the shore, induced the subscribers to the News Room, near the Law, at the lower end of South Shields, to turn their attention to the possibility of constructing a boat which should not be liable to be overset by the sea, and which also should retain its buoyancy when manned with a sufficient crew and nearly full of water. To a committee, which was appointed to devise the best means of accomplishing the object of the subscribers, two models were in a short time submitted; the one constructed by Mr. William Wouldhave, painter, of South Shields; and the other, by Mr. Henry Greathead, boat-builder, of the same place. Mr. Wouldhave's model was made of tin, and rendered buoyant by cork; and the inventor intended that his life-boat should be formed of sheet-copper. Mr. Greathead's model, which was made of wood, when over-turned would not right, but floated bottom up; while Mr. Wouldhave's, on being subjected to the same test, immediately recovered its proper position. Neither of these models were, however, approved of. Mr. Wouldhave received a guinea for his trouble; and Mr. Greathead was promised to have the building of the boat when the committee should decide upon a model. A short time afterwards, a model in clay was produced by Mr. Fairles and Mr. Rockwood, two members of the committee, and from this Mr. Greathead was directed to build a life-boat; and it is said that the only alteration suggested by Mr. Greathead was the curved keel, which some persons are pleased to consider as an error in its construction, although experience in this instance appears to be at variance with hypothesis. Although the invention has been confidently claimed for Mr. Wouldhave, yet the precise figure of his intended life-boat has never been clearly explained by any of his advocates. The life-boat built by Greathead was neither formed of copper, nor had she a straight keel; which were both peculiar to Wouldhave's invention; and the plan of casing and lining with cork, without which the life-boat would be comparatively valueless, unless provided with air-boxes instead, was proposed by Greathead when he produced his first model. A large Norway yawl, raised a streak in midships, having her sheer * increased towards the bow and stern, and cased and lined with cork, in the manner of Greathead's life-boat, would be likely to live in broken water as well as the latter.

The merits of the boat built by Mr. Greathead were soon put to the test; and the success which attended her first practical essay fully realised the expectations of the most sanguine promoters of the design. A vessel having struck on the Herd Sand, on the 30th January, 1790, the newly-built boat put off to her assistance. In the sight of crowds who were assembled on the shore, anxiously watching the result, she triumphantly made her way through a heavy sea to the stranded vessel, and brought the crew, whose destruction without her assistance was inevitable, in safety to the shore; thus proving herself a LIFE-BOAT indeed! Repeated trials, opportunities for which were but too frequently afforded, displayed yet further her excellence. It was found that she could proceed *athwart*, with as much safety as *against*, the sea; and that she could float with thirty men in her, and when nearly full of water.

---

* The *sheer* of a boat or ship is the upward curvature of her top line towards the stem and stern. The *rake* is the angular inclination of the stem or the stern towards the keel. Since the remarks in the text, respecting a Norway yawl, were written, which were founded on the writer's own experience, he has been much pleased to find the following passage, in Surtees's History of Durham, vol. ii. p. 96, written by N. Fairles, Esq., chairman of the committee which ordered the original life-boat to be built: —"The committee was unanimous that a boat, somewhat resembling a *Norway yawl*, with both ends alike, having great spring or elevation at the bow and stern, and with the bottom flatter, might answer the purpose. The description which Mr. Rockwood gave of a boat by which he had been saved at Memel, tended much to establish the opinion of the committee; and a model in clay was handed about, and altered from time to time, for the explanation of ideas; which, though like all creatures of clay, frail and transitory, yet contained a perfect germ (*la belle idée*) of the life-boat."

As the utility of the life-boat became known, Mr. Greathead received many orders for boats built on the same principle, and in the same manner, both from places in Great Britain and from abroad.   When her value had been thoroughly proved by the experience of twelve years, during which time several hundred lives had been saved by her means, Mr. Greathead, in 1802, petitioned parliament for a reward.   His petition was referred to a committee, which was instructed to inquire;—first, concerning the utility of the invention; secondly, concerning its originality; and, thirdly, if the petitioner had received any remuneration.   Upon the report of this committee, which examined witnesses touching the several heads of inquiry, the House of Commons voted Mr. Greathead a reward of £1200; and in the same year, the Society of Arts presented him with a gold medal and the sum of sixty guineas.

Mr. Greathead, in a brief account of the invention which he published, has stated that the idea of building the life-boat with a curved keel was suggested to him from the principle of a segment of a spheroid, the tendency of which is to swim with the convex surface downward.   The half of a wooden bowl affords a familiar illustration of this principle; and the sixth part of an orange, the pulp being extracted, and the sides slightly compressed, may give a person some idea of the form of a life-boat.   In the life-boat there is no distinction between the stem and stern, both extremities being formed alike, so that she can be rowed with equal facility either way; and when amongst broken water her direction can be immediately changed without turning round.   The following are the dimensions of the original life-boat, built by Mr. Greathead, at South Shields :—

	Feet.	Inches.
Length from stem to stem - - -	30	0
Breadth in midships - - - -	10	0
Depth in midships, from gunwale to keel - -	3	3
Depth in midships, from gunwale to floor - -	2	4
Height of each stem above the lowest part of the keel -	5	9

Her sides, from the floor-heads to the gunwale, " flaunched off," or extended outwards, in proportion to rather more than half the breadth of the floor, thus making her broad in the beam, compared with the fineness of her bottom.   Her breadth was well continued towards her extremities, thus giving her good bearings at the bows; and her sheer was considerably increased towards each stem, in order that they might the better divide an over-topping wave, and thus prevent the boat shipping water when rowed against a head-sea.   A casing of cork, sixteen inches deep from the gunwale, and four inches thick, extended for twenty-one feet six inches along each top-side, giving her at once additional buoyancy, and serving as a "fender," should her side come in contact with the side of a ship. The inside of the boat, from the thwarts to the floor, was also lined with cork in a similar manner. She was built of oak, and was copper-fastened; and the quantity of cork used in lining and casing her weighed 7 cwt. She had six thwarts for rowers, which, from her breadth, held two men each; and she thus rowed twelve oars, six on each side. The oars were not worked in "row-locks*" or between "thowls," as in most other boats, but a small ring of rope, called a "grummet," being passed loosely over the loom of each oar, was afterwards slipped over an upright iron pin, which thus formed the fulcrum for the rower's stroke. The rower, by this means, could occasionally leave his oar without its being broken or unshipped.

The oars used by the rowers are short, and of fir. The boat is usually guided by two steermen, one at each end, who use oars of a larger size. When the life-boat was first built, cork jackets were provided for the men, who, after a few trials being convinced of her safety, discontinued them. Experience, however, has shown that the crew of a life-boat are not perfectly safe without some such protection. On the 17th of February, in the present year, 1836, the Scarborough life-boat, when going off to a vessel, was upset by a heavy sea, and did not right again, in consequence, as is supposed, of part of her crew clinging to the thwarts. Out of her crew of fifteen, eleven were drowned. Had the boat been lined and cased with cork, quite up to her stems, she would have been more likely to right after having been upset; and had her crew been provided with cork jackets it is probable that not one of them would have been lost.

The original South Shields life-boat, which used to be much employed in assisting to save the stores and cargo of a wreck, was split upon the Black Middens, about seven or eight years ago. The boat which was built in her stead is provided with air-boxes, instead of being lined and cased with cork. There is also a life-boat kept at North Shields, which was presented to that town in 1798, by the late Duke of Northumberland, who also during his life gave the sum of £20 per annum, for the purpose of keeping her in repair, and rewarding her crew. The present duke, following the example of his noble father in every generous deed, still continues the subscription. The life-boat is usually manned by the pilots of South Shields, and half a guinea a man is paid to them when they succeed in saving the crew of a vessel, or even one man. It is believed that they have never yet put off without earning their reward, which is paid by the Port of Newcastle Association for the Preservation of Lives from Shipwreck.

---

* *Row-locks* are the spaces or notches in the upper line of a boat's side, within which the oars work. In many boats each "row-lock" is formed by means of two wooden pins, termed "*thowls*," or "*tholes*," that is fulcra or bearers, from the old verb "*thole*," to bear. The *thils*, or shafts, of a cart, may be traced to the same source.

Drawn by G. Balmer.

Engraved by W. Finden.

CULLERCOATS.

London. Published 1836. by Charles Tilt. 86. Fleet Street.

CULLERCOATS.

In the engraving, a view of Cullercoats is given, as seen from the southward. On the sand, in the fore-ground, is a coble, a light kind of boat generally employed by the fishermen on the coast of Northumberland; near the coble, to the right, is seen a *dand* or buoy, used by the fishermen to mark the place where they have cast their lines or nets. It is formed of an inflated bag of tanned skin, through which a light pole passes, and to which pole the ends forming the openings of the bag are tightly tied with cord. The lower end of the pole is sometimes rendered heavy by lead, so that the *dand* may float upright, and it has also a loop, or a ring, to which the rope connecting it with the nets or lines is fastened; and a piece of *bunting* *, or coloured cloth, is attached, as a small flag, to the upper end, in order that it may be more perceptible at a distance.

The village of Cullercoats, which lies about a mile to the northward of Tynemouth, is mostly inhabited by fishermen. The duties performed by the wives and daughters of the Cullercoats fishermen are very laborious. They search for the bait—sometimes digging sand-worms in the muddy sand at the mouth of the Coble-dean, at the head of North Shields; gathering muscles on the Scalp, near Clifford's Fort; or gathering limpets and dog-crabs among the rocks near Tynemouth;—and they also assist in baiting the hooks. They carry the fish which are caught to North Shields, in large wicker baskets, called *creels*, and they also sit in the market there to sell them. When fish are scarce, they not unfrequently carry a load on their shoulders, weighing between three and four stone, to Newcastle, which is about ten miles distant from Cullercoats, in the hope of meeting with a better market. The fish principally caught by the fishermen of Cullercoats are codlings, cod, ling (*Gadus molva*), holibut, usually called turbot in Northumberland, haddocks, and whitings. Herrings are also taken in the season; and the colesay (*Gadus car-*

---

* *Bunting*, the thin woollen stuff of which ship's colours are made.

bonarius), is not unfrequently caught, but it is a fish which is hardly worth the bait, as it is scarcely saleable at any price. The most valuable sea-fish caught by the fishermen of Cullercoats, is the *bret*, or turbot proper of the London market. But this fish, when caught by them, is mostly sold to the bret smacks, by which it is conveyed to London. Gentlemen residing at Cullercoats or Tynemouth during the bathing season, may often obtain excellent sport in fishing for whitings, in fine weather, off the north-eastern end of the Herd Sand. The best time is in the evening, towards high-water; and the best bait is sprats cut into small pieces. It is no extraordinary feat for a party of three, with half a dozen lines, to take twelve or fifteen dozen of whitings in three hours, on a summer's evening.

For the amateur sea-fisher, in the neighbourhood of Tynemouth, there is no bait generally so good when fishing within six or eight miles of the shore, as the small dog-crab, called in the neighbourhood of Shields a *pillan*. It is known from the common dog-crabs by the facility with which its shell may be stripped off; for instance, in breaking the shell round one of its claws, the broken portion may be withdrawn from the member as a glove from the hand; and the shell of the back may also be stripped off in the same manner. From this facility of *peeling*, it is probable that the crab derives its local name of *pillan*. Pillan, however, are not plentiful; and when such are not to be got, then sand-worms, muscles, and common dog-crabs are the most likely bait. Codlings and rock-codlings are plentiful a little to the eastward of Tynemouth; but haddocks and cod, the staple of the Cullercoats fishermen, are not often caught in any great quantity within seven miles of the shore. The young of the colesay, called a *hallan*, a beautiful little fish, is frequently caught with a rod, from the rocks in the neighbourhood of Tynemouth. The weaver, (*Trachinus draco*,) or stinging-fish, as it is called at Shields, is often caught when fishing off Tynemouth Bar; and strangers, who are unacquainted with the formidable character of this little fish, are sometimes pricked by it when taking it off the hook. The men who are employed in the salmon fishery, at the end of the Herd Sand, have sometimes their bare feet stung by it when hauling their nets. The average length of this fish, as caught at the mouth of the Tyne, is about five inches; though some are occasionally caught there three or four inches longer. The dangerous spines are those of the first dorsal fin; and the best remedy for the wound is to rub it well with sweet oil.

The township of Cullercoats, according to the population returns of 1831, contained 89 houses, which were inhabited by 145 families, consisting of 542 persons. Cullercoats is a kind of land-mark for vessels leaving Shields Harbour; for as soon as the man at the helm can see the village opening behind Tynemouth Cliff, the ship is over the bar.

Drawn by G. Balmer.

Engraved by W. Finden

ENTRANCE TO SHIELDS HARBOUR.

London, Published 1836, by Charles Tilt, 86, Fleet Street.

SHIELDS.—ENTRANCE TO THE HARBOUR.

THE view of the entrance to Shields Harbour is taken from the bank a little below the Spanish Battery, on the north side of the Tyne, and about a quarter of a mile to the south-westward of Tynemouth lighthouse. To the left, a part of South Shields is seen, with a vessel "dropping up" the Narrows, just before entering the harbour. Towards the middle of the engraving are the two light-houses at North Shields—distinguished by their flag-staffs—which, when taken in a line, are a guide for vessels in passing the bar. To the right of the low light-house is Clifford's Fort—distinguished by the line of embrasures—which commands the entrance to the harbour. To the right are the banks, of clay, which extend from the Spanish Battery to the Low Lights, and upon which the sea is every year gradually making encroachments. The present engraving, independent of its beauty as a work of art, possesses the merit of containing the only correct view of the entrance to Shields harbour which has hitherto appeared.

That portion of the river Tyne which may be considered as Shields Harbour, is about a mile and a half in length, supposing it to commence at the Low Lights, on the north side, and to terminate at the lower end of Jarrow Slake, at the head of South Shields; its direction is from east by north to west by south; and the towns of North and South Shields are built on the banks and by the shore on each side of it. As the Low Lights are about a mile within the bar, the swell of the sea is not felt within the harbour.

The river is of unequal width, being in some places not more than 400 yards broad, while in others, when the sands are covered with the tide, its width is upwards of 600. From the shoals and varying width of the river, the velocity of the current is different in different parts of the harbour. Opposite to the New Quay at North Shields, the average velocity of the current in the middle of the tide-way is, at half flood, about three miles an hour; and, at half ebb, about three miles and three quarters an hour. As the easterly wind blows directly into the harbour, vessels formerly were often hindered from getting out to sea, even in fine weather, when the wind was in that quarter, more especially if they were of considerable draught of water; for frequently before such a vessel could drop down with the ebbing tide as far as the bar, there was not sufficient depth of water on it to allow her to proceed to sea. The general introduction, within these last ten years, of steam boats for the purpose of towing vessels out to sea, when the wind is shy or contrary, has, however, in a great measure, remedied this inconvenience; and vessels can now proceed to sea at any time, in favourable weather, when there is a sufficient depth of water on the bar.

Though there are staiths both at South and North Shields, where ships are loaded with coals directly from the spout, yet the greater number of colliers which bring up in Shields Harbour are loaded from keels—a kind of river craft of about twenty-two tons burden—which bring the coals from the upper parts of the river. The coals are cast by the keelmen into the vessel, and are "trimmed" in her hold by men called "trimmers," who gain their living by such work, and by casting the ballast brought by light ships, into ballast keels, by which it is conveyed to the ballast quays. There are quays both at North and South Shields, where keels cast the ballast which they bring from ships, into small wagons, which are drawn up an inclined plane by machinery, and unloaded at the top of the heap. There are also one or two ballast quays at South Shields, where the ballast is craned up at once from the vessel's hold, in large tubs, without being previously cast into a keel. The greater number of ballast quays are, however, higher up the river, between Shields and Newcastle. The Corporation of Newcastle have the regulation of the different ballast quays upon the Tyne; and from the tonnage duty, which they are empowered to levy, according the quantity of ballast brought by each ship, they derive a considerable revenue.

In loading ships and keels, and from loaden keels coming into violent contact with each other or with ships, a considerable quantity of coals falls into the river. But such coals, though lost to their proper owners, are not entirely lost to the public; for a great portion of them is washed by the tide upon the Dotwick sand, on the north side of the river, and upon the In-sand, at the lower end of South Shields. Every working day, at low water, a number of poor people, young and old, and of both sexes, may be seen gathering coals on those sands; and the annual value of the coals thus obtained, and from dredging in the harbour, cannot be less than £600; and is probably much greater. Were it not for the Dotwick and the In-sand, it is likely that the poor-rates of North and South Shields would be much more heavy than they are.

The towns of North and South Shields having only risen into commercial importance within the last sixty years, their early history is extremely meagre, and their modern annals contain few incidents which are likely to interest the general reader. The town of South Shields is in the county of Durham, and, as its name imports, on the south side of the river Tyne. From antiquities which have been dug up at the Law *, at the east end of the town, it is certain that there had been a Roman station at South Shields, although its name has not been discovered. The name Shields is derived from the *Shiels*, or *Sheles*, as the word is written in old manuscripts, the huts or cottages of the fishermen which were built there. In the seventh year of Edward I.. 1279, the burgesses of Newcastle, jealous of their privileges, instituted a suit against the prior of Tynemouth and the bishop of Durham, for building houses at North and South Shields, and there establishing markets, and loading and unloading ships, to the injury of the said burgesses and the rights of the King. The prior of Tynemouth was charged with having sixteen large fishing vessels employed for gain only ; and he had also twenty-six houses at North Shields, the inhabitants of which were in the habit of loading and victualling ships which ought of right to have gone up to Newcastle. He was also charged with obstructing the free towage of boats and ships proceeding up or down the river ; not suffering the persons towing to enter upon his land, whereby many had nearly lost their lives. In this cause the prior of Tynemouth was worsted. He was fined five marks on account of the four ovens which he had erected at North Shields, and he was forbidden to hold any fair or market there in future, for the sale of provisions or wares to ships. All quays or wharfs erected by the said prior, within high-water mark, on the King's soil, were also ordered to be removed. It would appear, that the burgesses of Newcastle had not been successful in their suit against the bishop of Durham ; for, upon a *Quo Warranto*, brought in 9 Edward I., 1281, the bishop's liberties were allowed by John Delavale and his companions, the King's justices itinerant in the county of Northumberland. By two several inquisitions taken in 21 Edward I., 1293, and 10 Edward II., 1317, the bishop's claim to a mediety of the waters of Tyne was allowed. In 1334, Edward III., by his writ, dated at York, on behalf of the bishop of Durham, Richard de Bury, prohibited the mayor and bailiffs of Newcastle-upon-Tyne from hindering the applying of ships on the south of the river belonging to the bishop.

Notwithstanding the patronage of the bishops of Durham, South Shields increased very slowly. From the reign of Henry VIII. till that of George I. a great quantity of salt appears to have been manufactured at South Shields ; but, as the town has increased in commercial importance, that branch of manufacture has declined. In 1696 there were 143 salt-pans, and ten years ago there were

* The " Law " is a bank, at the lower end of South Shields, which rises from the sands. This word, according to the Rev. John Hodgson, who spells it " *Lawe,*" " is a Saxon term applied to fortified places, as well as to tombs and conical hills." In Northumberland, and on the borders of Scotland, the term law is frequently given to a hill. For instance, Heifer-law, Dunse-law, North Berwick Law, and Wirb-law.

only five. The article now chiefly manufactured at South Shields is glass, of which a considerable quantity is sent to London, both as bottles and as window-glass. There are thirteen dry docks for repairing ships at South Shields, with building yards to each; and the opening of the Stanhope and South Shields railway, which was commenced about three years ago, is likely to add considerably to the trade of the latter town.

About a hundred years ago, it is said that there were only four ships belonging to South Shields: at present the number is 286, the registered admeasurement of which is 66,747 tons. Most of those vessels are employed in the coal trade between London and Shields Of those employed in the foreign trade the greater number are chartered from various ports in the kingdom, as the shipping of the Port of Tyne is much greater than is required for its own trade.

The town of South Shields is very irregularly built; and the principal street for business extends from the market-place to the lower end of the town. The market-place, in the centre of which stands the town hall, is spacious, but the market is very indifferently supplied with every thing except fish. Westoe, anciently Wivestoe, is a pleasant village about a mile southward of South Shields, where several ship-owners and persons of property reside. Jarrow, so famous in days of yore for its monastery, is about a mile and a half to the west-ward of Westoe; and in the vestry an old chair is still preserved, which is said to have been the seat of the venerable Bede.

Persons who judge of the population of the *town* of South Shields, from that of the *township*, as given in the parliamentary returns of 1831, will form an erroneous opinion. What is there called the township of South Shields, is that part of it only which consists of a long slip of land, lying near the water side, and which does not contain more than half the inhabitants of the *town*. As a great part of the town of South Shields is included in the township of Westoe, the population of the latter township is given as consisting of 9682 persons; though about nine-tenths of that number are properly inhabitants of the town of South Shields, whose population will be more correctly represented as follows ·

Township of South Shields	9074
Township of Westoe	9682
	18756
Deduct for the village of Westoe and outskirts . .	1500
Leaving for the *Town* of South Shields . . .	17256

By the Reform Bill, South Shields, with Westoe, returns one member to parliament. The present member is Robert Ingham, Esq., son of the late William Ingham, Esq., an eminent surgeon of Newcastle-upon-Tyne. Mr. Ingham, who is a barrister of extensive practice in the northern circuit, has a country house at Westoe, and is personally known to the constituency which he represents.

The town of North Shields, which lies on the north side of the river Tyne, is in the county of Northumberland. The principal street for business, and which may be considered as forming the greater part of the old town, is the Low-street, running nearly parallel with, and at a short distance from, the river, and extending from the New Quay to the Low Lights. The greater part of the town which is built on the bank top, extending in regular streets towards the north, has been erected within the last forty years.

At the New Quay there is a commodious wharf, with warehouses at each end, where trading vessels load and unload, and where steam-boats leave for Newcastle every half-hour between eight in the morning and eight at night. A little above the New Quay is the landing for the steam ferry-boat, which plies between North and South Shields, and leaves each place four times an hour, from seven in the morning till dusk, carrying passengers across the river at the charge of a penny each. This ferry, which was only established in 1829, is a great accommodation to both the towns. Previous to its establishment, the conveyance of sheep, cattle, and horses across the Tyne, in an awkward flat-bottomed boat, managed by a single man, was attended with great inconvenience. The large steam ferry-boats now employed are surrounded with a strong railing; and sheep, cattle, and horses can be driven on board with little trouble, and conveyed across the river without risk.

The Market-place at North Shields lies immediately behind the New Quay, but, as it is open towards the river, the situation is bleak and cold in winter; and until either the market be removed to a better situation, or some shelter afforded by building a wall on the south side, near the quay, it is not likely to be well attended. The fish-market is held in a kind of to-fall, built against one of the warehouses at the foot of the New Quay, in a situation where there is little risk of the fish being spoiled by the rays of the sun.

The town of North Shields consists of the township of that name, and of part of the township of Tynemouth; a distinction which has caused the poor rates to fall most heavily upon the inhabitants of the lower part of the *town*. By the Parliamentary Return of 1831, the population of the township of

Tynemouth is given as	-	-	-	10,182
North Shields township	-	-	-	6,744
Total -	-	-	-	16,926

Deducting from this total 2,000 for the population of the village of Tynemouth and outskirts—which is perhaps too much—there remains 14,926 for the population of the town of North Shields. The number of ships belonging to the town is 270, the register admeasurement of which is 62,934 tons.

D

BERWICK.—THE BRIDGE, FROM THE NORTH-WEST.

THE view of Berwick Bridge from the north-west, looking towards Spittal and Holy Island, by Harding, is taken from a bank a little beyond the old town-walls, and to the right of the road in coming from Kelso and Dunse. The prospect from this bank is extremely beautiful and interesting; and the artist, who knows so well how to represent such a view with effect, has done it ample justice. To the left is seen part of the old town-walls, beyond which appear the tops of the houses and the spire of the Town-hall. To the right is " Tweed's fair river," hastening with rapid current—for the bare shoal in the midst of the stream informs us of its being ebb-tide—to mingle its waters with the briny sea. The houses seen to the right, at the end of the bridge, are part of the village of Tweedmouth. Towards the middle of the engraving, beyond the bridge, is the village of Spittal, built

" Upon the beachèd verge of the salt flood."

Following the line of coast to the southward, where here and there a light sail gives relief to the prospect, the land view is terminated by Holy Island, which, in consequence of the main land being seen beyond it to the south-west, appears like a promontory extending into the sea. The high ground which rises immediately behind the village of Tweedmouth, is Sunny-side Hill, over which the great north road used to pass, with a very steep rise on each side, but which has, within these last five or six years, been materially improved by cutting through the top of the hill, and by reducing the slope to the southward. The distant mill is that of Scremerston, a well-known land mark to the Tweedmouth fishermen.

Near the edge of the bank from which the view was taken, there is a fall of more than 100 feet nearly perpendicular to the shore of the Tweed. In 1798, Mr. Anthony Hindmarsh, of Alnwick, who was unacquainted with Berwick, in approaching the town at night time, on horseback, from the north-west, mistook his

Drawn by J. D. Harding.

Engraved by W. Finden.

BERWICK BRIDGE.

London, Published 1836, by Charles Tilt, 86, Fleet Street

road, and supposing the lights of Tweedmouth, on the opposite side of the river, to be those of Berwick, he rode over the edge of the bank; the horse was killed from the fall, but the rider most miraculously escaped unhurt. Like a thrifty man, when he found that his horse was dead, he took off the saddle and bridle, and, carrying them with him, scrambled up another part of the bank where the declivity was less precipitous.

From an early period there appears to have been a bridge across the Tweed at Berwick, though not on the same site as the present one. A wooden bridge, which stood about a hundred yards higher up the river, was carried away by a flood in 1199. It was re-built by William, King of Scotland, who then held possession of Berwick, after some objections on the part of the Bishop of Durham, to whom the south shore belonged. It was again carried away " with great force of water," says Leland, " bycause the arches of it were too narrow," after it had stood scarcely nine years. The present bridge of stone, after having been upwards of twenty-four years in building, was finished in October, 1634. It is 17 feet wide; and its length, from shore to shore, is 1164 feet. At each of the piers on both sides there is a recess for the convenience of foot passengers, who otherwise would often be exposed to danger at the meeting of carts and carriages. The Bishop of Durham's jurisdiction extends to the sixth pier from Tweedmouth, on the south side; and the coping stones of the recess there are always covered with turf, as a guide to bailiffs and constables, that they may not execute writs or warrants beyond the jurisdiction of their respective courts.

The village of Tweedmouth,—as well as the whole coast south of it as far as Bule-bay, with Norhamshire on the south of the Tweed,—though within the geographical limits of Northumberland, is yet held to belong to the county pala-tine of Durham, as part of the extensive possessions acquired through the fame of St. Cuthbert, whose bones to that see were worth more than

> " Nine kings' rents,
> For seven hundred year."

In 1204, King John began to erect a castle at Tweedmouth, in order to overawe that of Berwick, but it was destroyed before it was finished by William, king of Scotland. Tweedmouth is an irregularly built village, with a chapel, dedi-cated to St. Bartholomew. In 1831, the population, including Spittal, was 4971. Spittal, which is about a mile to the eastward of Tweedmouth, derives its name from a hospital which formerly stood there. It is mostly inhabited by fishermen; and on account of the convenience which the fine sandy beach in its vicinity affords for sea-bathing, it is much visited by families during the summer season.

BERWICK.—FROM THE SOUTH-EAST.

THE view of Berwick from the south-east is taken from the Tweedmouth shore, at low water, about a quarter of a mile below the bridge. In the fore-ground is a group of salmon-fishers on the shore, examining the produce of their last haul; while two others in a coble are shooting the net. To the left are seen the chapel and some of the houses of Tweedmouth; to the right a few ships are perceived lying on the shore near Berwick quay, where the smacks usually take in and discharge their cargoes. The spire which towers above the houses, like the steeple of a church, is that of the Town-hall. As Berwick church, which stands towards the north side of the town, is without a steeple, it would seem that the inhabitants had determined to make amends for the deficiency by giving their Town-hall a steeple like a church.

The town of Berwick stands on the north side of the Tweed, by which it is separated from the county of Northumberland, and about half a mile from the mouth of that river. It is 336 miles north by west from London, and 54 south by east from Edinburgh. As a great part of the town is built on a declivity, which slopes down towards the river, and as most of the houses are covered with red tiles, the view that is first obtained of it, in approaching from the south, on a clear bright day, is very striking, though not very grand. It is almost the only town on the Scottish side of the Tweed in which the houses are so covered; in all the others the houses being, for the most part, roofed with slate.

Chalmers, in his Caledonia, vol. 2. p. 217, speaking of Berwick, says, " this place, lying at the mouth of the Tweed, on a dubious frontier, has an origin obscure, undignified, and recent." That its origin, like the origin of most other towns in Great Britain, is obscure, may be admitted; but the term " recent" can scarcely be applied with propriety to a town which was of such consequence in the reign of David I., as to be appointed one of the " *Four Boroughs* *," which, by their

* The other three were Roxburgh, Stirling, and Edinburgh.

Drawn by G. Balmer.

Engraved by W. Finden.

BERWICK.

FROM THE SOUTH-EAST

London. Published 1836, by Charles Tilt, 86. Fleet Street.

Commissioners, met annually at Haddington, where, under the presidency of the King's Chamberlain, they formed a Court of Appeal from the jurisdiction of other boroughs, and exercised an authority in commercial affairs. As nothing is positively known respecting the origin of Berwick, it is impossible that an uninspired antiquary should be able to decide whether it was " undignified" or not. Its first " kirk and mill"—the primary conditions of a town—were more likely to be founded by a noble than by a serf.

Berwick is not mentioned by Bede; and the name does not occur in the list of churches enumerated by Hoveden as standing on the banks of the Tweed in 882. These facts may therefore be admitted as negative evidence of its being at those periods a place of little importance, even supposing that it might then consist of a few fishermen's houses by the river side.

Although the name, according to Chalmers, first occurs as " Berewyk," in a foundation charter of Earl David, brother of Alexander I., whereby he establishes a monastery at Selkirk, yet the place must then have been of considerable importance. In the charter of David, mention is made of the church and mill of Berwick; and during his reign—he succeeded his brother, Alexander I., in 1124—he occasionally resided at the Castle of Berwick. William of Newbrig, an English Historian, who flourished about the year 1200, calls Berwick " Nobilis vicus"—a noble village; and at that period it was one of the most populous and flourishing towns in Scotland.

If the origin of the town of Berwick be obscure, the derivation of the name is no less uncertain. Leland supposed it to have originally been " Aber-wic," from the British " Aber"—the mouth of a river, and " wic," from the Latin vicus—a village. Camden, disapproving of this derivation, thus expresses his own opinion of the meaning of the word: " They will best understand the true etymology of it who know what is meant by the word in the charters of our kings, wherein nothing is more common than ' I give the townships of C and D cum suis Berwicis.' For my part, what it should mean I know not, unless it be a hamlet or some such dependency upon a place of better note; for, in the grants of Edward the Confessor, Tothill is called the Berwicus of Westminster; Wandlesworth the Berwicus of Patricksey; and a thousand like *." In the glossaries of Lye and Somner, referred to by Chalmers, Berewic is said to have the same meaning as Beretun—villa frumentaria, a grange, a village; from Bere, a species of barley, here used for corn generally; and tun or ton, an assemblage of houses, a town.

* Camden's Britannica, Gibson's translation, vol. ii. p. 215. Edit. 1771. F. Tate, in his Exposition of the obscure words in Domesday-book, says that Berwica signifies a corn-farm.

As the barn of a monastery or of an individual proprietor would most likely be surrounded by the dwellings of persons engaged in agricultural labour, the name *Berewic* would be most appropriately given to such a place : at once expressive of its original use, and of the nature of its dependency on a " place of better note," whether lay or ecclesiastical. The derivation of the name of Berwick, from *Berewic*, without reference to its being the grange of a monastery, appears to receive a certain degree of support from the fact of the town being, at the present time, a place where a considerable quantity of corn from the adjacent district is stored, and afterwards exported to different places in England, as well as in Scotland.

Chalmers, discarding the previously enumerated etymologies, derives the name from the Anglo-Saxon *bar*, bare, naked, which he supposes to have been characteristic of the eminence on which the castle is built; and *wic*, which he loosely interprets " *vicus, castellum, sinus,*" a village, a castle, the winding reach of a river.* This mode of derivation is, however, something like firing at a covey of birds, without marking one ; for he thus lets fly his *bar* at village, castle, and winding reach, although it is difficult to conceive how it could be appropriately applied to any. Although *bar* might be characteristic enough of a naked bank by a river side, yet it by no means follows that the same term would be equally appropriate when applied to the castle erected on its top, or the village built on its declivity. On the contrary, its bareness and want of verdure would be less apparent as it began to be covered with buildings. It is also questionable if the word *wic* ever does signify the winding reach of a river; and, if it did, there seems very little reason to suppose that Berwick derived its name from such a source. In concluding his etymological speculations respecting the name of Berwick, Chalmers thus expresses his deliberate opinion, which scarcely seems to correspond with what he had previously stated concerning the " recent and undignified" origin of the town :—" On the whole, it is more than probable that the *wick* in the name in question was originally applied by the Northumbrian Saxons to the *castle* on the *bare* knoll, which was built by some Northumbrian Baron before the memorable epoch of 1020, A.D."†

* This etymology savours a good deal of the ingenuity which derives the name *Winchilsea*, from *wind*, *chilly*, and *sea*. Abraham Fraunce, in his Lawiers Logike, 1588, gives the following amusing specimens of etymological induction :—" A woman is a woe-man, because she worketh a man woe. Agreamentum, quasi *aggregatio mentium*. But all the sport is to heare the Monkish notions of wordes, both Greeke and Latine, whereof they knew neither sense nor signification : as *Diabolus*, of *dia*, that is two, (say they,) and *bolus*, which signifieth a morsel ; because the devill maketh but two morsels of a man : one of the soule, and another of the body."

† This epoch, 1020, is called memorable by Chalmers, because, in that year, Eadulf, Earl of Northumberland, ceded Lothian, which had formerly appertained to the Northumbrian Saxons, to Malcolm II., King of Scotland. The territory then ceded probably comprised the present counties of Berwick and Haddington, with a considerable portion of West and Mid-Lothian.

As the name *Berwick*, or, as it is often spelled by old writers, *Barwick*, does not appear to have been known until subsequent to Earl Eadulf's cession of Lothian to Malcolm II., its derivation from *Bar*—a barrier, and *wick*, seems most probable ; this name being expressive of its situation as a frontier or barrier town.

In 1174, Berwick, with the castles of Jedburgh, Roxburgh, Stirling, and Edinburgh, was delivered up to Henry II. as security for payment of the ransom of William the Lion, King of Scotland, who had been taken prisoner when besieging Alnwick ; and it remained in the possession of England until 1189, when Richard I. restored it with the other castles to William for the sum of 10,000 marks. In 1216, Berwick was plundered and burnt by King John, but in a short time was rebuilt by the Scots, in whose uninterrupted possession it continued until 1296, when it was taken by Edward I. at the commencement of the Scottish war of independence, which was first waged by Wallace, and afterwards by Bruce, against Edward and his successor: who, laying claim to the sovereignty of Scotland, endeavoured to reduce that country to a state of vassalage, and to compel her kings to do homage to England for their crown. From this war may be dated that jealous and hostile feeling with which the two countries continued to regard each other for nearly three centuries afterwards, which became modified in the reign of Elizabeth,—when there was a prospect of a Scottish king succeeding to the English throne, and when open warfare was succeeded by political intrigue,—but which was not wholly extinct at the Union of the two kingdoms in 1707.

After the battle of Stirling, in 1297, Berwick opened its gates to the victorious arms of Wallace, but the castle held out until relieved by Edward in the following year, who at the same time recovered possession of the town. In 1312, Berwick was unsuccessfully assaulted by Bruce ; but in 1318 it was betrayed to his nephew, Randolph, Earl of Murray, by the governor, Sir Pierce Spalding, who received certain lands in Angus in reward of his treachery. Bruce being aware of the importance of Berwick, as the key which opened to the English a ready entrance to the south-eastern parts of Scotland, strengthened the place by raising the height of the walls, and building additional towers. After the defeat of the Scots, in 1333, by Edward III., at Halidon Hill, about two miles to the north-west of Berwick, that town again fell into the hands of the English. In 1355, the town, but not the castle, was taken by the Scots, but was re-taken by the English in the following year. In 1377, the castle of Berwick was surprised by a small party of Scots, who held it for only seven days. In 1384, they obtained possession of the town, which was recovered by the English in the same year. In the rebellion of Percy, Earl of Northumberland, against Henry IV., in 1405, Berwick being garrisoned by his retainers, a numerous army was despatched by Henry, in order to recover possession of so important a place. At this siege of Berwick, cannon, according to Walsingham, were first used in this country A discharge from a large cannon of the besiegers having nearly demolished one of the towers, the garrison became alarmed, and immediately surrendered the town. The truth of this account appears to be corroborated by the fact of a large cannon ball, weighing 96lb., being dug out of the old walls, near to a tower, in 1811. In 1461, Henry VI., after the battle of Towton, delivered up Berwick to the Scots, who retained possession of it until 1482, when it was recovered by Edward IV. From 1482, to the Union of the two crowns in 1603, Berwick continued in the possession of the English. From 1296—when Berwick was first besieged oy Edward I.—to 1482, when it was finally gained for England by Edward IV., perhaps there is no instance in the history of Modern Europe of a town being so often lost and won.

In 1484, it was agreed on, by commissioners appointed by the two kingdoms, that the debateable ground in the neighbourhood of Berwick should remain without culture, buildings, or inhabitants; and by a treaty, concluded at Norham, 10th June, 1551, between Edward VI. and Mary Queen of Scots, Berwick was declared to be a free town, independent of both kingdoms. Notwithstanding this declaration, Berwick continued subject to English authority, and, during the reigns of Mary and of Elizabeth, was garrisoned with English soldiers. At the Union of the two kingdoms in 1707, Berwick, as a salvo to national pride, was considered as a separate and independent territory ; and it is to this cause that, in Public Acts and Forms of Prayer, the " Town of Berwick-upon-Tweed" is especially mentioned*.

From the commencement of the reign of David I., in 1124, to 1296—when the town was seized by Edward—it is certain that Berwick was a place of considerable importance and increasing trade ; and from chartularies and old monastic records we may learn, that in the above period it had become of some note as a place for the export of corn, and that the salmon fisheries in its neighbourhood were valuable. David granted fishings in the Tweed, near Berwick, to the monks of Selkirk ; and he also granted to the monks of Dunfermline "tractum de Aldstelle"—the draught of the Old Stell †, also near Berwick. Notwithstanding the

---

* By the 20th of Geo. III. it was enacted that all public acts relating to England should be considered as extending to Berwick-upon-Tweed, although that town should not be expressly named.

† " *Stell*-fishing," says Chalmers, Caledonia, vol. 1, page 785, " probably meant a stationary fishing ; perhaps from the Anglo-Saxon, *Steal*—signifying, as we know from Somner, *locus, statio.*" Stell-fishing, which is at present generally practised in the Tweed, from its mouth to near Norham, is thus explained by Mr. James Innes, in the Report from the Select Committee on the Salmon Fisheries, 1825 :—" This species of net [the stell-nett] is either stretched across the river or in the sea, and fixed by means of an anchor at one end, with the other resting on the bank ; a man in a boat is stationed near the extreme outward end, holding in his hand the top line of the net, and the instant a fish touches the net he feels it, and calls to the people on shore, who immediately pull the anchor and net to the land, and the salmon are secured. While they are performing this operation, another boat and net are launched to occupy the

vicissitudes to which Berwick had been exposed for nearly two hundred years, it appears that in 1480 the monks of Dunfermline had not lost the evidence of their grant, for in that year, Berwick being then in possession of the Scots, a jury at Edinburgh found that the brethren were entitled to employ two " *cobils*" and two nets at the fishery of the Aldstelle, which is the number required for stell-fishing at the present day. It appears from the chartulary of Kelso that, in the period previously referred to, a fishing at Berwick let for 20*l.* yearly,—a large sum, considering the value of money at that time; the fishing at " Wudehorn," near Tweedmouth, for fourteen marks; and the fishing of " Northariun," at the same place, for two marks. From the same document we learn that the tenants of the abbot of Kelso were obliged to carry on each horse to Berwick, the usual place of export, three bolls of corn in summer, and two in winter; and that they brought coals and salt in return.

In the early part of the reign of Edward III., Lord Henry Percy had 500 marks per annum secured to him out of the customs of Berwick; and, by an act passed in the twenty-second year of the same king's reign, certain persons are appointed to " ordain remedy touching the buying and selling of stock-fish of St. Botolf, and *salmon* of *Berwick*." While this town was the subject of frequent contention between the English and the Scots, it is not likely that it would be of much consequence as a place of trade; and there seems reason to believe that at the Union of the two crowns in 1603, it was not more populous than in 1296, when it was taken by Edward I. During the above period, we have little account of its commerce; which would probably be of very limited extent, as the Scottish counties of Berwick and Roxburgh would neither ship their produce of corn, wool, or hides at an English port, nor receive through it their foreign supplies.

About the middle of the last century, Berwick salmon used chiefly to be conveyed to London by small vessels of about forty tons burthen, belonging to Harwich and Gravesend, engaged by the London dealers; the fresh-caught salmon and gilse were conveyed in wells in the hold, but a large portion was sent pickled in kits. About 1787, the practice of packing salmon in pounded ice was suggested by George Dempster, Esq., of Dunnichen, then M. P. for Cupar, to Mr. John Richardson, a salmon dealer, of Perth, who immediately adopted it; and the next year the salmon dealers of Berwick followed his example.

About the beginning of August there is a perceptible enlargement of the milt and the roe of salmon, and they then begin to make their appearance in the upper parts of the Tweed and its principal tributary streams, and they continue to ascend

same ground as the former, so as to intercept the shoal of fish as they pass upwards. This process goes on incessantly, and the success attending it is such, that, at stations near the mouth of the river, sixty and one hundred salmon are caught by two boats in one day."

for the purpose of spawning during the three succeeding months. When full of spawn, they are termed *red fish*, and are then out of condition. Salmon that have recently spawned are called *kelts*; they are then lean, sickly, and unfit for food; and they do not recover their strength until they have visited the sea. The spawn is deposited chiefly during the months of November, December, and January, in shallow streamy places, with a gravelly bottom; and about the latter end of March the fry begin to make their appearance. During April they descend the river; and by the first week in May they generally reach the sea. About the latter end of June they begin to return to the river, as *gilse*, or *grilse*, when they weigh from one and a half to two pounds. From the middle of July to the middle of August, when the gilse fishing is at its height, they are usually caught weighing from three to four pounds. The salmon fishery in the Tweed commences on the 15th of February, and continues till the 15th of October. From the latter date till 15th of February is called *close time*, when it is illegal to take salmon.

Most of the salmon sent from Berwick to London are caught between the mouth of the Tweed and Norham, which is about eight miles up the river, and the highest point to which the tide flows. In 1799, the yearly rental of the fisheries within this distance, on both sides of the river, was estimated at £10,000; and in 1817 it was nearly double that sum. In consequence of the decline of the salmon fishery since 1820, it does not at the present time exceed £9,000. Various causes have been assigned for the decline of the salmon fishery in the Tweed; such as the building of the New Pier at the north side of the Harbour; with the draining of lands and the destruction of fish in close time towards the upper parts of the river. How the building of the New Pier, and the draining of lands in Selkirk and Roxburghshire affect the breed of salmon, has not been clearly shown; and poaching in close time has not prevailed to a greater extent during the last twenty years than in the twenty years previous to 1816. The unremitting manner in which the river was *legally* fished between the mouth of the Tweed and Norham, from 1800 to 1817, is more likely to have been one great cause of the decline: but the proprietors of the fisheries seem unwilling to admit that a river may be over-fished, as well as land exhausted by over-cropping.

It can scarcely be said that there is a public market for salmon in Berwick, almost all that are caught being engrossed by factors or fish-curers, and sent to London; and salmon is generally as dear there as in the metropolis. The fish, as soon as caught, are packed in large boxes, between layers of pounded ice, and in this manner conveyed to London by the smacks, which are fast-sailing, sloop-rigged vessels, and the passage is usually made in about five days. In consequence of the mildness of the winter of 1833—1834, a sufficiency of ice could not be obtained in the neighbourhood of Berwick, and about 1,000 tons were imported from Norway. In the present year about 600 tons have been imported from the same place. The following is the average annual shipment of salmon from Berwick to London from 1800 to 1835 :—

From 1800 to 1809	.	.	.	8,550 Boxes.
1810 to 1819	.	.	.	7,720
1820 to 1829	.	.	.	4,779
1830 to 1835	.	.	.	4,090

The number of boxes, in the preceding account, must not be considered as affording a criterion of the decline of the salmon fisheries in the Tweed; for the weight of the boxes throughout the above period has not been the same. According to the evidence of Mr. John Wilson, given before the Select Committee on the Salmon Fisheries in 1824, a box of salmon, previous to 1816, used to contain only six stone and a half. In 1824, it contained eight stone. At present the average weight of a box of salmon is from nine to ten stone. Notwithstanding the outcry which has been made respecting the decline of the salmon fisheries in the Tweed, the account of the quantities shipped within the last twenty years proves that it is not so great as has been stated by interested parties. The decline of the great rents which were derived from them in 1815—16—and 17, has been often erroneously represented as indicating the decrease in the quantity of salmon caught.

In 1835, there were shipped from Berwick, to various places in England and Scotland, the following quantities of grain, beside 21,340 sacks of ground corn :—

	Wheat.	Barley.	Oats.	Rye.	Beans & Peas.
Quarters:—	21,103	43,059	37,895	970	5,419

In 1801, there were sixty-two vessels belonging to Berwick, with a register admeasurement of 5,150 tons. In 1829, the number had decreased to fifty-seven, with an admeasurement of 4,984 tons; and, since then, the trade of the town has not been increasing.

Berwick is a corporate town, governed by a mayor, and other officers, whose election was regulated by a Charter of James I., granted in 1604, until the Municipal Reform Bill came into operation in December 1835. It has returned two Members to Parliament since the reign of Henry VIII. By the Reform Bill, the right of suffrage—which was formerly confined to burgesses by patrimony or by apprenticeship—has been extended to the 10l. householders of Berwick and its bounds, and also to those of Tweedmouth and Spittal. The present members are Sir Francis Blake, Bart., and Marcus Beresford, Esq. The population of Berwick, by the returns of 1831, was 8,920.

BERWICK.—LIGHT-HOUSE ON THE PIER.

THE view of the Light-house, at the head of Berwick Pier, is taken from the entrance to the Harbour, about half a mile below the bridge. This Pier, the building of which was commenced in 1810, stands on the north side of the river, and is chiefly erected on the foundations of an old one, which is said to have been built in the reign of Queen Elizabeth. From the Light-house, which was finished in 1826, two lights are exhibited at night, the one above the other. The upper one, which is of a pale, white colour, is lighted from sun-set to sun-rise; the lower one, which is of a bright red, is a tide light, and is only displayed during the time that there is ten feet water on the bar.

Berwick Harbour is not well adapted for vessels of large burthen, for the greater part of the shore, in front of the quay, is dry at low water. On the Tweedmouth side, near the Car Rock, is the best water within the bar; and a vessel drawing from sixteen to eighteen feet water may lie there at all hours of the tide without touching the ground. The entrance to the Harbour is narrow, as a bank of sand stretches out to the eastward, from the Spittal shore, to the extent of nearly half a mile, and approaches to within a cable's length of the rocks on the north. When the wind is from the eastward, there is always a swell on the bar; and the ebb tide—more especially when there is a *fresh* in the river, in consequence of rain—runs out with such velocity that it is impossible for a vessel to make head against it. Vessels bound for Berwick, which cannot take the Harbour in bad weather, usually seek shelter in Leith Roads.

At low water, at spring tides, there are only five feet water on the bar; at high water, from eighteen to twenty; at high water, at neap tides, about fourteen feet. At the full and change of the moon, it is high water on the bar at half-past two o'clock. The average rise of the tide on the bar is ten feet at neaps, and sixteen feet at springs. Berwick lies in latitude 55° 46′ 21″ north; longitude 1° 59′ 41′ west.

Drawn by G. Balmer.   Engraved by W. Finden.

ENTRANCE TO THE PORT OF BERWICK.

London, Published 1836, by Charles Tilt, 86, Fleet Street.

Drawn by G. Balmer

Engraved by E. Finden.

NEWCASTLE-UPON-TYNE.

London, Published 1836, by Charles Tilt, 86, Fleet Street

NEWCASTLE UPON TYNE.

THE view of Newcastle is taken from the Gateshead shore, on the south side of the river Tyne, about a quarter of a mile below the bridge. From the point chosen by the artist, a better and more *characteristic* view of the town is obtained than from any other station. The line of vessels, extending from the right of the engraving to the bridge, indicates the quay,—the longest in England, except that of Yarmouth; and which on a Saturday, when the country people come in to market, is one of the most crowded thoroughfares in the kingdom. The steeple, which rises above the houses to the right, is that of All Saints. Between All Saints and the Castle—which is distinguished by its modern turrets and battlements—is the famed steeple of St. Nicholas, which the Rev. Dr. Carlyle, vicar of Newcastle, in 1804, declared to be, in his opinion, " the most beautiful fabric existing in the world : surpassing the Cathedral of St. Sophia, at Constantinople ; the Mosque of Sultan Saladin, at Jerusalem ; the Church of St. Peter, at Rome ; and even the Temple of Minerva, at Athens*. The modern building, with a Grecian portico, in front of the Castle, is the County Court, where the assizes for the county of Northumberland are held. The Exchange is hidden by the sails of the large vessel, towards the middle of the engraving ; and the bridge excludes a view of the Mansion House, which stands in friendly neighbourhood with a glass-house and a soapery, in a narrow street, with a most expressive name—the " Close."

The town of Newcastle, though its present name is not older than the reign of William the Conqueror, claims to be a place of great antiquity. The Roman Wall—which extended from Wallsend, about four miles eastward of Newcastle, to Boulness on the Sands, in Cumberland—crossed the site of the present town ; and it is certain that there was a Roman station there, the southern wall of which had probably run along the high ground which overlooks the river in front of the old castle. In the list of stations, with their garrisons, on the line of the wall, as given

---

* Dr. Carlyle was a traveller, and had seen the different buildings which he thinks are surpassed by the steeple of his own church. It is, however, questionable if he would have deliberately and publicly expressed the above opinion which, in the warmth of his admiration, he communicated to the *Church-wardens* of St. Nicholas.

in the Notitia, *Pons Ælii* occurs as the next station to *Segedunum ;* and our best informed antiquaries appear to agree in assigning the latter name to the station at Wallsend, and the former to the station at Newcastle. The name Pons Ælii, however, occurs in no other ancient work as the name of a station on the line of the wall, and no inscription has been discovered which might confirm the opinion of its being the name of the station at Newcastle. Different writers also have interpreted the list of stations in the Notitia from different ends, and at the present time the situation of several places remains undecided.

The name Pons Ælii—the bridge of Ælius—wherever the place may have been—was evidently given from some bridge, which was probably so called in honour of the Emperor Hadrian, who was one of the Ælian family. Brand, and later historians of the town of Newcastle, have supposed that it was a bridge over the Tyne at Newcastle ; and it has even been conjectured that the reverse of one of Hadrian's coins is intended to commemorate the building of this very bridge. In removing the piers of the old bridge, in 1771, a coin of Hadrian was found, which has been considered as decisive of the fact of a bridge having been built there by that emperor. The coins of later emperors were, however, found at the same time ; and Pennant, who adopts the opinion of there being an " Ælian Bridge" at Newcastle, gets quit of the objection by supposing that they were " deposited there in some later repairs." The " Pons Ælii " rests, it must be admitted, on very slender foundations—the passage in the Notitia and the old coin of Hadrian ;—and the flood of negative testimony that assails it appears more than sufficient to sweep it away. It is by no means certain that the *Segedunum* of the Notitia—upon which the situation of Pons Ælii is supposed to depend—is the modern Wallsend ; and no road has been traced branching from the great Roman road southward to Newcastle, nor proceeding northward from that town. The station at Newcastle, therefore, was not on the line of any of the great Roman roads which traversed the island from north to south ; and, if there was no great military road leading northward through, or near to, such a station, it is extremely unlikely that a bridge should be built across the Tyne at such a place. The map in the Itinerary of Richard of Cirencester has been cited by writers, who ought to have been more careful in their examination, to prove that a branch of the Roman military road had extended from *Vinovium*, Binchester, to the Ælian Bridge. The road in Richard's map extends only to *Epiacum*, Chester-le-street, from whence it has been traced to South Shields, but not to Newcastle.

It has been supposed that Newcastle was the " Ad Murum " mentioned by Bede as the place where Peada, King of Mercia, was baptized by Finan, Bishop of Lindisfarn in 653. Bede, however, says that " Ad Murum " was twelve miles from the sea ; but in order to make this statement harmonize with conjecture, we are informed that Bede meant Roman miles; and it is thus proved that Newcastle and "Ad Murum * " are only different names of the same place.

Under the Saxon kings it is said that Newcastle was known by the name of Monkchester; which, according to Brand, "has generally been interpreted 'the fortified residence of persons of the monastic order'"—a very elegant periphrasis of the name. The principal authority for supposing that Newcastle was ever known by such a name, is Simeon of Durham†, who in his history gives the following account of the pious pilgrimage of three monks, in search of Monkchester, but who found not what they sought:—

In 1074, Aldwine, prior of Winchilsea, having gathered from ancient histories that Northumberland had been distinguished for its religious edifices, resolved upon visiting their remains. Accompanied by two monks of Evesham, he set out on his journey, and, on arriving at York, he desired a guide of the sheriff, Hugh, the son of Baldric, to conduct him and his companions to Monkchester, "which," says the historian, "is now called the New Castle." On arriving at the place, and finding no vestige of any monastic orders, they went to Jarrow, and in that ruined monastery rekindled the zeal for monastic life, which for about two hundred years had been nearly extinct in those parts.—

As the name, Monkchester, never occurs in any of our earlier historians, it seems most likely that Aldwine and his companions had been wrong in their topography. *Monkwearmouth* is celebrated by early ecclesiastical historians for its monastery; and as this place was within the ancient Saxon kingdom of Northumberland, the pious travellers from the south might very easily mistake its site. It has been conjectured that during the Heptarchy, and subsequently, Monkchester was the residence of the kings and the earls of Northumberland; and Brand says that there "are still both traditionary and printed accounts" of the Saxon kings having a palace there. The printed accounts and the tradition appear to owe their common origin to Grey's Chorographia, or Survey of Newcastle upon Tyne, which was first printed in 1649.

The earliest authentic written accounts which we have of Newcastle do not extend beyond the period at which it acquired its present name;—the evidence that the Romans had a station there, rests upon better authority than the simple notice of such a place in the pages of an ancient historian. The Castle, which gives

* The Rev. John Hodgson thinks that the "Ad Murum" of Bede was at Welton, near Harlow Hill, about twelve miles westward of Newcastle. The "Ad Murum" of Richard of Cirencester, which Brand— in his History of Newcastle, misled by Stukely—supposes to have been Newcastle, was most probably the "Hunnum" of the Notitia, now Halton Chesters, about three miles westward of Welton.

† Simeon of Durham was precentor of that cathedral in 1164. His account of Aldwine's journey in search of Monkchester is copied by Roger Hoveden, and other later historians.

name to the town*, though now " old and hoary," and with front somewhat rugged from the corroding touch of time, still rears its head with undiminished height, like a stalwart giant—of those days when there " were giants in the land"— whose brow the lapse of ages had wrinkled, but who retained the bulk and stature of his youth. According to the general testimony of annalists and historians, the New Castle upon Tyne was built by Robert, surnamed Curt-hose, eldest son of William the Conqueror, between 1079 and 1082. It stands on an elevated situation, within a short distance of the edge of the bank, which rises with a steep ascent from the end of the bridge. Its plan forms nearly a square ; the side from east to west being fifty-seven feet, and the side from north to south, sixty-two feet†. The walls at the top are fourteen feet six inches thick, and seventeen feet thick at the base. The original height of the keep—before the modern battlements were added—was about ninety feet. The castle was also surrounded by two outer walls, enclosing an area called the Castle-garth. As this castle formed an important barrier to the irruptions of the Scotch, the principal baronies in Northumberland were charged with a certain sum or duty, under the name of Castle-ward, for its maintenance and defence. In 1292, John Baliol did homage for the Scottish crown to Edward I., in the castle of Newcastle ; in 1644, it was surrendered by the mayor, Sir John Marley, to the Scottish army, under the Earl of Leven ; and in 1782, it was advertised to be let, by the lessee under the crown, John Crichloe Turner, Esq., as a place most suitable for a wind-mill. As it contained a good spring of water, the hydraulic capabilities of the property were not overlooked by the advertiser. " There is a good spring of water within the castle," saith he, " which renders it a very eligible situation for a brewery, or any manufactory that requires a constant supply of water." After the once hostile nations of England and Scotland had beat their swords into plough-shares and their spears into sickles, the converting of their border fortresses into wind-mills and breweries appears to follow as

* Brand, History of Newcastle, vol. i. p. 144, says : " Its having been called, on its erection, ' the New Castle,' seems strongly to imply that it arose from the site of some older fortress....Thus, as Dr. Plot, in his History of Staffordshire, informs us, in a similar instance, Newcastle under Lyme, or Line, in that county, had its name from the old castle of Chesterton under Lyme, which, at the time of its erection, was falling into ruin." Brand informs his readers, on the authority of the " English Morery," that Newcastle upon Line [under Line] is so called from the rivulet Line, upon which it is seated, to distinguish it from Newcastle upon Tyne. The person whom he is pleased to designate the " English *Morery*," he names not ; and the writer will not venture to guess. In the reign of Edward I. there is an instance of Newcastle in Northumberland being named " Newcastle under Tyne "—subtus Tynam. " Burgenses de Preston allocantur quamplurimas libertates in longo placito, scilicet, fales quales Burgenses Novi Castri *subtus Tynam* habent juxta cartam Regis Henrici II. et Regis Johannis."— Abbreviatio Placitorum, temp. Ric. I. ; Johan. ; Hen. III. ; Ed. I. ; et Ed. II. p. 233. Printed by his Majesty's command, 1811.

† The castle does not stand due east and west ; that which is called the east front rather fronts to the south-east ; and that which is called the south front, looks towards the south-west.

a matter of course. As the Castle-garth was held to be in the county of Northumberland, and exempt from the jurisdiction of the magistrates of Newcastle, persons committing offences within the town used to seek refuge within its precincts. By a clause in a charter of the 31st of Elizabeth, to the corporation of Newcastle, the same power within the Castle-garth, the dungeon only excepted, was given to the magistrates as in all other places under their jurisdiction. For many years after the date of this charter, the Castle-garth used to be frequented as a privileged place by petty dealers and chapmen, who, as non-freemen, were not allowed to open shops in other parts of the town; and to the present time it continues to be the great mart for the sale of old boots and shoes, and cast-off wearing apparel.

Under the protection of the *new* castle, the town in its vicinity appears, within a short period, to have become a place of importance. Henry I. granted certain privileges and immunities to the inhabitants, which were confirmed and enlarged by Henry II. King John, by several charters, granted between 1201 and 1217, confirmed and extended the liberties of the burgesses of Newcastle. In a charter granted in the seventeenth year of his reign to the Merchants Adventurers of Newcastle, constituting them a guild or free company, mention is made of the town-walls*. It is said that in 1239, Henry III., by letters patent, gave the burgesses liberty to dig *coals* and *stones* in the Castle Field and in the Forth; places of which they had the common right, and lying in the vicinity of the town. In 1251, the same king granted that the town should have a mayor, in addition to the four bailiffs by whom it had been previously governed. From an inquiry made in the ninth of Edward I., 1291, it was found that the fee-farm of the town was worth 200*l.* per annum, if in the king's hands; as its value, since the reign of King John,—when it was granted to the burgesses for 100*l.* per annum—had greatly increased through the working of coals. In 1283, Newcastle was summoned by Edward I. to send two of the most apt and intelligent burgesses to attend his parliament at Shrewsbury. In 1400, Henry IV. constituted Newcastle a county of itself, and directed that, instead of bailiffs, as formerly, a sheriff should be annually chosen by twenty-four of the most reputable burgesses. Six aldermen were also to be appointed, who, with the mayor, were to be justices of peace. In the second of Henry VIII., 1510, a decree was made in the Star-cham-

---

* Hardyng, in his Chronicle, says that the town-walls were built in the reign of William Rufus. It is said, though erroneously, by Leland, that the walls were first built in the reign of Edward I., in consequence of a wealthy person being seized in his house by the Scots, owing to the defenceless state of the town, and only recovering his liberty on payment of a large ransom. In 1307, the walls were repaired, and probably extended towards the east. According to Hutton's Plan of Newcastle, the circuit of the walls, on the land sides of the town, was 2,740 yards. By Mr. Thomas Aubone's measurement, in 1745, their whole circuit, including the distance between Sand-gate and Close-gate, by the river side, which was not reckoned by Hutton, was 3,759 yards: that is, two miles and 239 yards. The town having increased far beyond its old limits, most of the old walls are now pulled down.

F

ber regulating the manner in which the mayor, aldermen, and other officers of
the corporation were to be chosen; and in the fifth of Queen Mary, 1557, the
number of the aldermen was increased to ten.   In 1600, Queen Elizabeth granted
to the burgesses a new charter—called, by way of eminence, the Great Charter—
confirming all their former liberties, and appointing a new mode of choosing the
mayor and other officers of the town.   By the same charter, the Free Grammar
School was incorporated, which can boast of having had such a critic as Dawes
for master, and that such distinguished characters as Lords Eldon, Stowell, and
Collingwood received their early education under the fostering care of a Moises,
within its venerable walls *.

An alteration in the mode of electing the officers of the corporation was introduced by a charter of James I., in 1604; but, with this exception, the Great
Charter of Elizabeth continued to be the grand code of the mayor, aldermen, and
burgesses of Newcastle upon Tyne, until the Municipal Reform Bill came into
operation in December, 1835.   By this bill the town, with its suburbs, is divided
into eight wards, which elect forty-two town-councillors, who again elect a mayor
and twelve aldermen.   The mayor, aldermen, and town-councillors then appoint a
recorder, town-clerk, and other officers.

The annual revenue of the corporation of Newcastle, which, in 1826, amounted
to £42,959 9s. 9d., is chiefly derived from ballast dues; from the rents of lands
and houses, and the sale of building sites; and from tolls.   By prescription the corporation of Newcastle claim the exclusive right of receiving all ballast brought into
the river Tyne, and demand certain dues for its conveyance to the ballast wharfs
appointed by them at different places on each side of the river.   In 1826, the sum
of £16,861 13s. 2d. was paid by colliers and other vessels on account of ballast
dues; and in the same year the disbursements of the corporation for conveying
199,855 tons of ballast to different quays and wharfs, amounted to £7666 6s. 11d.
The claims set up by the corporation to certain land-dues and tolls were frequently
denied by persons who questioned their legality.   In an action for arrears of toll,
brought by the corporation of Newcastle in 1820, against J. G. Lambton, Esq.,
now Earl of Durham, it was elicited from a witness of the plaintiffs, in his cross-
examination by Mr. (now Lord) Brougham, counsel for the defendant, that they
claimed a toll on *potatoes*, by virtue of a prescriptive right enjoyed by them beyond
legal memory—that is, from the reign of Richard I.—although potatoes were first
brought to Spain as a dainty, from America, about 1530, and were not known in
England till 1586.   The plaintiffs, however, gained a verdict; but not wishing in

---

* The Grammar School of Newcastle owes its first foundation to Thomas Horsley, who was mayor of
Newcastle in 1533. The school-room was formerly the chapel of St. Mary's Hospital, which was suppressed by Henry VIII. in 1539.

future to trust their claims to the uncertain evidence of their prescriptive right, they in 1822 applied for and obtained an act of parliament, authorising them to collect certain tolls, specified in a schedule annexed to the bill, and to enforce payment by distress and sale.

From the reign of King John, when the company of Merchant Adventurers was established by charter, to that of Queen Elizabeth, Newcastle appears to have been only a second-rate port ; having fewer ships, and contributing less to the revenue in customs, than such places as Yarmouth, Lynn, Boston, and Southampton. Towards the latter part of the reign of Queen Elizabeth, the coal trade of New-castle received an additional impulse, in consequence of the increased demand for sea-borne coal in the London market ; and from that period the increase of the population of the metropolis affords an index of the extension of the coal trade, and of the progress of Newcastle to its present eminence as a maritime town.　In 1829 the aggregate tonnage of all the ships belonging to Yarmouth, Lynn, Boston, and Southampton, was only 74,972 tons ; and in the same year the tonnage of vessels registered in the port of Newcastle was 202,379 tons ; exceeding, by upwards of 40,000 tons, the tonnage of all the ships belonging to Liverpool, and being nearly equal to the tonnage of all the ships belonging to Hull, Bristol, Yarmouth, and Scarborough*.

From cinders and portions of coal having been found in the sites of old Roman stations in this island, and from a *celt*—a kind of axe-head used by the ancient Britons—having been discovered in a vein of coal in Monmouthshire, there can be little doubt of the ancient Britons being acquainted with the use of coal as an article of fuel ; and it is also likely that coals, in small quantities, might be consumed during the Saxon period, though there is no historical evidence to establish such a fact.　In a grant from the abbot of Peterborough to one *Wulfred,* A.D. 852, the land of " *Sempilgaham* "—Sempringham, in Lincolnshire—is conveyed to him for

* The following statement, extracted from a parliamentary return, ordered to be printed 29th April, 1830, will show the relative tonnage of the ten principal ports of England in 1829 :—

Name of Port.			Number of Ships.				Tons.				Average Tonnage of each Ship.
London.	.	.	2663	.	.	.	572,835	.	.	.	215
Newcastle.	.	.	987	.	.	.	202,379	.	.	.	205
Liverpoo .	.	.	805	.	.	.	161,780	.	.	.	201
Sunderland	.	.	624	.	.	.	107,628	.	.	.	172
Whitehaven	.	.	496	.	.	.	72,967	.	.	.	147
Hull	.	.	579	.	.	.	72,248	.	.	.	124
Bristol	.	.	316	.	.	.	49,535	.	.	.	157
Yarmouth	.	.	405	.	.	.	44,134	.	.	.	75
Whitby	.	.	258	.	.	.	41,176	.	.	.	161
Scarborough	.	.	169	.	.	.	28,070	.	.	.	166

It is to be observed, that ships belonging to North and South Shields, Seaton Sluice, and Blyth, are all registered at the port of Newcastle.

his life, on certain conditions; one of which is, to supply the monastery annually with "cᵽælᵹ ꝼoðuꞃ ᵹꞃæꝼæꞃ"—twælf fothur græfan—which Gibson, in his edition of the Saxon Chronicle, 1692, translates, though without sufficient authority, "duodecim plaustra carbonum fossilium"—twelve fothers or cart-loads of fossil coal. The word "ᵹꞃæꝼaꞃ"—græfan,—which is translated "fossil coals," simply means something *græfed*, that is, *graved*, or dug; and is much more likely to have signified turves, or peats, than fossil coal. With the former the vicinity of Sempringham abounds, but no seam of coal has hitherto been discovered there. In the "Boldon Buke," containing a survey of lands belonging to the Bishop of Durham, and compiled about the year 1190, the word *carbo*, the Latin name for charcoal, appears to be used to signify fossil or pit-coal.

To the coal trade of Newcastle an earlier date cannot be assigned than the reign of Henry III., who, in 1239, is said to have granted liberty to the burgesses of that town to dig for stones and coals, at certain places within their common soil, called the Castle-field and the Forth. Though this charter, which is referred to by Gardiner*, has not been discovered, yet there is positive evidence of fossil coal being known within a few years of its date; for in a writ of inquiry, issued in 1245, and preserved among the additions to Matthew Paris, it is expressly mentioned by the name *carbo maris*—sea-coal; and in the same document, the pits from which it is obtained are termed *fossata*. In 1291 it appears that the burgesses of Newcastle derived a considerable revenue from the coals obtained on their property; and in 1306 the consumption of sea-coal by brewers, dyers, smiths, and others who had occasion for large fires, appears to have increased so much, that parliament complained of it to the king as a nuisance, infecting the air with noxious vapours. In consequence of this representation, the king forbid the use of sea-coal; but the prohibition does not appear to have been very long enforced, for in 1321, Richard Hurst, of London, petitions parliament that they will order 10s. to be paid to him for sea-coals—*carboun de meer*—supplied by him to the royal palace at the time of the king's coronation.

In 1325 there is evidence of coals being sent abroad; for in that year one Thomas Rente, of Pontoise†, brought a cargo of corn to Newcastle, and returned with a cargo of coals. In 1330, the prior and convent of Tynemouth let a colliery at Elswick, a village near Newcastle, to Adam de Colewell, for the yearly rent of

---

* "England's Grievance Discovered, in Relation to the Coal Trade, by Ralph Gardiner," p. 9. Edit. 1796. The first edition of Gardiner's book, which is very rare, was printed, in 4to., in 1655. A copy was sold at the sale of J. T. Brockett, Esq.'s books, in 1823, for £20 9s. 6d. There is a copy, wanting the map of the Tyne, in the British Museum; and there *was* one in the library of the London Institution, but it has been stolen.

† Pontoise is the name of a small town upon the Oise, a small river which discharges itself into the Seine, about twenty miles below Paris.

five pounds; and in the chartulary of the same monastery, under the year 1338, mention is made of a *staith*, that is, the elevated stage—usually extending from the shore to low-water mark—from which the coals are put on board of ships or keels. In 1365, Edward III. issued an order concerning the measures to be used by venders of coals; and in 1379 a temporary duty of sixpence a ton was imposed on ships coming from Newcastle with coals, to protect the coast and the town of Scarborough from the attacks of the French. From the rolls of Whitby Abbey, it appears that in 1394-5-6*, coals were brought from Newcastle, to that town, in ships belonging to Sunderland, Shields, Newcastle, Barton, Lynn, and other places; a proof that the coasting-trade in coals had become of considerable importance previous to 1400, the year in which Newcastle was constituted a county of itself—probably on account of its increasing consequence as a commercial town.

In order to secure the king's dues of two-pence a chalder on all coals sold to persons not franchised in the port of Newcastle, an act was passed in the 9th year of Henry V., 1421, ordering that all keels conveying coals from the land to ships, in that port, should carry twenty chalders, and no more; and that they should be measured, and their portage marked by commissioners appointed by the king. This act was passed in consequence of the coal-owners loading the keels with twenty-two or twenty-three chalders†, and thereby defrauding the king of his due. From the household book of Henry Percy, fifth Earl of Northumberland, of the date of 1512, the best sea-coals appear to have been then sold at 5s. a chalder, and those of inferior quality at 4s. 2d. In 1536, coals were sold in Newcastle at 2s. 6d., and in London at 4s. a chalder. Of the progress of the coal trade during the reigns of Henry VIII., Edward VI., and Queen Mary, there are but few particulars; but from them it may be gathered that the use of fossil coal during that period was steadily increasing, though many persons were reluctant to employ it for culinary purposes, and who still preferred to see the log or the faggot blaze upon their social hearth. The increasing scarcity and consequent dearness of wood towards the latter end of the reign of Queen Elizabeth, contributed materially to remove the prejudice which had previously existed against the use of fossil coal in families; and the " black diamonds" of the North, whose brightness had hereto-

* In those years coals cost the abbey 3s. 4d. a chalder; and at the same period the brethren paid, for sixty fothers or cart-loads of turves—" pro 60 plaustris turbarum"—10s., being at the rate of 2d. a fother.—(Charlton's Hist. of Whitby, p. 260, quoted by Brand.)

† Either the chalders must have been less or the keels larger than at the present time. The legal burthen of a keel is now 8 Newcastle chalders, of 53 cwt. each, or 21½ tons. The medium weight of a London chalder—36 Winchester bushels—is 25½ cwt. From experiments made by Mr. Buddle, in 1830, it was found that a London chalder of Stewart's Walls End coals weighed 26 cwt. 0 qrs. 18 lbs. ; and the same quantity of Russell's Walls End only 25 cwt. Those were the highest and the lowest weights of seven different kinds that were tried.—(Report of the Commons' Committee on the Coal Trade, p. 341 and p. 392.)

fore been chiefly confined to the forge, the smithy, the brew-house, and the dye-house, or to the kitchen of the "vitailler and coke," were now allowed to display their light and heat in the parlours of noble lords and wealthy merchants; and high-born ladies and worshipful dames took their slice of the round or cut of the sirloin, without inquiring whether they were "sod or roasted with a sea-coale fire," or with a fire of wood *.

In 1582, Queen Elizabeth having obtained a lease for ninety-nine years, from Richard Barnes, Bishop of Durham, of the manors of Gateshead and Whickham, with their coal mines, common wastes, and parks, transferred it to her favourite, Dudley, Earl of Leicester, who assigned it, for the sum of 10,000*l.*, to Thomas Sutton, Esq., the founder of the Charter-house, who again assigned it to Sir William Riddell and others, for the use of the mayor and burgesses of Newcastle. The large sum paid to Sutton for this lease, whose chief value consisted in the privilege of working the mines, sufficiently proves the ardour with which the coal trade began to be prosecuted at that period. This lease, usually termed the Grand Lease, being again assigned to a company of coal-owners, who had engrossed several other collieries on the Tyne, a partial monopoly was thus created, and between 1582 and 1590, coals had advanced from 6*s.* to 9*s.* a chalder. In consequence of this advance in the price of an article which was daily becoming of greater necessity and more general use, the Lord Mayor of London complained to the Lord Treasurer Burleigh against the town of Newcastle, setting forth the manner in which the trade was engrossed by a few persons, and praying that all collieries might be opened and worked, and that the price of coals should not exceed 7*s.* a chalder. The lord mayor, who certainly asked for more than the treasurer could either grant or enforce, appears to have gained nothing by the application. Brand, in his History of Newcastle, vol. ii. p. 269, says that "in the latter end of the reign of Queen Elizabeth the duty of the town of Newcastle upon Tyne on coals, at four-pence per chaldron, appears to have brought in 10,000*l.* per annum to that corporation." This information, wherever he obtained it, is evidently incorrect; for the quantity shipped, to raise such a sum, must have been 600,000 chalders, London measure, which is 100,000 chalders more than was exported from Newcastle in 1699†, when the coal-trade had certainly much increased. In a subsequent page Brand says, that in 1624 the sum raised, at four-pence a chalder on all the coals sent from Newcastle, Sunderland, and Blyth, amounted to only 3200*l.*,

* "Within thirty yeares last past, the nice dames of London would not come into any house or roome where sea-coales were burned; nor willingly eat of the meat that was either sod or roasted with sea-coale fire."—(Stowe's Annales, or Generall Chronicle of England, 1615.)

‡ In 1699 the quantity of coals exported from Newcastle was 200,000 chalders, which is less than 400,000 chalders London measure; the proportion between a Newcastle and a London chalder being as 68 to 36.

which gives a total of only 192,000 chalders. In 1602 there were twenty-eight acting hoastmen, or fitters*, in Newcastle, who in that year agreed to vend 9080 *tens* of coals, and to find 85 keels for the purpose of conveying the coals to the ships. In 1616 the vend was 13,675 tens, and in 1622 it had increased 14,420 tens. A ten is a local term, signifying originally ten score of baskets or corves of coals, each score consisting of twenty or twenty-one. The ten of the present day is not a fixed quantity, but varies between seventeen and twenty-three chalders, Newcastle measure†. Supposing each corve in 1602 to have contained sixteen pecks, or four bushels; then each ten, consisting of two hundred corves, would be rather more than twenty-two London chalders; and the whole shipment of 9080 tens, in the above year, would amount to 199,760 London chalders, a quantity which appears to be too great.

In 1615, there were four hundred sail of ships in the coal trade, one half of which were employed in conveying coals to London, and the other half in supplying other places in England. In 1633, coals were sold at Newcastle, at 9s. a chalder, Newcastle measure; and in 1635, at 10s. a chalder. In 1638, a company of coal-monopolisers, incorporated in London by Charles I., were charged to sell their coals at a price not exceeding 17s. the London chalder in summer, and 19s. in winter.

In January, 1642-3, the counties of Northumberland and Durham, being then in the power of the king's party, the parliament prohibited ships from bringing coals or salt to London from Newcastle, Sunderland, or Blyth, which occasioned so great a scarcity of coals in the metropolis, that a chalder, in the latter end of that year, sold for 4l. The Scottish army under the Earl of Leven having advanced towards Newcastle, in August 1644, for the purpose of besieging it, the Marquis of Newcastle, the royalist commander, ordered the coal mines to be fired; but through the activity of the Scottish general, and probably through the relutance of the inhabitants to assist in destroying their own means of subsistence, his design was frustrated. In 1655, coals were sold in London at rather more

* A *fitter* is a person who keeps an office for the sale of coals to ships. In 1600 the fitters, or coal-salesmen, under the name of Hoastmen, were incorporated, by a charter of Queen Elizabeth.

† The evidence of Mr. Buddle, one of the most experienced viewers in the north of England, when explaining the meaning of a *ten* before the committee of the House of Commons on the coal trade, 1830, must have been misreported. After having explained that "the *ten* ranges from $17\frac{1}{4}$ chaldrons to about 22 to 23," he is made to say that "440 bolls, each containing 36 gallons Winchester measure, is the most usual ten," which does not agree with his previous statement; for, allowing a Newcastle chalder to be equal to 68 bushels, then 440 bolls, of 36 gallons or $4\frac{1}{2}$ bushels each, would be equal to $29\frac{2}{17}$ Newcastle chalders. In the same page Mr. Buddle is made to say, that "in the infant state of the coal trade, the ordinary size of a corf or basket was about two bolls," each boll containing 36 gallons, which can scarcely be correct. The largest corves now used contain only 24 pecks, or 48 gallons dry measure.—(Report of the Select Committee on the Coal Trade, 1830, p. 271.)

than 20s. a chalder; and in that year three hundred and twenty keels are said to have been employed on the Tyne, each of which carried during the year 800 chalders, Newcastle measure, to be put on board of ship, thus making the whole quantity vended equal to 256,000 Newcastle, or 480,000 London chalders, reckoning the Newcastle chalder to be to the London chalder as fifteen to eight. This account is either much exaggerated, or another, which Brand refers to, very much underrated. By the latter it appears that the average export of coals from Newcastle, between 1704 and 1711, was only 178,143 chalders, Newcastle measure; and the coal trade, between 1655 and 1711, had certainly not decreased, but on the contrary; for in 1704, there were four hundred keels employed on the Tyne, while in 1655 there were only three hundred and twenty. In 1703, the masters of the Trinity House of Newcastle, in answer to an enquiry of the House of Commons, stated that six hundred ships, each carrying eighty Newcastle chalders, and navigated by four thousand five hundred men and boys, were required for carrying on the coal trade; and they added that the above number, "both of ships and men, had been engaged therein for the three years last past."

According to Hutton's plan of Newcastle upon Tyne, published in 1772, there were then about four hundred and fifty keels employed in the coal trade; and the average export of coals about that period is given as follows:—

Coastwise.	Foreign.
330,200	21,690 Chalders, Newcastle measure.

The following return will show the progress of the coal trade from the Tyne, since the beginning of the present century. The chalders are Newcastle measure.

Years.	Coastwise.	Foreign.
1800	537,793	47,487 Chald.
1810	623,299	17,253
1820	756,513	44,826
1828	725,082	59,325

In 1835, the total quantity of coals exported from the Tyne was 2,558,571 tons, of which 297,170 tons were shipped for foreign ports *.

* The following account shows the proportion which the quantity of coals imported into London bears to the population of that city and its vicinity:—

	Population.	Coals imported.
1801	818,129	859,738 London chalders.
1811	953,276	993,182
1821	1,144,531	1,161,784

The average annual consumption was nine chalders for eight persons previous to the general establishment of gas works; and since it has increased to ten chalders.—(C. Perkins, Esq., evidence before the Lords' Committee on the Coal Trade, 1829, p. 101.)

In 1829, there were forty-one working collieries on the Tyne, twenty-three on the north side, and eighteen on the south; and the total number of persons employed in them, in working the coal, and conveying it to the water side, was as follows:—

	Men.		Boys.			Together.
Employed under ground	4,937	.	3,554	.	.	8,491
Employed above ground	2,745	.	718	.	.	3,463
Total			.	.	.	11,954

The pits lie on each side of the Tyne, from within two miles of its mouth, to sixteen or eighteen miles up the river. Some are within a quarter of a mile of the water side, and others are nearly eight miles distant. The coals are conveyed from the pits to the staiths by the river side, in waggons, containing 53cwt. each, and running upon rail-ways. In one colliery, Fawdon, which lies about four miles to the north west of Newcastle, and which delivers its coals at the river side about four miles to the eastward of that town, the rail-way, or as it is usually called, the waggon-way, is about ten miles long. This waggon-way is the longest on the Tyne; there are, however, several on both sides of the river, from four to eight miles long.

Waggon ways appear to have been first introduced about 1670, previous to which time the coals used to be conveyed from the pits to the water side in carts. Formerly the rails of the waggon-ways—that is, the parallel lines upon which the wheels of the waggon run—used to be made of wood; but latterly, cast-iron rails have been generally adopted. About twenty years ago, a steam carriage was first tried on one of the rail-ways, for the purpose of drawing the waggons from the pit-mouth to the water side; but it travelled so slowly, and was so often out of order, that the experiment, though it has led to such important consequences as steam carriages running at the rate of thirty miles an hour on the Manchester and Liverpool railway, could scarcely be called successful, since after a few months' trial, the steam carriage was laid aside on that waggon-way, and the old mode, of waggons drawn by horses, resumed. It was only in 1823, that Mr. George Stephenson succeeded in constructing a steam carriage for the Hetton Coal Company, that could travel at the rate of eight miles an hour; and in 1824, Mr. Nicholas Wood, a north country engineer, declared, in a work on rail-roads, that it was hopeless to expect a greater degree of speed than nine miles an hour. This gentleman, a friend of Mr. Stephenson's, was one of the umpires at the trial of the steam carriages on the Manchester and Liverpool rail-way in 1830; and while there as a judge received a practical proof of the fallacy of his own opinion, with respect to the maximum speed of locomotive engines.

G

From such staiths as are above Newcastle bridge, all coals are conveyed in keels to the lower parts of the river, chiefly to Shields, and there cast into ships; and it not unfrequently happens that three men and a boy row a loaden keel from Blaydon or Dunstan to Shields—a distance of about fourteen miles—and, after casting eight chalders or twenty-two tons of coal, into a ship, return to the staith with the next flood tide, completing the trip within fourteen hours. For strength and activity, the keelmen of the Tyne are perhaps the finest body of men in the kingdom. From the evidence of Mr. Buddle, given before the Lords' Committee on the Coal Trade in 1829, it appears that the keelmen of the Tyne have less per chalder for conveying the coals seven or eight miles, and then casting them into a ship, than the London lighterman or barge-owner has for merely carrying them from the ship's side to the wharf. Between Newcastle and Shields—more especially in the lower part of the river within six miles of its mouth, a considerable number of vessels take their coals on board direct from the staith, and thus save the charge of having them conveyed by keels. At some staiths, the waggon is lowered down to the ship's deck, and a bolt being withdrawn, its bottom, which moves upon hinges, falls outward, and the coals are shot at once into the hold. Another mode is to unbolt the bottom of the waggon at the top of the staith, and to allow the coals to run down into the vessel's hold by an inclined plane of wood, with a high ledge at each side, called a *spout*. In consequence of the practice of loading ships directly at the staiths becoming daily more general, the number of keelmen employed on the Tyne appears to be decreasing.

The amount of capital employed in the collieries which supply the coals vended on the Tyne was estimated by Mr. Buddle, in 1828, at a million and a half; and the value of the shipping, keels, and river craft employed in the coal trade of the Tyne, cannot fairly be estimated at a less sum. Supposing the annual return of this aggregate capital of three millions to be eight per cent. it would seem that the coal trade of the Tyne yields to the owners of collieries and of ships a yearly revenue of 240,000*l.* besides giving employment to about 22,000 pitmen, keelmen, coal-trimmers, and seamen.

> What more may heaven do for earthly man,
> Than thus to pour out plenty in their laps,
> Ripping the bowels of the earth for them,
> Making the sea their servants, and the winds
> To drive their substance with successful blasts ?

According to the conclusions of some of our most eminent geologists *, founded on data supplied by practical men, it appears probable, that in about four hundred

* Rev. Dr. Buckland, professor of Geology at Oxford, the Rev. Adam Sedgwick, Woodwardian professor of Geology at Cambridge, and Mr. Bakewell.

years, at the present rate of working, the most productive mines in the great coal field of Northumberland and Durham will be exhausted. It would be useless to speculate on what will be the condition of Newcastle when her coal-trade, at present her chief dependance, shall have become extinct. For an evil so far remote—if evil it shall then be—man's limited faculties neither enable him to foresee consequences, nor to provide a remedy; for by the time that this exhaustion shall have taken place, the active industry of the district will have doubtless sought another channel; and when Northumberland and Durham, ceasing to be exporting counties, shall derive their supply of coals from Wales by some great south-western railway—at present, wonderful to say, *unprojected*— their inhabitants, under the care of that Power " who made and loveth all," and who attends equally to the welfare of his creatures in all ages, will be as happy as those of the present generation.

The Tyne is navigable as high up as Newcastle, about ten miles from its mouth, for vessels of 250 tons burthen, though in some places between Newcastle and Shields, even in the middle of the stream, its depth does not exceed four feet at low water. A little below Hebburn quay, about half-way between Newcastle and Shields, it is not unusual to see three or four small steam-boats, which do not draw more than three feet water, lying aground in the very mid-channel at the last quarter ebb, and waiting for the flood-tide to set them afloat. A few years ago the corporation of Newcastle, as conservators of the river Tyne, employed a steam boat to *scratch* away the sand in shallow places, by means of a kind of harrow, which she towed after her. Since the accession of the present corporation to office, a dredging machine has been ordered, and if they proceed in their plans for the improvement of the river as they have begun, they will merit the thanks of every person interested in the trade of the town.

The principal exports from Newcastle, besides coals, are pig and sheet lead; anchors, and chain-cables, with other articles of wrought iron; bottles, plate and crown glass; brown and white paper; common leather gloves, manufactured at Hexham; leather; hams and butter; grindstones, obtained on Gateshead Fell; fire-bricks; alkalies; soap; and Epsom salts. The preceding list comprises the principal articles which constitute the cargo of a Newcastle trading vessel proceeding to London.

In 1835, there cleared from the Custom House at Newcastle for foreign ports:—

	Ships	Tonnage
British	1,077	178,907
Foreign	827	92,879

Entered from foreign ports during the same year:—

	Ships	Tonnage
British	609	102,035
Foreign	459	50,097

In 1835 there cleared coastwise 13,061 ships, the tonnage of which was 1,740,362; and the quantity of coals exported was 2,261,401 tons, coastwise; and 297,170 tons, foreign. In the same year the quantity of lead exported was 100,389 pigs, each weighing from 1 to 1¹ cwt.; with 2,087 tons of sheet lead, shot, and white lead for the use of painters.

In 1834, the sum received on account of customs was 286,000*l.*; and in 1835, 289,000*l**. The number of vessels registered in the Port of Newcastle in January 1836, was—   Ships, 1,076   211,173 tons.

	Ships	Tonnage
Deducting for North Shields	270	62,934
South Shields	286	66,747
Blyth & Seaton Sluice	84	14,450
	—— 640	———— 144,131
Leaving for the Town of Newcastle and its neighbourhood Ships,	436	67,042 tons.

In January, 1836, there were 87 Steam Boats belonging to Newcastle, with an aggregate tonnage of 1,781 tons. Of this number one is 87, and another 74 tons. Most of the others are from 16 to 24 tons each. The small boats are employed in conveying passengers between Newcastle and Shields, and in towing ships up and down the river and out to sea. A large steam-packet belonging to the General Steam Navigation Company usually runs between London and New-castle during the summer; and during the same season, the Ardincaple steam packet leaves Newcastle for Leith twice a week. Two other steam packets have this season plied regularly between Newcastle and Hull, and Newcastle and Stockton.

Within the last ten or twelve years the appearance of Newcastle has been much improved, by the formation of new streets, consisting of commodious shops and handsome dwelling-houses; and by the erection of several large public buildings, among which the library of the Literary and Philosophical Society, in Westgate-street; the Arcade, in Pilgrim-street; and the New Church, near the Barras Bridge, may be mentioned as the most conspicuous. The new market-place, which was opened last year for the sale of butcher-meat and vegetables, is one of the most elegant, convenient, and spacious in the kingdom. The tide of improve-

---

* The foreign import trade of Newcastle compared with the great tonnage of the port, is small. In 1835 there was paid on account of Customs at,

London	.	.	.	£11,773,000
Liverpool	.	.	.	4,273,000
Bristol	.	.	.	1,117,000
Hull	.	.	.	721,000

ment still continues to flow, and at the present time two or three new streets are in course of erection.   In 1829, an act of parliament having been obtained for the construction of a railway between Newcastle and Carlisle, the work was almost immediately commenced; and forty-three miles are already completed; that is, twenty-three miles, from Blaydon, about four miles above Newcastle, westward, to Haydon Bridge; and twenty miles, from Carlisle, eastward, to Greenhead.   The whole length of the line is sixty-one miles, and it is expected that the unfinished portion will be completed in little more than a year.   This railway, which will connect the eastern and western sea, and thus materially facilitate the commercial intercourse of Newcastle with Whitehaven and Liverpool, as well as with Ireland, appears likely to be of great advantage, not only to the two towns situated at its extremities, but also to every place within the vicinity of its line.

In 1831, the population of Newcastle was 42,760.   The present members of parliament for the town are, William Ord, Esq., and John Hodgson, Esq.; the latter gentleman having been returned in the room of Sir Matthew White Ridley, Bart., who died on the 15th July last, after having represented the town for twenty-four years; and who, during the whole of that period, never swerved from the principles which he professed at his first election.   He closed his parliamentary career as he began it.   He was a slave to no party; he truckled to no minister for place; and he sought not to catch the fickle breath of popular applause by the hypocritical disavowal of opinions which he believed to be true.   In private life he lived like what he was,—an English gentleman.   He was a warm patron of the fine arts, and he ever showed himself able to appreciate the productions of genius, and willing to assist in its promotion.

Newcastle lies about 372 miles to the northward of London, and 117 miles to the southward of Edinburgh, in 54° 58' 30" north latitude, and 1° 37' 30" west longitude.   It is high water at Newcastle bridge about an hour later than at Tynemouth bar.   The average rise of spring tides is about 11 feet 7 inches; of neaps, 7 feet 2 inches; and the tide flows there for about five hours, and ebbs for about seven.

The borough of Gateshead, which lies on the south side of the Tyne, and is connected with Newcastle by a bridge of nine arches, returns one member to parliament under the Reform Bill.   The present member is Cuthbert Rippon, Esq., of Stanhope Castle.   In 1831, the population of the borough and its precincts was 15,177.

BAMBROUGH CASTLE.—FROM THE SOUTH-EAST.

Sir Walter Scott, in his description of the voyage of the abbess of Whitby and her nuns to Holy Island, in the second canto of Marmion, thus speaks of them as noticing Bambrough Castle:

> Thy tower, proud Bambrough, marked they there,
> King Ida's castle, huge and square,
> From its tall rock look grimly down,
> And on the swelling ocean frown.

The view which Balmer, with his usual effect, has given of Bambrough Castle from the south-east, is that which the reverend mother and her five fair nuns might be supposed to contemplate on entering the channel between the great Farn island and the main-land, and when about half a mile from the shore. The stranded vessel, however, must not be supposed to be of the age of Henry VIII., when the abbess made her voyage; for she is evidently a light collier of the present day, whose captain, probably, in running for Skate Roads in a strong south-east gale, had stood too close in-shore in passing through the Fare-way, and laid her snugly up on Bambrough Sands. The Holy Island fishing-boats that are seen—for no fishermen dwell at the village of Bambrough—would seem to indicate that their owners expect a job in assisting to get her off.

Bambrough, which is now a small village, was a place of considerable import-ance during the Saxon period. King Ida, who ascended the throne of Bernicia in 559, first built a castle there, which he is said to have named Bebban-burgh, in honour of his queen, Bebba. It has been conjectured by Wallis, in his history of Northumberland, that the Keep, or great tower, is of Roman original; but Grose, with greater probability, considers it to have been built by the Normans. In 1095 Robert Mowbray, Earl of Northumberland, having rebelled against William Rufus, retired to Bambrough Castle, whither he was followed by Henry, the King's brother, and closely besieged. After the siege had continued some time, Mowbray left the castle in the charge of his kinsman Morel, who continued to defend it with great bravery. The Earl being afterwards seized at Tynemouth, where he had taken sanctuary, Henry caused him to be brought to Bambrough, and there showing him before the walls of the castle, he threatened to put out his eyes if it were not immediately delivered up—a proceeding which caused Morel to surrender the place forthwith.

Drawn by G. Balmer.

Engraved by W. Finden.

BAMBOROUGH.

FROM THE SOUTH EAST.

London, Published 1836, by Charles Tilt, 86, Fleet Street.

Drawn by G. Balmer.

Engraved by E. Finden.

BAMBOROUGH.

FROM THE NORTH WEST.

London, Published 1836, by Charles. Tilt. 86. Fleet Street

BAMBROUGH CASTLE.—FROM THE NORTH-WEST.

From the reign of William Rufus till about the middle of the fifteenth century, Bambrough Castle, as if it were a place too important to be in the hands of a subject, appears to have continued in the possession of the crown, by whom a governor was appointed. In the frequent contests between the houses of York and Lancaster, it sustained great damage; and as it was not repaired either by Henry VII. or his successor, it ceased about the beginning of the sixteenth century to be a fortress of importance. In 1575 Sir John Foster, warden of the Middle Marches, was governor of Bambrough Castle; and one of his descendants received a grant of the old building from James I. It continued in the possession of this family till the commencement of the reign of George I., when it was forfeited through the treason of Thomas Foster, Esq., M.P. for Northumberland, better known as General Foster, who in 1715 took up arms in favour of the Pretender.

The Manor and Castle of Bambrough were afterwards purchased of the crown by Nathaniel, Lord Crewe, Bishop of Durham, who was married to Foster's aunt. Lord Crewe, at his decease in 1720, left the above property, with other valuable estates, to trustees to be applied to charitable uses. In compliance with the intentions of the testator, a noble charity is established at Bambrough for the succour of shipwrecked seamen, the education of children, and the relief of indigent persons. In 1757 part of the Keep being ready to fall down, the Rev. Thomas Sharp, Archdeacon of Northumberland, and one of Lord Crewe's trustees, caused it to be repaired, "merely because it had been a sea-mark for ages, and as such beneficial to the publick." The Rev. Thomas Sharp being succeeded in the trusteeship as well as in the archdeaconry by his son, the Rev. John Sharp, D.D., the latter, who was also perpetual curate of Bambrough, continued to make further repairs; and he also caused an immense quantity of sand, which had accumulated in the castle-yard, to be cleared away. To this gentleman, who was a brother of the amiable Granville Sharp, the present arrangements of the charity are chiefly owing. At the castle, blocks and tackles, anchors, cables, warps, and other articles, are kept for the use of stranded vessels. In stormy weather two men patrol the coast for eight miles, day and night, in order to look out for vessels in distress, and during a fog a bell is rung at intervals from the castle, and a gun fired every quarter of an hour, as a warning to such ships as may be near the coast. Flour and groceries are sold to poor families at a reduced rate, and twenty poor girls are boarded and educated within the castle.

CASTLE OF HOLY ISLAND, AND LINDISFARN ABBEY.

In the engraving which is marked " Holy Island Castle," the view is taken from the eastward on entering the harbour. To the right is the castle; beyond which, towards the centre of the view, are seen the ruins of the abbey. The setting sun sheds a warm yet mellow light over land and sea; and as evening is approaching, and the breeze freshening with the flood tide—for it is evident from the inward swell that the tide is flowing—the fishermen are seen making for the shore. The boats bound merrily before the wind, and

> —— the waves, that murmur in their glee,
> All hurrying in a joyful band,
> Come dancing from the sea.

The painter when he made his sketch must have thoroughly felt the beauty of the scene, and been touched with the influence of the hour :—

> O Hesperus, thou bringest all good things!

and inspirest poets to sing, and artists to paint the charms of eve's sweet hour in words and colours that never die—for once felt and communicated, they become impressed on the heart and soul of man, and live and bloom there for ever.

Holy Island, which is about two miles and a half long, and about two miles broad, lies off the Northumberland coast. On the south it is separated from the main-land by a deep channel about a mile broad. To the north-west it is connected with the main-land by a sand, which is dry at low water, and by which carts and passengers can pass to and from the island. Speed says that the Britons named it " Inis Medicante, for that, in manner of an island, it twice every day suffreth an extraordinarie inundation and overflowing of the ocean, which, returning unto her watery habitation, twice likewise makes it continent to the land, and laies the shoare bare againe, as before." It was called Lindisfarn by the Saxons; and in after times, from the celebrity of its monastery, and the holy men who had lived there, it acquired the name of Holy Island.

About 635, a church, of wood and thatched with reeds, was first built at Lindisfarn, by Aidan, a Scottish monk from the Isle of Iona, who exercised the office of bishop in Northumberland. It was afterwards built of stone, and gave title to a bishop, until the see was removed to Durham in 995. The monastery continued as a cell, dependent on Durham, till it was suppressed by Henry VIII. A considerable part of the old church, with circular arches in what is termed the Saxon style, is yet standing, and forms, with the adjacent ruins, a most picturesque object.

Drawn by G. Balmer.

Engraved by E. Finden.

HOLY ISLAND CASTLE.

London. Published 1836. by Charles Tilt. 86. Fleet Street.

Drawn by G. Balmer.

Engraved by E. Finden.

CASTLE OF HOLY ISLAND.

FROM THE WEST.

London Published 1836 by Charles Tilt 86 Fleet Street.

CASTLE OF HOLY ISLAND.—FROM THE WESTWARD.

THE Castle of Holy Island stands on a steep rock, about half a mile to the eastward of the Abbey. It is wholly inaccessible, except by a winding pass cut through the rock on the south side. The date of its foundation is unknown; but it is supposed to have been first built by the monks, as a place of refuge against the piratical attacks of the Danes, who frequently annoyed them, and twice burnt their abbey. The most memorable event in the meagre history of this castle is its capture for the Pretender, by two men, Launcelot Errington, and his nephew Mark, in 1715. The garrison at that time consisted of a serjeant, a corporal, and ten or twelve men. Errington, who was master of a little vessel then lying in the harbour, invited the serjeant, and such of his men as were not on duty, to drink with him on board of his ship. The invitation being accepted, he plied them so well with brandy, as to render them incapable of opposition. Framing an excuse for going ashore, he proceeded to the castle with his nephew, and succeeded in turning out the old gunner, the corporal, and two soldiers, being all that were on duty. He then shut the gates, and hoisted the Pretender's colours; but being disappointed in the succour which he expected, and a party of the king's troops arriving from Berwick, he and his nephew made their escape over the castle walls, and endeavoured to conceal themselves among the rocks and sea-weed, to the south-eastward of the castle, till it was dark, when they intended to swim to the main-land. In consequence of the rising of the tide, they were obliged to swim while it was yet light, and being perceived by the soldiers, they were taken, and conveyed to Berwick gaol; from which however they broke out before they were brought to trial, and escaped to France. On the suppression of the rebellion they took the benefit of the general pardon, and returned to England.

Holy Island is of an irregular form. Its greatest length, including a low sandy point, which stretches out towards the west-north-west, is about two and a half miles. Its mean breadth does not exceed a mile and a half. The village, or as it is usually called, " the town," lies at a short distance to the northward of the ruins of the monastery, and is chiefly inhabited by fishermen, about two-thirds of whom are also licensed by the Trinity-house at Newcastle to act as pilots for their

H

own harbour and the adjacent coast.   In 1831 the population of Holy Island was
836.

The fishery for cod, ling, and haddock is usually carried on in cobles*, of which
there are about sixty belonging to the island.   A great quantity of the fish thus
caught is sent to London in smacks, employed by fishmongers or salesmen there,
who annually contract with the fishermen to pay them so much per score for all the
fish sent during the season.   From December to April many lobsters are caught
off Holy Island, nearly the whole of which are sent to London by contract at
twelve shillings a score.

For the herring-fishery boats of a larger size are employed.   They are from
thirty to thirty-six feet long, about eleven feet broad, and from four and a half to
five feet deep.   They carry two lug sails, and have no deck.   The herring-fishery
commences off Holy Island about the twentieth of July, and usually terminates
about the first week in September.   Many herrings are caught in the Fare-way,
between the Farn islands and the mainland; but the principal fishery for them is
generally a little to the southward of the Staples, a cluster of small islands which
lie from two to three miles to the eastward of the Farns.   Most of the herrings
caught by the Holy Island fishermen are taken to Berwick to be cured, and are
thence chiefly exported to London, Hull, and Newcastle.

On the beach to the westward of the island the fossils called St. Cuthbert's
beads—the *entrochi* of naturalists—are found.   They are also to be observed in
the cliff to the north-east.   A rock which lies at a short distance from the south-west
point of the island is called St. Cuthbert's rock, where in former times superstition
feigned that the saint was wont to sit and

" frame
The sea-born beads that bear his name."

This article of popular credulity has, however, been long exploded, and the fisherman when he hears the stones rattle on the beach from the force of the waves,
no longer imagines that the sound proceeds from the saint's hammer.

Holy Island harbour is a small bay or haven on the south side of the island,
between the castle and the ruins of the monastery.   On the bar, which is about
a mile distant from the town, there is about nine feet at low water at spring
tides.   The flood at spring tides sets with a strong current in the channel between

---

* Cobles are very generally employed in the coast fishery from the Tweed to the Humber.   They
are sharp and wedge-shaped at the bow, and flat-bottomed towards the stern.   They have only one mast,
stepped close forward, on which a lug sail is set.   They are excellent sea-boats, and, for their size, carry
a large sail, which they are in a great measure enabled to do from the length of their rudder, which
extends about three feet perpendicularly below the line of the boat's bottom.   The usual length of a
Holy Island coble is from twenty-five to twenty-seven feet over all.

the island and the mainland; and at high water there is twenty-four feet on the bar. There is no light-house on Holy Island, but there is a beacon on the " Heugh,"—a hill between the town and the harbour—on which, in bad weather, when pilots cannot get off, a flag is hoisted during the time of tide that ships may safely enter. In gales of wind from the eastward, coasting vessels sometimes seek shelter in Holy Island harbour, and find good anchorage before the town in three fathoms at low water. It is high water in Holy Island harbour at half-past two at the full and change of the moon; and the rise of spring tides is eighteen feet; of neaps eleven.

The Staples and Farn islands, with the rocks and shoals between them and Holy Island, render the in-shore navigation of the coast of Northumberland, from North Sunderland point to the mouth of the Tweed, extremely intricate and hazardous; and the corporation of the Trinity House, London, caution all masters of ships, and especially strangers to the coast, not to attempt sailing within those islands and shoals; more particularly on account of the various settings of the rapid tide which runs in the different sounds between the islands.

On the Longstone, one of the most easterly of the Staples, there is a revolving light to warn the seaman of his danger; and there is another of the same kind on the great Farn island, which is the one nearest to the shore. These lights, which appear in their greatest brightness once a minute, and are seen all round, bear from each other W. S. W. and E. N. E., and when seen in a line, lead directly over the Naivestone, the easternmost of the Staples, and which is not visible until two hours after high water. Near the northern extremity of the Great Farn there is also another light, which is stationary, and only visible from the north. When the two lights on this island are seen in a line, bearing nearly S. by E., and N. by W. they lead through the sound, between the Goldstone and the rock called Arthur's Seat, near Holy Island, and directly over the Megstone, a rock which lies about a mile north by west of the Great Farn.

A visit to the Farn and Staple islands, from Bambrough or Holy Island, forms a pleasant excursion in fine weather, more especially when the eider ducks are sitting, which is from about the middle of May to the latter end of July. These birds, which are seldom seen, and do not breed, to the southward of the Farn islands, are also known in the neighbourhood by the name of St. Cuthbert's ducks. Their eggs, and the fine down with which they line their nests, are collected and sold by the person who rents the islands, which are also the haunt of several other species of water-fowl, such as the sheldrake, the cormorant, and the shag, with auks, guillemots, terns, and gulls. Solan geese also visit the Farn islands, but do not breed there, commonly making their appearance early in spring, and departing before May.

H 2

DUNSTANBROUGH CASTLE.—FROM THE EASTWARD.

In the above-named engraving a view is presented of the principal remaining tower of Dunstanbrough Castle, as seen from the sea at the distance of about a mile; and whoever has seen it at that distance in a blustering day, towards the latter end of October, will immediately acknowledge the fidelity of the artist's delineation *. Though the Abbess of Whitby and her nuns, in their fabled voyage to Holy Island, passed the place in summer, and in fine weather, yet they seem to have been near enough to be sensible of the danger of too close an approach to its " wave-worn steep," for Sir Walter Scott, in Marmion, Canto II., relates that,

> " They crossed themselves, to hear
> The whitening breakers sound so near,
> Where, boiling through the rocks, they roar
> On Dunstanborough's caverned shore."

Dunstanbrough Castle, in the county of Northumberland, is situated about seven miles north-east of Alnwick, and about two miles north by east of Howick, the seat of Earl Grey. Of the keep there are no vestiges remaining; and it is even questionable if it had ever been completed. Thomas, Earl of Lancaster, who is generally considered to have been the founder of the present castle, only obtained the king's licence to crenelate, or fortify, his house at Dunstanbrough in 1316; and as he was beheaded at Pontefract in 1321, and in the intermediate years had been much engaged, in the south, in rebellion against Edward II., it is not unlikely that the keep might be unfinished at his decease, and never afterwards completed. Of Dunstanbrough Castle history records little that is interesting. In 1464 it was held, after the battle of Hexham, for Henry VI., by Sir Peter de Bressy, and a party of Frenchmen; but was taken, after a vigorous defence, by Ralph Lord Ogle, Edmund and Richard de Craster, John Manners, and Gilbert de Errington, all Northumbrians, and partisans of Edward IV. From this period, the castle, which was dismantled by the victors, is never mentioned in the history of the county as the scene of any memorable event. It was in the possession of the crown in the 10th of Elizabeth, but was granted by James I. to Sir William Grey, afterwards Lord Grey of Wark. It is now the property of the Earl of Tankerville, whose ancestor, Charles Lord Ossulston, became possessed of it in 1701, through his marriage with the daughter and heiress of Ford Grey, Earl of Tankerville, son of Lord Grey of Wark.

* Through an oversight, this view, in the Engraving, is said to be drawn by " G. Balmer," instead of " J. D. Harding;" and a similar mistake has been made in the view of Blyth.

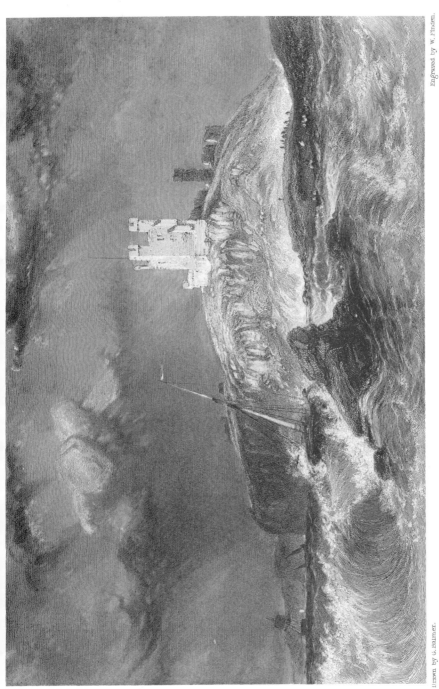

Drawn by G. Balmer.

Engraved by W. Finden.

DUNSTANBOROUGH CASTLE.

FROM THE EASTWARD.

London, Published 1836, by Charles Tilt, 86, Fleet Street.

Drawn by G. Balmer.   Engraved by F. Finden.

DUNSTANBOROUGH CASTLE.

London, Published 1836, by Charles Tilt, 86, Fleet Street.

DUNSTANBROUGH CASTLE.—MOONLIGHT.

In the vignette engraving of Dunstanbrough by moonlight, the incident of a wreck coming ashore among the rocks at the foot of the castle is introduced with striking effect. The masts of the vessel are seen dashed against the rocks. To the left are fishermen assisting such of the crew as have escaped to ascend the cliff; while to the right are seen people with torches from the adjacent country hastening towards the scene of destruction. The moon appears as if " wading* " through the clouds, and the old tower, itself the wreck of time, appropriately occupies the centre of the view.

" On the brink of the cliff to the sea," says a writer describing Dunstanbrough Castle, " appear the remains of a very strong wall; indeed it is probable the whole area was originally so enclosed. The heavy seas which break upon the rocks of the north-west point have torn them much, and it appears as if the area had been originally of greater extent than at present, many separate columns of rock standing near the cliffs, which, some ages ago, may have been joined to the mainland. . . . . Immediately below this tower [that which is seen in the engraving] is a gully or passage, of perpendicular sides, formed in the rocks, about sixty yards in length, and forty feet deep, where the sea makes a dreadful inset, breaking into foam with a tremendous noise: the spray occasioned thereby is driven within the castle walls. This place is called by the country people the *Rumble Churn*†." It is to this chasm that Sir Walter Scott alludes when he speaks of " Dunstanborough's caverned shore," in the lines quoted from Marmion in a preceding page.

In the neighbourhood of Dunstanbrough there is a legendary tale yet current, though no longer at its ancient value, of a knight who, many centuries ago, discovered a place of enchantment in the vaults of the castle; but who, failing to break the spell, through inattention to certain mysterious instructions given to him, is doomed to seek for ever amid the ruins for the entrance to the enchanted apartment. M. G. Lewis, in the " Tales of Wonder," has versified this story under the title of " Sir Guy, the Seeker," adding to it certain embellishments of his own, and, among other matters, introducing a description of the Rumble Churn.

The principal parts of Dunstanbrough Castle at present standing are the outer walls to the south and west, with the tower overlooking the sea, and a gateway towards the south, defended by two circular towers. The area inclosed by the walls and the cliff is about nine acres. It is under cultivation; and in the additions to Camden it is said to have produced in one year two hundred and forty bushels of corn, besides several loads of hay.

* The moon is said to " wade " when she seems as if toilfully making her way through a succession clouds, which flit rapidly past her.

† History of Northumberland, vol. i. p. 594. Edit. 1810.

BLYTH.

THE view of Blyth, or more properly of the entrance to the harbour, is taken from the north side of the river, and looking towards the south-east. The cottages seen in the fore-ground are in North Blyth, which consists only of a few houses, chiefly occupied by fishermen and pilots. On the opposite side of the river are seen the lighthouse of stone, and the " basket light " to the left of it, in which lights are exhibited at night when there is eight feet water on the bar.

Blyth, which is a small sea-port town, on the coast of Northumberland, and about thirteen miles north-east of Newcastle, derives its name from the river Blyth, on the south side of which it is built. The principal trade of Blyth is in coals, of which about 120,000 tons are now annually exported. The earliest notice of Blyth as a harbour occurs in Bishop Hatfield's Survey in 1346, from which it appears that the Bishop of Durham claimed fourpence for every ship which anchored there, and that the sum received for that year was 3s. 4d. At what time the coal-trade was first established there is uncertain, but so early as 1610 a complaint appears to have been made to Parliament on account of a late imposition of a shilling a chalder, levied on coals shipped at Blyth and Sunderland, " not by virtue of any contract or grant, as in the coals of Newcastle, but under the mere pretext of his majesty's royal prerogative." In 1624, Blyth is again mentioned, in a proclamation, as a place exporting sea-coals; and in 1643 an order of Parliament prohibits ships from bringing coals or salt from Newcastle, or Blyth, as those places were then in the hands of the Royalists.

Within the last forty years the trade of Blyth has much increased in consequence of the opening of new collieries in the neighbourhood. A commodious dry dock was formed in 1811; and there are three or four slips for the building and repairing of ships. A considerable quantity of articles of cast and malleable iron, manufactured at Bedlington, about three miles up the river, are shipped at Blyth.

Blyth is a member of the port of Newcastle; and the number of vessels belonging to persons residing there, but registered at the latter port, are sixty, with a tonnage of 8,872 tons. Nearly the whole of Blyth is the property of Sir M. W. Ridley. In 1831 the population, with that of the adjacent township of Cowpen, was 3,877. It is high water at Blyth at a quarter before three o'clock at full and change of the moon. At spring tides there is about fourteen feet water on the bar; and about twelve at neaps. At low water the bar is nearly dry.

BLYTH.

Drawn by J.D. Harding.

Engraved by W. Finden.

London. Published 1836. by Charles Tilt. 86. Fleet Street.

Drawn by C. Palmer.

Engraved by E. Finden.

SUNDERLAND.

THE LIGHT HOUSE ON THE SOUTH PIER.

London, Published 1836, by Charles Tilt, 86, Fleet Street.

SUNDERLAND.—THE LIGHTHOUSE ON THE SOUTH PIER.

THE view of the Lighthouse on Sunderland South Pier is taken from the south-east. The entrance to the harbour lies beyond the pier-head, to the right, on which a crane, and a capstan used in warping out ships, are perceived. The large D on the fore-topsail of the collier lying within the pier is a distinguishing mark adopted by the owner that his vessels may be more readily known. To the left is seen the higher lighthouse, of stone, which stands on the north pier, on the opposite side of the river.

The erection of a pier on each side of the entrance to Sunderland harbour, has been rendered necessary in consequence of the constant tendency of the bar of sand at its mouth to accumulate. The piers, by contracting the channel of the river, have deepened the water, and increased the velocity of the current at ebb tide, which thus scours the entrance to the harbour, and prevents the accumulation of sand upon the bar.

In 1669 Charles II. granted letters patent to Edward Andrew, Esq., empowering him to build a pier, erect lighthouses, and cleanse the harbour at Sunderland, and also to raise funds for these purposes by a tonnage-duty on ships. At a subsequent period commissioners were appointed for the same purposes by an act of parliament; and under their authority 333 yards of the north pier were built, between 1716 and 1746. From a report of the commissioners made in 1765, it appears that £50,000 had been expended on the south pier up to that time, and it was estimated that to finish it would cost as much more. It is now extended to the length of 625 yards. The north pier, which is entirely of stone, was commenced about 1785, and additions are still making to its eastern extremity.

The lighthouse on the north pier was erected in 1803. The light, which is stationary, is exhibited from sun-set to sun-rise, and is visible in clear weather at the distance of twelve miles. The light on the south pier is a tide-light, and is only shown when there is sufficient depth of water on the bar for ships to enter. This light is of a red colour, and for these last two years has not been shown from the lighthouse, but from the top of a long pole, which is fixed at the extremity of the South pier. By day a flag is hoisted during tide-time. At full and change of the moon it is high water at Sunderland bar at three o'clock; and the average depth of water at spring tides is about sixteen feet; at neaps about twelve.

SUNDERLAND.—THE BRIDGE FROM THE WESTWARD.

UNDER the general name of Sunderland, the three townships of Monk-Wear-mouth, Bishop-Wearmouth, and Sunderland, are usually comprised. Monk-Wearmouth is situated on the north side of the river Wear, at a short distance from its mouth. Sunderland and Bishop-Wearmouth, which form one continuous town, lie on the south side of the river; Sunderland, properly so called, extending from the line of junction of the two parishes, eastward to the sea; and Bishop-Wearmouth extending towards the west. Sunderland—which has given its name to the port and to the borough—is 269 miles distant from London; fourteen from Durham; and thirteen from Newcastle-on-Tyne.

Monk-Wearmouth owes its distinctive name of " Monk " to a monastery which formerly stood there, and which on its first erection was one of the most splendid religious structures in England. Its founder, Benedict, who is frequently called Benedict Biscop by ecclesiastical historians, before he turned monk had been a soldier, and held an office in the court of Oswy, king of Northumberland. At the early age of twenty-five he retired from the court in order to devote himself entirely to religion. He performed his noviciate in the monastery of Lerins, in Provence, where he received the tonsure and assumed the religious name of Benedict. Soon after he had taken the monastic vows he proceeded to Rome, which he had visited twice before, from whence he was sent by Pope Vitalian, in company with Theodore and Adrian, two pious and learned ecclesiastics, as a missionary to his own country. After residing two years at Canterbury as abbot of the monastery of St. Peter and St. Paul in that city, he proceeded a fourth time to Rome, from whence he returned to England in 672, bringing with him a large collection of books, and, according to the opinions of that period, a no less valuable collection of reliques. Having, through the fame of his literary and sanctified stores, obtained a grant of seventy hides of land from Egfrid, king of Northumberland, he, in 674, founded the monastery of St. Peter's, Wearmouth, on the north side of the river Wear. The next year Benedict, who seems to have been fond of travelling, took a journey into France, from whence he soon returned, bringing with him skilful masons to build the church of the new monastery, after the Romish style, with glaziers to glaze the windows.

Bede, who relates the foregoing particulars respecting Benedict Biscop, says that he was the first who introduced glaziers into England. On his return from a

Drawn by G. Balmer.

Engraved by W. Finden.

SUNDERLAND.

(THE BRIDGE FROM THE WESTWARD)

London, Published 1836. by Charles Tilt, 86, Fleet Street.

subsequent visit to Rome, Benedict brought with him brother John, an arch-chanter or leader of the choir of St. Peter's at Rome, who instructed the monks of Wearmouth in the whole order of psalmody, and the complete ceremonial of the Church of Rome; not only instructing them *viva voce*, but pricking them out a course for the whole year*. This more perfect mode of singing introduced by Benedict was the "Gregorian chant;" which had been established at Rome by Pope Gregory I., about eighty years before. Monks from other abbeys came to Wearmouth to hear and to receive instruction from "brother John," and thus an improved manner of chanting mass and of singing became diffused throughout the whole province. Benedict in his last visit to Rome brought over an additional store of books, with several paintings, representing the Virgin and the twelve apostles, sacred subjects from the Evangelists, and visions from the Revelations. Bale, who had been a Carmelite friar, censures Benedict for being the first who introduced into England "painters, glaziers, and such-like artists, whose works promote only pleasure."

Benedict having died in 690, and his successor, Sigfried, four months afterwards, the care of the abbey of Wearmouth devolved upon Ceolfrid, the friend and co-adjutor of Benedict, who at the same time presided over the monastery of Jarrow†,

---

* Surtees's Hist. of Durham, vol. ii. p. 3.

† The following inscription, the original of which is still preserved in Jarrow church, marks the date of the dedication of *some* part of the monastery:

```
DEDICATIO  BASILICAE
SCI PAVLI VIIII KL MAI
ANNO XV ECFRIDI REC
CEOLFRIDI ABB EIVSEMQ
Q ECCLES DO AVCTORE
CONDITORIS ANNO IIII
```

"I translate it as follows, taking in the two QQ's," says Brand, in his Hist. of Newcastle, vol. ii. p. 51: 'The dedication of the church of St. Paul on the 9th of the Kalends of May, in the fifteenth year of King Egfrid [685] *and* the fourth of Ceolfrid, abbot, and under God founder of the said church.''— This translation will not hold unless we presume that the two different words Basilica and Ecclesia— which are both rendered "church" by Mr. Brand—mean the same thing. There seems reason to suppose that the "Basilica" mentioned in this inscription was the chancel at the eastern extremity of the church. From authorities cited by Du Cange, it appears that in France, in the sixth and seventh centuries, the church attached to a monastery was called "Basilica;" while parochial churches and cathedrals were termed "Ecclesiæ." The word Basilica was also used to signify that part of a church which was considered more particularly sacred. It seems probable that this "Dedicatio" refers to the consecration of the chancel at the time when the altar was erected. In later times we know that the altar, which always stood in the chancel, was separately consecrated; and the space within the rails con-sidered as a βασιλικὸν χωρίον—a royal place, within which only kings, nobles, and eminent persons, were permitted to sit.

I

which appears to have been founded jointly by those two religious brethren, shortly after the erection of the monastery of Wearmouth. Bede, who in 684, being then seven years old, was sent to be educated at Jarrow, states that at one period while Ceolfrid was abbot there were 600 monks belonging to the abbey of St. Peter at Wearmouth; a number which appears surprising, and which shows how prone men were at that period to avail themselves of the monastic habit in order that they might lead an indolent life.

About the year 800 the abbey of Wearmouth was plundered by the Danes; and about 870 it was burnt to the ground by another band of those piratical invaders. It would, however, appear to have been rebuilt after this misfortune, though probably upon a small scale, for it is mentioned as one of the religious houses destroyed by Malcolm IV., King of Scotland, in his hostile incursion into England in 1070. About 1074 Aldwine, prior of Winchelsea*, under the patronage of Walcher, bishop of Durham, repaired the ruinous monasteries of Wearmouth and Jarrow, and established in each a fraternity of monks. Those two places, so famed during the Saxon period, did not recover their former state under the Norman dynasty; for in 1083, William de Carilepho, bishop of Durham, removed most of the monks to the abbey of Durham, to which he annexed Wearmouth and Jarrow as cells On the suppression of the monasteries, by Henry VIII., the revenue of that of Wearmouth was found to be £25. 8s. 4d. The monastery, of which no part is now remaining, stood at a short distance to the north-eastward of the present church. Monk-Wearmouth hall—which was built in the reign of James I., and burnt in 1790—is supposed to have been erected on a part of its site, and with materials obtained from its ruins.

Monk-Wearmouth consists of two separate townships. That which is known as Monk-Wearmouth Town is chiefly built on the elevated ground which forms the left bank of the Wear. Monk-Wearmouth Shore, as its name denotes, lies by the water-side, being built on the low ground between Monk-Wearmouth proper and the river. Monk-Wearmouth Shore is chiefly inhabited by persons employed upon the river, or as shipwrights, boat-builders, mast-makers, and smiths; and the whole township is the property of Sir Hedworth Williamson. In 1831 the population of Monk-Wearmouth was 1,498; of Monk-Wearmouth Shore 6,051.

In 930 King Athelstan gave the lands of South Wearmouth to the see of Durham; and hence the town which was built there came to be called Bishop-Wearmouth, by way of distinction from Monk-Wearmouth on the opposite side of the river. About 1164, Hugh Pudsey, bishop of Durham, granted a charter to his burgesses of Wearmouth, conferring upon them the same privileges as were enjoyed by the burgesses of Newcastle. In the survey called the " Bolden

---

* In Surtees's History of Durham, this Aldwine—who is mentioned at page 31 as coming from the south accompanied by two monks to seek for Monkchester—is called the prior of *Winchcombe*.

Book," compiled about the year 1190, South Wearmouth and the adjacent township of Tunstall are mentioned together. Among other entries relating to Wearmouth in that curious record is the following: " The smith has twelve acres for the iron work of the carts, and finds his own coal.*" At the time that Bishop Pudsey's charter was granted, the town appears to have been also called Sunderland; and in subsequent grants, between that period and 1719, it appears to be indiscriminately called both by the latter name and that of Bishop-Wearmouth. Neither Leland nor Camden mention Sunderland, though this name was very generally applied to the town on the south side of the Wear long before either of them wrote. In their notice of the place they seem to have considered it as included under the general name of " Weremouth." In 1719 an express distinction was made by an Act of Parliament, which constituted Sunderland a separate parish from that of Bishop-Wearmouth, in which it had formerly been included. This act was passed on the petition of the inhabitants of Sunderland, who, between 1712 and 1719, had built a new church. The old church of Bishop-Wearmouth— which was pulled down and rebuilt in 1808—was probably founded shortly after the date of Athelstan's grant. The rectory of Sunderland is but slenderly endowed ; that of Bishop-Wearmouth is one of the richest in the kingdom, and is at present held by the Rev. Dr. Wellesley, a brother of the Duke of Wellington. Dr. Paley—whose " pigeon illustration," in his Moral Philosophy, of the basis of political authority, is said to have kept him out of a bishopric—was rewarded by Dr. Barrington, bishop of Durham, with the rectory of Bishop-Wearmouth, where he died in 1805.

Since the year 1200—and probably from a much earlier period—the harbour at the mouth of the Wear appears to have been generally known as that of Sunderland, the present name of the port and of the parliamentary borough. " Various conjectures," says Mr. Surtees, " have been formed as to the derivation of this name: the simplest and most obvious seems to be, that it marked the original situation of the place on a point of land almost insulated by the Wear and by the sea, which has probably flowed much higher than at present up some of the deep gullies on the coast, particularly Hendon-Dene, which, it seems, contained as late as 1350 water sufficient for vessels to ride at anchor in the bay.†"

* Surtees's Hist. of Durham, vol. 1, p. 224. The original passage stands thus : " Faber xii. acr. p ferrament' caruc' & carbones qm' invenit." The smiths at Escombe and at Sedgefield, also held lands on the same conditions.

† Hist. of Durham, vol. 1, p. 253. Hutchinson, in his Hist. of Durham, gives the original passage, upon which Mr. Surtees founds his opinion, thus : " Thomas Menvill tenet quandam plac. vocat. Hynden [Hendon] pro *applicatione* navium." In Spearman's extract from the same document, Bishop Hatfield's Survey, 1346, the words are " locum pro *ædificando* naves ;" a place for *building* ships, and not a place where ships are moored or ply, as in Hutchinson.

The grand source of the prosperity of Sunderland, and the means by which the town has attained its present importance, is the coal-trade. The period at which coals first began to be exported from Sunderland has not been clearly ascertained; but there seems to be reason to believe that the trade in coals, though probably to a very small extent, commenced on the Wear not long after its establishment on the Tyne. In 1394, coals were brought to Whitby in ships belonging to Sunderland, which very likely were loaded at their own port. In a writ issued by Bishop Neville, in 1440, commanding certain yares* in the Wear to be removed, because they interrupted the navigation, and prevented salmon and trout from ascending, " keeles," the craft in which coals are brought from the upper to the lower part of the river, are expressly mentioned. In the reign of Queen Elizabeth it seems that a considerable quantity of salt was manufactured at Sunderland; and in the reign of her successor it is certain that the coal-trade was carried on there to a considerable extent. In 1634, when Bishop Morton incorporated the burgesses under the title of " the Mayor, twelve Aldermen, and Commonalty of the Borough of Sunderland," sea-coal, grind-stones, and rub-stones, or whetstones, are mentioned in the charter as the principal articles of export †. During the siege of Newcastle in 1644, when no coals from the Tyne were allowed to be brought to London, the export of coals from Sunderland, which was then in the possession of the Parliament, was very greatly increased. Between 1704 and 1711 the average annual export was 65,760 Newcastle chalders. The increasing importance of Sunderland as a place of trade was viewed with extreme jealousy by the corporation of Newcastle. In 1706, when a proposal was submitted to the House of Commons for the improvement of the entrance to the Wear, and of Sunderland harbour, it was opposed by the master and brethren of the Trinity House at Newcastle; and when a bill for the said purposes was introduced in 1716, the mayor, aldermen, and common-council of Newcastle petitioned against it. Notwithstanding the opposition that was thus made to it, the bill was passed, and commissioners appointed, who were charged with the conservancy of the harbour, and empowered to raise money by a tonnage-duty for the purpose of clearing the river of sand, building a pier, and other purposes. By subsequent acts the power of the commissioners was continued and enlarged; and to their exertions the present improved state of the harbour is entirely owing. While the inhabitants of Sunderland have been diligently improving their harbour, the state of the river

---

* A yare is a kind of hedge formed of stakes and wicker work, extending from the bank towards the middle of a river for the purpose of catching fish. An extract from the original writ of Bishop Neville is given in Spearman's Enquiry, p. 30.

† During the civil war, when the bishops were deprived of their sees, this charter was suffered to expire, and was not afterwards renewed.

Tyne has from year to year been suffered to get worse, through the indifference of its conservators, the corporation of Newcastle. Under the new order of things it is to be hoped that the reproach will be removed.

From a curious map of the Wear, published in 1737*, a part of the south pier appears to have been then erected. On the north side, extending eastward from the lower part of Monk-Wearmouth, there is a sand marked the "Ham-sand," between which and a sand named the "Canch," extending from the south side, the main channel appears extremely contracted. Between the "Canch" and the south pier there is another channel termed the "Sledway." Between the mouth of the river and New Bridge, about a mile to the north-east of Chester-le-Street, there appear to be as many staiths as at present; from which we may infer that though the coal-trade of Sunderland has been greatly extended within the last hundred years, yet the number of coal-owners has not been increased. The trade, in fact, at present appears to be in fewer hands.

The great boast of Sunderland is the beautiful iron bridge, of a single arch, which connects it with Monk-Wearmouth. This noble structure, which is at once highly ornamental and useful, was projected by Rowland Burdon, Esq., of Castle Eden, who in 1792, he being then M. P. for the county of Durham, obtained an act of parliament empowering him to raise money for its erection; the sums advanced to be secured on the tolls, with five per cent. interest, and all further accumulation to go in discharge of the capital. The abutments from which the arch springs are nearly solid masses of masonry; twenty-four feet thick; forty-two feet broad at bottom, and thirty-seven feet broad at top. That on the south side is founded on a solid rock, which rises above the level of the Wear; the foundation of that on the north side, owing to the unfavourable nature of the ground, was obliged to be laid ten feet below the level of the river. The arch, which is a segment of a large circle, is of 236 feet span, and its centre is 94 feet above the level of the river at low water. From the height of the arch and its comparative flatness—its versed sine, or perpendicular height from its centre to a line joining its extremities, being only 34 feet—ships of 300 tons burthen can pass underneath not only directly below the centre, but also to the extent of fifty feet on each side. The navigation of the river thus remains unobstructed—for many vessels proceed to the staiths above the bridge for the purpose of taking in their coals—while the inhabitants on each side enjoy all the advantages of facilitated intercourse. The breadth of the bridge at the top is 32 feet, including the footpaths on each side;

* " A plan of the river Wear from Newbridge to Sunderland Bar, as it appeared at low water. By Burleigh and Thompson. 1737." This plan, which is in four sheets, contains the names of all the proprietors of land on each side of the river between its mouth and Newbridge, the names of the staiths and sands, with the depth of water, and sundry other particulars.

and the carriage-way is formed of lime, marl, and gravel, above a flooring of timber, which is laid across the iron ribs of the arch. The iron ribs and blocks were cast and prepared at the foundry of Messrs. Walker, at Rotheram, near Sheffield. The whole weight of the iron is 260 tons; of which 46 tons are malleable, and 214 cast. The foundation-stone* was laid on the 24th September, 1793, and the bridge opened to the public on the 9th August, 1796, having been completed, under the superintendence of Mr. Thomas Wilson, of Bishop-Wear-mouth, in less than three years. The total expense was £26,000*l.*, of which sum £22,000*l.* was subscribed by Mr. Burdon †.

Except the bridge, there is but little in the shape of public or private buildings at Sunderland to claim the attention of the stranger. The more wealthy inhabitants do not yet seem to be inspired with that " architectural taste " which prompts the erection of streets of elegant shops, with large dwelling-houses above them,—highly ornamental indeed to the town in which such goodly buildings rise, but scarce likely to suit the means of the tenants who are to occupy them. At Sunderland, if we do not behold such choice specimens of the Grecian style of architecture as at Plymouth, neither do we read there, as at the latter place, the singularly *appro-priate* sign—in letters, according to the act of parliament, white on a black ground, and not less than two inches long — of " M. N., licensed dealer in wine, foreign spirits, beer, and tobacco," on entering a " tetrastyle portico, constructed in the chastest style of the Illissus Ionic‡." Such " music of the eye " is ex-ceedingly provocative of a cachinnatory accompaniment of the voice.

Although many ships are loaded direct from such staiths as are at a short distance above the bridge, yet the greater part of the coals are brought down in keels from staiths situated higher up the river. The keels of the Wear, though of the same tonnage as those of the Tyne, are somewhat differently built, being flatter in the bottom and of a lighter draught of water. The Sunderland keels are managed by only one man, who usually has a boy to assist him. In the Wear the coals when in bulk are cast from the keel into the ship by men called coal-casters ; while on the Tyne, where the crew of each keel consists of three men and a boy, the coals are always cast by the keelmen. Within the last seven or eight years, a consider-able quantity of coals, in order to prevent the breakage occasioned by discharging them into the keels from the spout, and then casting them into the ship, have been

* The inscription on the foundation stone contains a bad pun : " Quo tempore civium Gallicorum ardor vesanus prava jubentium gentes turbavit Europeas *ferreo* bello, Rolandus Burdon armiger, meliora colens, Vedræ ripas, scopulis præruptis, ponte conjungere *ferreo* statuit."

† Surtees's Hist. of Durham, vol. 1, p. 226.

‡ See the east front of the building at Plymouth, which under one roof contains assembly rooms, a theatre, and a hotel.

put on board of keels in *tubs,* which are afterwards raised by machinery to the vessel's deck, and then discharged into the hold. These tubs are exactly like coal-waggons without their wheels, and contain the same quantity, one Newcastle chalder, or fifty-three cwt *. Each keel carries eight of such tubs. The number of keels employed on the Wear is about 500.

The ship-owners of Sunderland have long been distinguished for their enterprising spirit, and for their unremitting exertions to improve their port and extend its trade. In this spirit a rail-road between that town and Durham has lately been constructed; and other lines to communicate with the Stanhope railway, and with Gateshead, have also been projected. At present a large wet dock is in course of construction at the eastern end of Monk-Wearmouth Shore; and it is extremely probable that at no distant period a similar work will be commenced at Sunderland.

With respect to the number of its ships, and their amount of tonnage, Sunderland is the fourth port in the kingdom; the three by which it is exceeded being London, Newcastle, and Liverpool. In 1829 there were 624 ships belonging to Sunderland, with a tonnage of 107,628 tons; at present there are 713, with a tonnage of 122,000 tons.

The quantities of coals exported at the following periods from Sunderland will show the progress of the trade since the commencement of the present century. The chalders are Newcastle measure.

YEARS.	COASTWISE.	FOREIGN.
1800	298,837	4,622 chalders.
1810	370,312	1,919 do.
1820	415,972	14,425 do.
1828	509,567.	22,941 do.
1835	928,998 tons.	154,536 tons.

From Seaham, a new harbour, about five miles to the southward of Sunderland, which was first opened in July, 1831, the following quantities of coals were exported between that date and the 10th October, 1835 :—Coastwise, 1,088,691 tons; foreign, 14,498 tons. A large proportion of the coals now shipped at Seaham are from the Marquis of Londonderry's collieries, from which, previous to the formation of the new harbour, all the coals used to be shipped at Sunderland.

In 1831 the population of Sunderland parish was 17,060; of Bishop-Wearmouth, 14,462; which, with 7,549 for Monk-Wearmouth and the Shore, makes an aggregate of 39,071 for the united townships, usually known as Sunderland. In 1832 the privilege of returning two members of Parliament was conferred on the borough of Sunderland. The present members are William Thompson, Esq., chairman of Lloyd's, and an alderman of London; and David Barclay, Esq., the head of the great mercantile firm of Barclay, Brothers, and Co., of the same city.

* Evidence of Sir Cuthbert Sharp before the Lords' Committee on the Coal Trade, 1829. p. 23.

ROBIN HOOD'S BAY.

THE above is the name of a fine bay on the Yorkshire coast, between Whitby and Scarbrough, and also of the fishing village, situated towards its northern extremity. In the view, which is taken from the north, several of the houses are seen standing upon the very edge of the cliff. The promontory to the left is called Ravenhill, and forms the south-eastern extremity of the bay. From an inscription dug up at Ravenhill in 1774, it appears that there had formerly been a Roman camp there.

The ancient name of the bay was Fyling, and from what reason or at what period it first received the name of Robin Hood's Bay is uncertain. That it ever was the resort of the famed outlaw of that name is extremely questionable; although two or three tumuli on the moor, about two miles to the southward of the village, are said to be the butts, in shooting at which he exercised his men in archery. Near Whitby Lathes, about five miles to the north-west of Robin Hood's Bay, are two upright stones, which are said to mark the spots where the arrows of the bold robber of Sherwood Forest, and of his man Little John, fell, when, in a trial of strength, they discharged them from the top of Whitby Abbey in the presence of the abbot. As the distance from these stones to the abbey is rather more than a mile and a half, it is evident that a *long* bow must have been drawn by some one, if not by Robin Hood. It has been supposed that the place was originally called Robin Wood's Bay, from a fisherman of that name, who formerly resided there; but this conjecture rests on no better ground than the fact of two or three fishermen of the name of Wood having lived there in modern times. A family of fishermen of the name of Wood, with whom "Zebedee" appears to have been a favourite "fore-name," have resided at Runswick, a fishing village, about seven miles northward of Whitby, for several generations.

Leland, in his Itinerary, written about three hundred years ago, calls the village by its present name, Robin Hood's Bay, and describes it as "a fisher townlet of twenty boats." It is still, as in his time, almost entirely inhabited by fishermen. The houses forming the principal street are built on each side of a steep road, leading down to the shore; while others, as may be seen in the view, are built upon the very extremity of the cliff. The approach to the village is by a steep descent, which is extremely inconvenient for carriages. It is about fourteen miles north-west of Scarbrough, and seven south-east of Whitby; and the population is about a thousand.

Drawn by G. Balmer.

ROBIN HOOD'S BAY.

Engraved by E. Finden.

London. Published 1836, by Charles Tilt, 86, Fleet Street.

Robin Hood's Bay, Filey, Runswick, and Staithes, are the principal fishing villages on the Yorkshire coast. Filey is about eight miles south of Scarborough; Runswick, as has been previously observed, is about seven miles northward of Whitby; and Staithes is about three miles northward of Runswick. At each of those places the fishery is carried on both by cobles and by five-man boats. At most of the other fishing stations on the Yorkshire coast, cobles only are employed.

The principal fishing ground for the cobles, is from eight to sixteen miles from the shore. In winter, however, they do not venture so far out as in summer, but usually shoot their lines between six and ten miles from the shore. There are usually three men to a coble. When the wind is not favourable, and they cannot set their sail, they use their oars; the two men seated nearest the head of the boat row each a single large oar, while the man on the thwart nearest the stern rows a pair of smaller size. The fish are not caught, as on some parts of the south-western coast of England, by hand-lines, which are suspended over the side of the boat, and pulled up when the fisherman feels that he has a bite. The mode of proceeding is to make fast a number of lines together, and shoot them across the tide; and after they have lain extended at the bottom of the sea for several hours—usually during the time of a tide's ebbing or flowing, that is, about six hours—they are hauled in. While the lines are shot one man keeps a look out, and the other two usually wrap themselves in the sail and go to sleep in the bottom of the coble. Each man has three lines, and each line is from 200 to 240 fathoms long. The hooks, of which there are from 240 to 300 to each line, are tied, or *whipped* as the fishermen term it, to lengths of twisted horse-hair called *snoods;* each snood is about two feet and a half long, and they are fastened to the line at about five feet apart. Each man's lines, when baited, are regularly coiled upon an oval piece of wicker work, something like the bottom of a clothes-basket, called by the Yorkshire fishermen a *skep;* at Hartlepool, in the county of Durham, the same thing is called a *rip.* In this mode of fishing the hooks are all baited, generally by the fishermen's wives and children, before the coble proceeds to sea. The lines when shot are all fastened together; and when each is 240 fathoms long, the length of the whole is nearly two miles and a half. There is an anchor and a buoy at the first end of the line; and the same at the end of each man's set of lines. There are thus four anchors and four buoys to each coble's entire line. The buoys at the extremities of the line are usually formed of tanned dog-skin, inflated in the manner of a bladder, and having a slight pole, like the handle of a mop, passing through them, to the top of which a small flag is attached to render them more conspicuous. The intermediate buoys are generally made of

K

cork. The anchors for sinking and holding the lines are mostly large stones ; as an iron anchor, with arms like a ship's, is liable to get fast among the rocks at the bottom of the sea, and be lost in consequence of the buoy rope being too weak to force it loose.

The following description of a coble and her crew is from a letter apparently written about the latter end of the reign of Queen Elizabeth, or the beginning of the reign of James 1.; and probably addressed to Sir Thomas Chaloner, of Guisborough, in Yorkshire *.

"Truly yt may be sayd of these poor men, that they are lavish of theyr lives, who will hazard twenty or forty myles into the seas in a small troughe so thinne that the glimse of the sunne may bee seene through yt; yet at eleven or twelve of the clocke in the morninge, when they come from the sea, they sell theire whole boaty's lading for 4s., or if they doe gette a crowne, they suppose to have chaffered fayre. Three commonly come in one boate, each of them having twoe oares, which they governe by drawinge one hande over the other. The boate ytself is built of wainscott, for shape excels all modeles for shippinge ; twoe men will easily carrye ytt on lande betweene them, yet are they so secure in them at sea, that some in a storme have lyved aboarde three dayes. Their greateste danger is nearest home, when the waves breake dangerouslye ; but they, acquainted with these seas, espyinge a broken wave reddy to overtake them, suddenly oppose the prowe or sharpe ende of theyre boate unto yt, and mountinge to the top, descende downe as yt were unto a valley, hoveringe untill they espye a whole wave come rowlinge, which they observe commonly to be an odde one; whereupon mountinge with their cobble as it were a great furious horse, they rowe with might and mayne, and together with that wave drive themselves on lande."

In the same account mention is made of a " five-man coble," which was con-siderably larger than the other, and doubtless the original of the modern fishing vessel called a " five-man boat." " It was my fortune," says the writer, describing the coast in the neighbourhood of Redcar, " to see the cominge in of a five-man coble, which in one night had taken above twenty-one score of greate fishe, of a yearde or an ell in length. Happie were that country yf a generall fishinge were entertained by building vessels and store of fish boats."

The vessels now called five-man boats, though their crew always consists of

---

* This letter, which is signed " H. Tr.," and contains some account of the lordship of Guisborough, is in the Cottonian Collection of MSS. It is referred to by Graves in his History of Cleveland, as being in the volume marked " Julius F. C. ;" and the Rev. G. Young in his History of Whitby, and Sir C. Sharp, in his History of Hartlepool, both cite the volume under the same title. It is, however, contained in " Julius F. vi.," and the account of a Redcar coble, given above, occurs at folio 433 b.

seven persons, are about forty-six feet long, sixteen feet eight inches broad, and six feet three inches deep. They are clinker-built*, sharp at the bows like a coble, and have a deck with a large hatchway in midships, and a cabin towards the stern for the men. They have three masts, on each of which they carry a lug sail. Their other sails are a jib, and, in fine weather, a topsail set on a shifting top-mast, above the main-mast. As the sails are all tanned, a five-man boat forms a picturesque object at sea, more especially when viewed in contrast with a square-rigged vessel with whit esails. The crew of each five-man boat consists of seven persons; five of whom, called *shares-men*, have equal shares of the proceeds of the voyage, or the season, after the boat's share is paid. The sixth person is often a young man who receives half a share, and is a kind of apprentice to the captain or owner of the boat. The seventh is generally hired at a certain sum per week, and not sharing in the profits of the fishery.

To each five-man boat there are two cobles, which in proceeding to the fishing ground are generally hauled up on the deck. On arriving at the place where it is intended to fish, the boat is anchored, and the cobles being launched, three men proceed in each to shoot the lines, while one remains on board. The lines used for this more distant fishery are called *haavres†*. They are about the same length as those used in the coble fishery nearer the shore, though thicker, and having the hooks placed at greater intervals. As the six men who fish have each two sets of lines, they are thus enabled to shoot one set immediately after they have hauled the other. In the five-man-boat fishery the hooks are always baited at sea. The boats usually sail from the place to which they belong on a Monday morning, and return home on Saturday. They mostly fish near the outer edge of the Dogger Bank, and the principal kinds of fish which they take are cod, halibut, skate, haddock, codfish, and ling. Part of the fish thus caught is sold to smacks, which are constantly lying off the fishing ground, for the supply of the London market; and the rest is brought by the fishermen to the shore, where it is either cured or sold to persons who dispose of it in inland places. The cod which is not immediately sold, is, in summer, mostly dried; but in winter, salted in barrels.

The five-man boats, which are all laid up during the winter, are generally fitted out again about the beginning of March. About the middle of August, part of them engage in the herring fishery, which then commences off their own coast, and

* Boats and vessels are said to be clinker- or clincher- built, when the planks overlap each other in the manner of slates on the roof of a house. The flat tiles used in covering houses are called clinkers, and from them the term "clinker-built" is probably derived. A vessel is said to be caulker-built when the planks do not overlap each other, but have their edges brought close together, and the seams caulked.

† This word is derived from "Haaf," which in the Swedish language signifies the main sea. The fishermen of Shetland call their fishing ground "the Haaf."

about the middle of September they all proceed to Yarmouth, and continue to fish for herrings off the coasts of Norfolk and Suffolk till the latter end of November, when the fishermen return home and the boats are laid up for the winter. The herrings which they catch at the Yarmouth fishery are sold to the curers there, who contract with them for all that they take during the season at a certain sum per last of ten thousand. On their return home from Yarmouth after a successful season, they indulge in festivity, which is shared by the humbler class of trades-people of the village, who then generally receive payment of the little debts con-tracted by the families of the fishermen during their absence. In winter, when the large boats are laid up, most of their crews employ themselves in coble fishing.

Five-man boats, like most lugger-rigged vessels, sail well upon a wind in smooth water; but in running before the wind in a rough sea they are not very safe, as their sails are then so liable to "jibe,"—at a time when, above all others, it is of the greatest consequence that they should be kept steady. Most of them, however, have now a storm square-sail, which they set in running for the land before a gale of wind from the eastward. On perceiving the approach of a storm from the eastward, when fishing, they immediately haul in their lines with all speed, and make directly for the land. When a storm comes on suddenly, raising a heavy sea on the shore before they can arrive, five-man boats are sometimes lost in attempting to gain their own harbours. In a violent storm, on the 14th of April 1815, four five-man boats, three belonging to Runswick, and one belonging to Staithes, were lost in approaching the shore.

> " Ye who dwell at home,
> Ye do not know the terrors of the main !
> When the winds blow ye walk along the shore,
> And, as the curling billows leap and toss,
> Fable that Ocean's mermaid shepherdess
> Drives her white flocks a-field, and warns in time
> The wary fisherman."—*Southey's Madoc*, book iv.

Drawn by J. D. Harding.

Engraved by W. Finden.

WHITBY.

WHITBY.

THE engraving of Whitby, from a drawing by Harding, presents a view of the entrance to the harbour, as seen from the northward. Towards the middle of the engraving is seen the end of the east pier; on the top of the cliff are the ruins of the abbey and the parish church; while, farther to the right, part of the town is perceived.

Whitby is in the North Riding of Yorkshire; and lies about 246 miles north of London; 22 north-north-west of Scarborough; and 47 north-east of York. It is chiefly built on the sloping banks of the river Esk, by which it is divided into two parts; that on the west side being the most populous. The opposite parts of the town are connected by means of a bridge, the middle of which is moveable for the purpose of allowing ships to pass through. In the old bridge, which has been recently pulled down, the opening in the middle was upon the principle of a draw-bridge, in which the road-way is raised and lowered by means of beams and chains. At high water the river above the bridge expands into a spacious harbour, where ships can lie in perfect security; but at ebb tide, except in the mid-channel, the harbour is nearly dry. In the outer harbour, as it is called, below the bridge, vessels cannot ride with safety in gales of wind upon the land.

The piers at the entrance to Whitby harbour are not built and maintained at the sole expense of the place, but by a duty on coals shipped at Newcastle, Sunderland, Blyth, and their dependencies, Yarmouth vessels only being exempt; and the sum thus raised amounts to upwards of £2000 per annum. It is doubtless a great advantage to the people of Whitby to have their piers built and kept in repair at the expense of other ports; but it is equally certain that the same sum might be employed more to the advantage of those by whom it is paid in improving other places—Scarborough and Burlington, for instance—as harbours of refuge on the eastern coast. In a gale of wind from the eastward, Whitby is perhaps one of the most dangerous harbours that a vessel can attempt to take between Yarmouth roads and the Frith of Forth, and captains of coasting vessels cannot be too frequently warned to avoid it. As the flood tide sets strong to the southward across the entrance of the harbour, vessels in attempting to enter with a gale of wind from the north-east are extremely liable to be driven on the rocks and wrecked at the foot of the cliff beyond the east pier.

WHITBY.—FROM THE NORTH-WEST.

THE view of Whitby from the north-west, by Balmer, is taken from the sands near Upgang, between Whitby and the village of Sandsend. From this point nearly the whole of the west pier is seen, extending directly from the shore, and having a light-house near its outer extremity. Beyond the pier, and on the other side of the river, are seen the houses built on the sloping side of the cliff, and on its top the ruins of Whitby abbey, which

> " In solemn grandeur, calm and still,
> O'erlook the restless flood."

The first authentic notice that we have of Whitby, is contained in Bede's Ecclesiastical History. In the time of the venerable historian it was called in the Anglo-Saxon language *Streoneshalh*, a name which he interprets in Latin by the words *Sinus Fari ;* that is, in English, " Light-house bay." Subsequently it received from the Danes its present name of Whitby, a word which is probably derived from *hvit* or *whit*, white; and *by*, a dwelling, or, in its more extended sense, a village or town. It has been supposed that this name might be given to the village in consequence of its being built chiefly with stone taken from the ruins of the monastic buildings; but the supposition is untenable, unless we at the same time presume that the stones, which were taken from buildings which had been destroyed by fire, were rendered white by being burnt. In Domesday Book the place appears to be called *Prestebi*—Priestby—as well as *Witebi*—Whitby. The name Priestby, which soon became obsolete, probably denoted that part of the village which lay on the east side of the Esk, and was more immediately dependent on the monastery.

The authentic history of Whitby commences from the foundation of the abbey of Streoneshalh in 658, by St. Hilda, a lady of royal descent, who had previously exercised the office of abbess at Hartlepool, and who was highly famed for her knowledge and piety. The new monastery, which was for monks as well as nuns, prospered under her rule; and in a short time it became so famous, that a synod for settling certain religious disputes was held there in 664, about six years from the date of its foundation. The principal point to be discussed related to the time of celebrating Easter; Colman, bishop of Landisfarn, and several other monks, contending that the British churches were not to be regulated by the practice of the

Drawn by G. Balmer.

Engraved by E. Finden.

WHITBY.

FROM THE NORTH WEST.

London, Published 1837, by Charles Tilt, 86, Fleet Street.

church of Rome; while Wilfrid, abbot of Ripon, and others, argued in favour of the authority of the Pope.

Oswy, king of Northumberland, who was present at the synod, hearing Wilfrid, who was insisting on the authority of St. Peter, cite the text, "I will give unto thee the keys of the kingdom of heaven," understood the words literally, and decided in favour of the Romish party. The reason he gave was, that "he did not like to offend St. Peter by refusing to sanction his rule, lest, when he should present himself at the gates of heaven, the saint would not let him in."

Of the monks who were educated at Streoneshalh under the care of St. Hilda and her successor Ælfleda, no less than six attained to the dignity of bishop. While under the care of St. Hilda, the monastery had also the honour of being the abode of Cædmon, the earliest Anglo-Saxon poet whose name has been handed down to the present age. Cædmon was an unlettered peasant, who knew nothing of poetry or verse until he was well stricken in years, when the gift was miraculously communicated to him one night as he lay asleep in an ox-stall, to which he had retired from a jovial meeting, because he could not sing a song when it came to his turn. In his sleep Cædmon composed a hymn; and the gift of verse-making being continued to him when awake, he became an object of attention. St. Hilda hearing of his wonderful talent, sent for him to the monastery over which she presided, where having proved his vein, and found it good, she prevailed on him to abandon the dress and the toil of a labourer, for a monk's habit and retired leisure at Streoneshalh; where he is supposed to have died about the beginning of 680. St. Hilda herself died on the 17th November in the same year, aged 66. For many ages after her death the memory of St. Hilda was cherished with veneration by the inhabitants of the eastern coast of England from the Humber to the Tweed; nor was superstition slow in ascribing to her such deeds of marvellous power as constituted at once the title and the proof of sanctity. The sea-shore and the cliffs in the neighbourhood of Whitby abound in those petrifactions, now called by geologists and oryctologists *ammonites*, but better known to those who remain in happy ignorance of the *ologies* by the name of *snake-stones*. As those stones, at the time that the Royal Society was first instituted, and subsequently, were believed by many of its members to be really petrified headless snakes, the uneducated of a former age may be excused for entertaining a similar opinion. To account for those headless snakes was, however, a difficulty with the philosopher, but none with the superstitious enthusiast; who, knowing that a saint had dwelt at the top of the cliff at the foot of which those supposed hardened reptiles were found, had a ready clue to the mystery. A miracle evidently must have been wrought, and of course by the saint who dwelt in the vicinity: the manner how is as easily conceived, as the following tradition is recorded. "The ground on which the abbey of Streoneshalh stood being much infested with snakes, St. Hilda determined to destroy them. Providing herself, therefore, with holy water, she, through its potency and the efficacy of her prayers, drove them all from their holes to the edge of the cliff, where, with the asperge-rium or holy-water sprinkler, she cut off their heads and swept them over on to the shore below; where, in perpetual remembrance of the miracle, they were converted into stone." The fact of migratory birds, when wearied with their flight across the sea, occasionally alighting within the precinct of the monastery, was also placed to the credit of St. Hilda by imaginative superstition, which professed to believe that the birds, in passing over the place, were obliged to check their flight and sink to the ground in reverential homage to the holy woman by whose presence it had been sanctified.

St. Hilda was succeeded in the office of abbess by Ælfleda, the daughter of king Oswy, who presided over the monastery till her death, which happened in 713. From this period, at which Bede's notice of the two first abbesses of Streoneshalh ends, to 867, nothing certain is known respecting the history of the monastery, except that in the latter year it was totally destroyed by the Danes; who, about the same time, also destroyed the monasteries of Jarrow and Wearmouth. After having continued in ruins for upwards of two hundred years, it was, about the year 1075, re-established by Reinfrid, one of the monks of Evesham, who had accompanied Aldwine, prior of Winchelsea, or rather of Winchcomb, in his pil-grimage to the north in search of the ruined monasteries of Monk-chester. Wil-liam de Percy, a powerful Norman baron, who had known Reinfrid before he became a monk, as a soldier in the army of William the Conqueror, was the principal contributor to the new foundation, which was dedicated to St. Peter and St. Hilda, and appropriated solely to monks. Under a succession of abbots, two of whom were of the Percy family, the monastery of Whitby continued to flourish till the period of its suppression in 1539, when its revenues were found to be 505l. 9s. 1d., according to Speed; but only 437l. 2s. 9d. according to Dugdale. At the dissolution, Richard Cholmley, Esq. obtained a lease for twenty-one years of the site of the abbey and several parcels of its lands. In 1550 those lands were sold by the crown to John, earl of Warwick, who again sold them to Sir John Yorke, of whom they were purchased by the original lessee, then Sir Richard Cholmley, in 1555. Since that time the property has continued in the family of Cholmley, who enjoy many valuable rights and privileges as lords of the manor of Whitby. On the dissolution of the monastery, the abbey was stripped of every thing that was valuable. The bells were taken down, and the church was unroofed for the sake of the timber and lead. The walls only were spared, as the cost of taking them down would probably have been greater than the value of the stones. Though time has destroyed much of Whitby Abbey, yet the ruins still form a conspicuous and interesting object when viewed from the sea. The tower, which for several preceding years had been in a tottering state, fell down 25th June 1830. The parish church, a plain structure, probably founded about the beginning of the twelfth century, stands at a short distance to the north-westward of the abbey. The direct foot-way to the church-yard from the town is by a steep ascent of one hundred and ninety steps.

A singular customary duty, called " making the penny-stake hedge," is annually performed at Whitby, by certain tenants of the Lord of the Manor. It consists in driving a certain number of stakes, which, according to the ancient prescribed form, were to be cut with a knife of the value of one penny, on the shore of the South side of the Esk, at low water mark, at nine o'clock of the morning of the day before Ascension day ; while a man with a horn blows " Out on you! Out on you !" to the shame of the persons whose duty it is to drive the stakes. When it shall be full sea or high water at nine o'clock on the day of performing this service, it was to cease, but as Ascension day is regulated by the change of the moon this can never happen. This custom is of great antiquity, as the *horngarth*, the enclosure formed by the stakes, is mentioned about 1315 in the registers of the Abbey, in an account of certain disputes between the abbot, Thomas de Malton, and Alexander de Percy, of Sneaton. Tradition reports that this custom was imposed as a penance on three persons of the families of Percy, Bruce, and Allatson, who held lands of the Abbey, for having killed a hermit in the chapel of Eskdale-side, when hunting a wild boar which had there taken refuge. The penance imposed was the tenure by which they and their successors were to hold the Abbey lands.

Leland, who visited Whitby a few years before the suppression of the monastery, describes it as a " great fisher town," and he mentions that when he was there a new quay and pier were in course of erection. Until the establishment of the alum works in its neighbourhood, towards the latter end of the reign of Queen Elizabeth, Whitby appears to have been a place of little trade. As this new branch of commerce became extended, the trade and population of Whitby increased. About 1650 the number of inhabitants was nearly 2000, and there were twenty small vessels belonging to the place engaged in the coasting trade. In 1676 there were 76 vessels belonging to the port; in 1700 they had increased to 113 ; and in 1734 the number was 130. The period in which the shipping of Whitby increased most rapidly, was from 1734 to 1776. In 1755

L

their number was 195; and in 1776 they amounted to 251*. In 1830 there were 258 ships belonging to Whitby, the tonnage of which was 41,176 tons. The number of ships registered at Whitby by no means affords a criterion of the trade of the place, for the greatest part of them are freighted to and from other ports. Perhaps no port in the kingdom presents so great a difference as Whitby between the number of ships registered at the port, and the number annually entered and cleared. This discrepancy between the trade and the tonnage of the port arises from the circumstance of many wealthy persons who live there having their ships built and registered at Whitby, but chiefly employed, on freight, in the trade of other places. When speaking of the shipping of Whitby, it would be unpardonable not to mention that Captain James Cook, one of the most distinguished of British circumnavigators, served an apprenticeship in a vessel belonging to that port.

The principal trades carried on at Whitby, are ship-building, and the manufacture of sail-cloth. Its principal imports are coals from Newcastle and Sunderland, and timber, hemp, flax, tar, iron, and tallow, from the Baltic. Alum manufactured in the neighbourhood is shipped at Whitby, but the principal article of export is at present stones for building, of which great quantities are sent to London. In 1833 a bill having been obtained for constructing a railroad between Whitby and Pickering, the work was almost immediately commenced, and prosecuted with such spirit that it was opened for general traffic on May 6, 1836. What advantages those two towns may hereafter derive from the railway cannot at present be known; but there can be little doubt of the original shareholders being losers, unless there should be a considerable rise in the present market price of the shares.

Whitby, by the Reform Bill of 1832, was constituted a parliamentary borough, returning one member to parliament. The total population within the limits of the borough is about 10,000. In 1831 the population of the town of Whitby was 7769. The present member for the borough is Aaron Chapman, Esq., a native of Whitby, and as a merchant and a ship-owner closely connected with the place.

From the light-house, on the western pier, a tide-light is displayed at night time, as long as there is eight feet water on the bar. The light is stationary, and is visible at the distance of two leagues in clear weather. During the same period of tide, in the day, a flag is hoisted on the west cliff. It is high water at Whitby pier at forty minutes past three o'clock at the full and change of the moon.

---

* The tonnage of these 251 ships was estimated at 55,000 tons, an amount which is certainly too large. There is in the British Museum a vellum roll containing a view of the Yorkshire coast from Robin Hood's Bay to Runswick, with views of Whitby Abbey, drawn about 1782, by Francis Gibson, Esq. afterwards collector of the customs at that port. In this roll a most exaggerated account is given of the population shipping, and trade of Whitby. The population of the town, for instance, is stated to be 18,000; and the number of ships to be 320, with an estimated tonnage of 78,000 tons.

Drawn by J. D. Harding.

Engraved by W. Finden.

SCARBOROUGH.

SCARBOROUGH.

In the view of Scarborough by Harding, which is taken from the southward, the most conspicuous object is the light-house on the Old Pier, or, as it is sometimes called, Vincent's Pier, from the name of the engineer, by whom the outer portion was erected about the year 1750. Beyond the pier are seen the masts of vessels lying in the harbour; to the left are the houses which are built near the shore between West Sand-gate and Bland's Cliff; and on the height are the barracks, with the ruins of the old castle a little further distant, to the left.

Though the name of Scarborough appears to be of Saxon origin *, yet as the place is not mentioned in any author who wrote before the Conquest, nor in the Domesday book, we cannot reasonably suppose it to have been of much importance, either during the Saxon period, or at the time when the Conqueror's survey was made. The castle of Scarborough was built about 1163, by William le Gros, Earl of Albemarle and Holderness ; and from that period the authentic history of the town commences. The castle is situated to the north-eastward of the town, and is built on the isthmus of a peninsula, which comprises an area of about sixteen acres, and is bounded on the north, east, and south by inaccessible cliffs, whose summits are about 300 feet above the level of the sea. The western boundary, overlooking the town, is also formed by an elevated rock ; and the only means of approach to the castle is by a steep path near the edge of the cliff which forms the north side of the isthmus. On passing through a gateway, and over a draw-bridge, we arrive at the castle, which, previous to the introduction of cannon, must have been almost impregnable. The keep, or principal tower, which is ninety-seven feet high, though greatly dilapidated, is yet a striking object, more especially when viewed from the sea, at about two miles' distance from the north cliff. The castle of Scarborough, since the period of its erection by William le Gros, has frequently been the scene of strife :

* The name, which in former times was written *Scearburg*, is derived from *scear* or *scar*, a rock; and *burg*, a castle or fortified place. Skinner, in his Etymologicon, as cited in Hinderwell's History of Scarborough, p. 29, second edition, explains the word scar as " *collis petrosus et asper*, a rocky and rugged hill." The idea of ruggedness is generally conveyed by the word *scar*. The coarse rough lumps of scoriæ, which form part of the refuse of glass-houses and iron-foundries, are in the neighbourhood of Newcastle on Tyne called *scars*.

" Since first by Albemarle its crest
In war's accoutrements was drest,
How many a gallant corse unblest
Has bleached the walls around ! " *

In 1212, Piers Gaveston, the favourite of Edward II., was besieged in Scarborough castle by the army of the confederate nobles under the Earl of Pembroke; and though he gallantly repulsed several assaults, he was at length obliged to capitulate through scarcity of provisions.   In 1536, during the insurrection called the " Pilgrimage of Grace,"—which seems to have been chiefly fomented by the monks in order to compel Henry VIII. to restore such of the lesser monasteries as he had then suppressed, and to dismiss Thomas Cromwell, and other heretical persons of " villayne blood," from his counsels,—Scarborough castle was besieged by the Yorkshire insurgents under Robert Aske; and though it was weakly garrisoned and badly supplied with military stores, yet Sir Ralph Evers, who was then governor, made so brave a defence that the besiegers were obliged to retire without accomplishing their object. In 1554, Thomas Stafford, second son of Lord Stafford, participating in the sentiments of Sir Thomas Wyatt,—who wished to prevent the marriage of Queen Mary with Philip of Spain,—with a few adherents, gained possession of the castle in the following manner :— On a market day, Mr. Stafford came to Scarborough, having his followers disguised as countrymen, and having thus with thirty of them gained admission into the castle, as if for the purpose of viewing the place, they knocked down and secured the sentries, and afterwards admitted the rest of their party.   The rapidity with which this enterprise was executed is said to have given rise to the proverbial phrase : " A Scarborough warning,—a word and a blow, but the blow first."   The triumph of the captors was, however, of but short duration, for in three days the place was retaken by the Earl of Westmorland.   Mr. Stafford and four others, who were the principal leaders in this affair, being made prisoners, were sent to London, where they were tried and executed for high treason.   About the commencement of the war between Charles I. and the Parliament, Sir Hugh Cholmley, who was then governor of Scarborough castle, and had previously held it for the parliament, declared himself in favour of the king.   Though the town and castle were threatened with a siege by the parliamentary forces under Sir Thomas Fairfax, shortly after the battle of Marston Moor in 1644, yet the place was not invested

---

* Poetical Sketches of Scarborough, [by the Rev. Francis Wrangham, Archdeacon of Cleveland, —— Papworth, Esq., and William Combe, Esq., author of the " Tour of Dr. Syntax,"] 8vo., 1813. Some of those Sketches are of rather a warm tint, and the book is now scarce.

until February 16$\frac{44}{45}$*. On the 18th of that month, Sir Thomas Meldrum, a Scottish general in the service of the parliament, assaulted and took the town, and immediately proceeded to lay close siege to the castle. Several assaults made by the besiegers were gallantly repulsed by the garrison, in one of which, on 17th May 1645, Sir Thomas Meldrum was so severely wounded that he died on the 3d June following. Sir Matthew Boynton, who succeeded to the command, continued to press the siege with unabated vigour; and the garrison being weakened through fatigue and the effects of scurvy, the castle was surrendered on 25th July 1645. Lady Cholmley, the wife of the governor, was in the castle during the whole of the siege, and displayed a most heroic spirit. "When Sir Thomas Meldrum," says Sir Hugh Cholmley in his Memoirs, "had sent propositions, with menaces that if they were not accepted he would that night be master of all the works of the castle; and in case one of his men's blood was shed, would not give quarter to man or woman, but put all to the sword; she, conceiving that I would relent in respect of her being there, came to me without any direction or trouble, and prayed me that I would not for any consideration of her do aught which might be prejudicial to my own honour or the king's affairs." In July 1648, the town and castle of Scarborough being then under the command of colonel Matthew Boynton, a kinsman of Sir Matthew Boynton, to whom the place surrendered in 1645, revolted from the parliament and declared for the king; whose cause, however, was too much depressed to derive any benefit from this testimony of loyalty. The town was recovered by the parliamentary forces on 15th of September following; and on 19th December the castle capitulated. Since that period no hostile force has assailed its crumbling walls.

Within fifty years from the erection of the castle, Scarborough appears to have become a place of some importance, for in 1181 Henry II. granted to certain of the inhabitants a charter of incorporation; and the privileges thus granted were confirmed and further extended by king John in 1200. In 1252, Henry III. granted to the bailiffs and burgesses of the town the power of levying sixpence on every merchant ship entering the port, fourpence on every fisherman's ship, and twopence on every fisherman's boat entering with fish, in order to aid the inhabitants in making "a new harbour with timber and stone towards the sea." This work to be made towards the sea was undoubtedly a pier. The grant was subsequently renewed by the king for the further term of three years;

---

* Hinderwell, the historian of Scarborough, in his account of the siege, does not appear to have been aware that February 1644 was, according to our present mode of beginning the year from the 1st January, February 1645. His account of the siege is therefore extremely confused; and he says that it lasted upwards of a year, though in truth it did not last quite six months.

and in subsequent reigns the corporation frequently received similar grants to enable them to improve the harbour and keep the pier in repair. In the year 1546, 37th Henry VIII., an act was passed, imposing a duty to repair the pier, which was then very much injured from the violence of the sea. Among the reasons for the grant, recited in the preamble, it is expressly stated, " That from an early period this port or haven had afforded safe harbour at all tides, and every full sea, to ships, boats, and vessels in any adversity, tempest, or peril on the north coast; and that they had ever been accustomed to resort thither, for the safeguard and assurance, as well of men's lives, as of vessels, goods, and merchandise*." The act passed in 1547 has been renewed with modifications at subsequent periods ; and at the present time, the duty of keeping the pier in repair, and attending to the improvement of the harbour, is vested in a body of commissioners, appointed by the authority of an act of parliament.

There is no river at Scarborough ; and the harbour, which is formed by the piers, is only accessible towards high water. It is high water at Scarborough at forty-five minutes past three o'clock at the full and change of the moon ; and at spring tides there is about twenty-two feet water at the end of the pier. At night a light is shown from the light-house as long as there is twelve feet water at the entrance to the harbour ; and during the same period a flag is hoisted by day. From lists transmitted to the Lord High Admiral of England in 1638, it appears that Scarborough then possessed twenty ships of large size, and that the others were small barques between twenty and sixty tons burthen. In 1730 there were twenty large ships belonging to the port, of about 200 tons each, and seventy smaller ones, of from 60 to 150 tons each ; and the estimated tonnage of the whole was 12,000 tons. In 1796 there were 165 ships, with a tonnage of 25,000 tons ; and in 1830, 169 ships, with a tonnage of 28,070 tons. In 1831 the population of the town was 8760. Scarborough has enjoyed the privilege of sending two members to parliament since 1282. By the Reform Bill, the right of suffrage, which had previously been confined to the members of the common-council, was extended to the ten-pound householders. The present members are Sir F. Trench and Sir J. Johnstone.

About 1620 the sanative virtues of the Spa well were discovered by Mrs. Anne Farrow, who "sometimes walked along the shore, and observing the stones over which the water passed to have received a russet colour, and finding it to have an acid taste different from the common springs, and to receive a purple tincture from galls, thought it probably might have a medical property." The

* Hinderwell's History of Scarborough, p. 164.

lady having tried the water herself, and persuaded others to do the same, it was in a short time pronounced an all-heal, and the people of the place took it as their usual physic. Before 1670 these waters had become celebrated, and many persons resorted to Scarborough for the sake of drinking them. Medical men, however, disagreed both as to their composition and effects; and the opinions of Dr. Witty, a resident physician, who recommended them in every case, were controverted by Mr. Simpson and Dr. George Tonstall. The latter says of the Spa water, "The essence is fit for the cup of a prince; the *caput mortuum*, which is sand and clay, is fit for nothing but the bricklayer's trowel. Hence it doth follow that those who are weak in their digestive faculties and strong in their distributive, may find good by drinking this water, but those who are weak in both will experience the contrary. To all those who have a petrifying character seminated in them, I say of Scarborough water: *Procul ite, citò abite, nunquam redite*.*" From the following anecdote related by the doctor, we may infer that the spa-drinkers of that period were accustomed to indulge in rather copious draughts. "Mr. Westro came to us at Scarborough only to visit his friends, and the two or three days he drank the waters (*not above two quarts at a time*), did so far put him out of tune, that he made his complaint to me he could neither eat nor sleep; and it took me a week's time before I could reduce him to the state of health which he had before he meddled with the waters." He would have been a person of strong constitution indeed—a brazen-bowelled man—not to have been "put out of tune" by such drenching; and it is no small proof of Dr. Tonstall's skill that he should have been able to restore to Mr. Westro the blessings of sound sleep and a good appetite in so short a time as a week. From the double advantage which Scarborough presents to visiters, of drinking the waters and enjoying the benefit of sea-bathing, it is much frequented during the summer season; and a more agreeable place is not to be found on the coast betwixt the Humber and the Tyne.

> " Believe me, ma'am, a daily dip
> Will mollify the cheek and lip:
> If you're too fat 'twill make you thin;
> And if the bones invade the skin,
> 'Twill in a month their sharpness cover,
> And clothe them well with flesh all over.
> The sea's the mill that people mean
> To make the old grow young again."
>
> *Poetical Sketches of Scarborough.*

* Scarborough Spaw spagyrically anatomised, by G. Tonstall, Doctor of Physick, 1670.

FLAMBOROUGH HEAD.

THE view of Flamborough Head, drawn by Balmer, is taken from the cliffs to the north-west. To the left is the promontory properly called " The Head," at a short distance from which stands the lighthouse. Between the Head and the nearer cliffs is a small haven, which is used as a landing place by the fishermen of the village of Flamborough, which lies about a mile to the south-west of the lighthouse.

Flamborough Head, which lies about eighteen miles southward of Scarborough, and four and a half miles northward of Burlington, is one of the most remarkable promontories on the eastern coast. It projects about five miles into the sea, from a line drawn between Burlington Quay and Filey; and its southern side forms the northern boundary of Burlington bay. The cliffs, which are of limestone rock, are from three hundred to four hundred feet high, and their crumbling sides form the haunt and the breeding place of innumerable flocks of sea-birds; among which are cormorants, puffins, razor-bills, and guillemots, with gulls and terns of several species. Guillemots, which are here extremely numerous, are known to the seamen of Shields and Newcastle by the name of " Flamborough-head pilots," as their presence in considerable numbers is almost a certain indication of the ship being " off the Head." Great numbers of those feathered denizens of the cliff are killed every year by " parties of pleasure," from Burlington, Scarborough, and other places, who visit the " Head" for the sake of indulging in the heartless sport, which requires neither skill nor courage, of killing birds by wholesale. At the foot of the cliff, which to the north-west is much indented, there are several caverns and large insulated masses of rock. The largest of those caverns, called Robin Lyth's Hole, has two openings, the one communicating with the land and the other exposed to the sea. The roof, though low at the landward entrance, is in some places fifty feet high; and the view, looking through the rocky vault towards the sea, is extremely grand.

Flamborough Head, which is a most important land-mark for vessels navigating the eastern coast, lies in 54° 8' north latitude; longitude 2' 30'' west. A revolving light is displayed from the lighthouse from sun-set to sun-rise, and presents, first the appearance of two lights on the same tower, and next a brilliant red light. Each of those lights appears at intervals of two minutes; and after gradually attaining their greatest lustre, they in the same manner decline and become eclipsed.

n by G.Balmer.   *Engraved by E.Finden.*

FLAMBOROUGH HEAD.

London, Published 1837, by Charles Tilt, 86, Fleet Street.

Drawn by G. Balmer.

Engraved by J. Stephenson.

BURLINGTON QUAY.

BURLINGTON QUAY.

THE engraving of Burlington Quay, from a painting by Balmer, presents a view of the entrance to the Harbour from the eastward. To the right is seen the inner part of the Old Pier, as it appeared about three months after the great storm of 17th and 18th February, 1836. In front are the houses at the end of Quay Street, and to the left is the South Pier; between which and the shore two ships are perceived aground at the entrance of the inner harbour, which is nearly dry at low water. In the storm above alluded to, great injury was done to the old North Pier, and part of one of the houses to the right was washed down by the violence of the sea.

Burlington Quay lies about a mile to the north-east of the market town of Burlington, and at the bottom of a bay of the same name. It is in the East Riding of Yorkshire, and is about 208 miles from London, 40 from York, and 20 from Scarborough. The earliest mention of it as a harbour occurs in a mandate of King Stephen, addressed to the Sheriff of Yorkshire, commanding him to allow the Prior of Burlington to hold the harbour on the same terms as Walter de Gaunt, and Gilbert, his ancestor, had held the same. During the time that it was in the possession of the Priors of Burlington, it seems to have been an inconsiderable place; but subsequently, as the coal trade between London and the northern parts of the kingdom increased, it began to be of greater importance as a harbour, in consequence of its affording shelter in stormy weather to vessels engaged in that trade. In 1546, an act was passed imposing a duty for erecting the piers and keeping them in repair; and in 1614, a second act was passed, upon a petition from the merchants and ship-owners of the eastern coast, imposing a duty, for the same purposes, on all coals shipped at Newcastle. Since 1614, several other acts have been obtained, authorising the levy of duties and tolls for the purpose of improving the harbour and repairing the piers; and since 1816, the sum thus collected has averaged about £1,750 per annum.

The harbour at Burlington Quay is almost entirely the work of art, as the small stream which there runs into the sea is scarcely sufficient to turn a mill. Its locality seems to render it one of the most appropriate stations for a harbour of refuge between the Frith of Forth and Yarmouth Roads, more especially in gales of wind from the north-eastward; but unfortunately it can only be entered by comparatively small vessels, as the depth of water at the entrance is only from ten to twelve feet at neap tides, and from fourteen to sixteen feet at springs.* The harbour is also so small, that fifty sail of colliers taking shelter there would render it extremely crowded. A few years ago a plan for enlarging the harbour and increasing the depth of water, was submitted to the Commissioners by Mr. Goodrick, who conceived that those desirable objects might be obtained by extending the piers, and deepening the inner part of the harbour by dredging. This plan was approved of, and about sixty yards of the outer end of the new North Pier are already finished; but as one hundred and forty yards more of masonry are required to complete it, and as a new South Pier would cost about £38,000, there seems little chance—considering the annual cost of repairs, and the limited funds of the Commissioners—of the present generation of north-country seamen enjoying any benefit from the proposed improvements. From the Report of a Committee of the House of Commons, appointed in 1836 to inquire into the propriety of levying passing tolls for the maintenance of harbours of refuge on the north-eastern coast of England, it would appear that the owners of vessels employed in the coal trade are generally opposed to the payment of any additional charge for the establishment and maintenance of such harbours. " The Ship-owners' Club and the owner of the ship," says Mr. B. S. Sawden, " are quite willing to risk the ship ; he does not consider about the lives of the men being in danger." † This statement appears to be confirmed by the evidence of Mr. George Booth, of Sunderland, and Mr. Joseph Straker, of Tynemouth, who, speaking for the ship-owners of the Tyne and the Wear, declared that they " were decidedly averse to any increase of toll for the establishment or improvement of harbours of refuge on the eastern coast."

Burlington Bay, between Burlington Quay and Flamborough Head, is a secure road-stead in north-east gales ; and, during the prevalence of such gales, it is not unusual for three hundred ships to be riding there at the same time, sheltered from the violence of the wind and sea by the lofty promontory of Flamborough Head. On the south-east, the Bay is partially sheltered from the violence of the sea by the Smithwick Sands, which run nearly in a line with the coast, from Burlington Quay to Flamborough Head. At each extremity of those sands there is a channel leading into the Bay ; that towards the Head is called the North Sea ; and the other, towards Burlington, the South Sea. Though the Smithwick Sands effectually break the violence of the sea at low water, yet at high water, when they are

---

* It is high water at Burlington Quay at half-past four o'clock, at the full and change of the moon.

† Report from the Select Committee on Harbours of Refuge.—Evidence of Mr. B. S. Sawden, of Burlington, p. 65. Ordered to be printed 16th June, 1836.

covered to a considerable depth, the protection which they afford, in gales of wind from the south-eastward, is not to be depended on. Vessels, therefore, leave the Bay as soon as the wind changes to east or south-east, as it no longer affords them sufficient security; the protection of the Smithwick Sands not being equivalent to the risk of the lee-shore, to which they would be exposed in a gale from the south-east. Were the harbour of Burlington, which is situated to the westward of the Bay, enlarged and deepened, its importance, as a place of refuge for vessels compelled to leave the Bay from the wind changing to the eastward, would be very greatly increased. Could it be so enlarged as to admit one hundred vessels, of from 200 to 300 tons each, it would, with the Bay, afford a place of refuge in all storms from north-east to south-east, which are generally the most destructive on the eastern coast.

The history of Burlington Quay, considering it as a separate place from the town of Burlington, is extremely meagre. The most remarkable event which its annals record, is the landing there of Henrietta Maria, Queen of Charles I., on her return, in 1643, from Holland, whither she had been to conduct her newly-married daughter to her husband, the Prince of Orange, and where she pledged part of the crown jewels in order to obtain money to purchase arms for the Royalists. The Queen, who was attended by a convoy of Dutch men-of-war under the command of Admiral Van Tromp, landed at Burlington Quay, on the 22nd February. The Parliamentary admiral, Batten, who had been cruising, with four ships, for the purpose of intercepting her, having received intelligence of her arrival, sailed into the Bay and began to cannonade the town. Several of the shot struck the house in which the Queen was lodged, so that she was obliged to leave it and take shelter in a ditch in a neighbouring field. A serjeant was killed near her, and the Parliamentary admiral continued his fire until the reflux of the tide and the threats of Van Tromp compelled him to desist.

Burlington Quay is much frequented in summer as a bathing-place; and many persons prefer its quiet and retirement to the greater gaiety of Scarborough. The beach, to the northward of the Quay, affords excellent opportunities for bathing, and the walks and rides in the vicinity are extremely pleasant. A visit to Flamborough Head, which is only about five miles distant, forms a highly interesting excursion either by land or water.

The market-town of Burlington, or, as it is frequently spelled, Bridlington, is situated about a mile to the north-westward of the Quay. In the Domesday Survey, the manor of "Bretlinton" is mentioned with its two "berewicis," or granges, of Hilderthorpe and Wilsthorpe. At the time of the Conquest it formed part of the possessions of Morcar, by whom it was forfeited, in 1072. It subse-

M 2

quently was granted to Gilbert de Gaunt, a Fleming, and one of the followers of the Conqueror. Walter de Gaunt, son of Gilbert, founded, in the reign of Henry I., a monastery at Burlington, for Black Canons of the order of St. Augustin. The monastery having been frequently assailed by enemies who entered the harbour, the prior and canons obtained from Richard II., in 1388, permission to surround it with walls and fortifications, but of which nothing is now remaining, except an arched gateway which leads to the church. William Wode or Wold, prior of Burlington, having been engaged in Aske's rebellion, was executed, for high treason, in 1537, and in the following year the monastery was suppressed, when, according to Speed, its revenues were found to be 682*l*. 13*s*. 9*d*.; or, according to Dugdale, 549*l*. 6*s*. 1*d*. The church, when entire, must have been a large and noble structure, judging from the size of the western part or nave, which is all that remains; the choir and transepts probably having been destroyed by the commissioners of Henry VIII. William of Newbridge, the historian, who flourished about the year 1200, was born at Burlington, although he took his surname from the monastery of Newbridge, in Yorkshire, of which he was a member; and William Kent, who is better known as an architect and landscape-gardener, than as a painter, was a native of the same place. Kent was born in 1685, and served an apprenticeship to a coach-painter at Hull. In 1710 he went to Rome, where he studied landscape and historical painting. On his return to England he was patronised by Richard, third Earl of Burlington, for whom he built Chiswick House, after a design by Palladio, and also laid out the ornamental grounds in the vicinity of that pleasant villa.

Burlington at present gives the title of Earl to a branch of the Cavendish family. Richard Boyle, Earl of Cork, was created an English Peer, by the title of Earl of Burlington, in 1664. On his death, in 1698, he was succeeded by his grandson, Charles, second Earl of Burlington, who died in 1705, and was succeeded by Richard, third Earl, the friend of Pope, and the patron of Kent. He died in 1753, leaving three daughters, one of whom, Lady Charlotte Boyle, was married to William, fourth Duke of Devonshire, whose second son, Lord George Cavendish, was created Baron Cavendish and Earl of Burlington, 7th September, 1831. On his death, on 9th May, 1834, he was succeeded by his grandson, William, the present Earl. His Lordship, who was born in 1808, took a degree with great honour at Cambridge in 1829, and is at present Chancellor of the London University.

According to the returns of 1831, the population of Burlington, Town and Quay, was 4,972; and in 1830 there were forty ships belonging to the port, with a tonnage of 6,290 tons.

Drawn by G. Balmer.

Engraved by W. Finden.

H U L L.

London, Published 1837, by Charles Tilt, 86, Fleet Street.

HULL.

HULL, though one of the most considerable ports of the kingdom, is also one of the least picturesque. From its low situation, little more of the town can be seen than the modern houses near the banks of the Humber; and though jetties, dock-gates, and pier-heads, are sometimes useful as accessaries in a picture, yet where such occupy almost the entire line of the fore-ground, with a row of brick buildings behind them, the painter must manage his subject as he best can, and be content with giving correctly that which his art cannot improve :—" Res ipsa negat ornari." The view of Hull, from a painting by Balmer, is taken from the Humber, looking towards the north. Beyond the river-craft, which are seen in front, is the entrance to the Humber dock; and the jetty to the right, which appears crowded with people, is a favourite promenade with the inhabitants of Hull, who some-times assemble there in crowds to watch the sailing and arrival of the steam-packets. The most distant building to the right is the citadel, at the entrance of the river Hull, which there discharges itself into the Humber. Towards the middle of the engraving is seen the tower of Trinity Church, the only object which at the distance of a mile commands the attention of the stranger, and gives an individual character to the river.

The town of Hull, or, as it is sometimes called, Kingston-upon-Hull, is in the East Riding of Yorkshire, and lies about one hundred and seventy miles north-ward of London, and about thirty-nine to the south-east of York. On the south it is bounded by the Humber, and on the eastward by the small river Hull. The old town, which was formerly protected on the north and west by a wall running from the Hull to the Humber, is now wholly insular, as a line of wet-docks occupies the site of the old fortifications. The suburbs, of Sculcoates on the north, and Drypool on the east, may be considered as forming, with the old borough of Hull, but one large town, the population of which is about 50,000.*

The Hull, which is but a small river, has its source near the village of Lissett, about five miles from Burlington, and after running about twenty-six miles, in a southern direction, discharges itself into the Humber on the east side of the town to which it gives name. It is navigable for small craft as far as Elmotlands,

---

* The parliamentary borough of Hull, as enlarged by the reform act, comprises a large portion of the parishes of Sculcoates and Drypool.

about sixteen miles from its mouth. It contains many fish, such as roach, perch, gudgeon, eels, and pike; and Driffield Beck, one of its tributaries, is famed for the size and excellence of its trout.

The Humber, which opposite to Hull is nearly three miles broad, and about six fathoms deep in mid-channel, is formed by the junction of the Trent and the Ouse, about sixteen miles above Hull, and it discharges itself into the sea about twenty-four miles below that town. From the rapidity of the current, which at spring tides runs at the rate of five miles an hour, and from the numerous sandbanks which are in the river, the navigation of the Humber is both intricate and dangerous; for should a vessel get aground on one of the sands, she is extremely liable to be overset by the force of the tide. Such accidents are, indeed, by no means uncommon, for almost every year affords instances of vessels, both ships and river-craft, being lost in the Humber in this manner. In the upper part of the Humber, in the Trent, and in the Ouse between Trent-Falls and Selby, the flood tide, more especially in a strong easterly wind, frequently rushes up the river like a wave, considerably raised above the water which it meets. This tidal wave is called by the people of Hull and its vicinity the " *Ager*,"—the *g* being pronounced hard; and from the murmuring sound which it makes as it rolls onward and dashes against the shore, it has been supposed that the river was called the " *Humber*." Drayton, in his Poly-Olbion, thus notices the " *Ager*," or, as he spells it, the " *Higre*,* " in his description of the Humber :—

> " For when my Higre comes, I make my either shore
> Ever tremble with the sound that I afarre doe send."

The name of Hull does not occur in Domesday-book; but Myton, now one of the wards of the town, is there mentioned as a " berewic" in the manor of Ferriby. In a grant, probably dated about 1160, to the monks of the abbey of Meaux or Melsa, in Holderness, and five miles distant from Hull, it appears to be called the Wyke of Myton.† About the same time it seems also to have been called Hull, for between 1160 and 1260 the names of persons frequently occur with the addition of " *de Hull*." In the Pipe-roll of 6th of King John, 1205, containing

---

* Taylor, the water-poet, observed this tidal wave in the estuary of the Wash below Boston :—
> " It hath lesse mercy than beare, wolfe, or tyger,
> And, in those countries, it is called the Hyger."

Dryden, who had noticed it in the river Trent, calls it the " *Eagre* " :—
> " But like an Eagre rode in triumph o'er the tide."

† At that period there is reason to believe that the river Hull discharged itself into the Humber further to the westward than it does at present; probably a little above the spot where the Humber-dock basin has been formed. The site on which the *town* of Hull is now built would then be situated on the *left* bank of the river. At what time the course of the Hull was changed does not seem to be clearly ascertained.

the receipts from various places on account of custom, a large sum is entered as received from Hull. In 1207 Hull is distinctly mentioned as a town; and, in 1269, it is noticed as one of the places from which wool was illicitly exported to Flanders and elsewhere. In 1278, the abbot of Meaux presented a petition to Edward I., praying that he and his successors might have a market every Thursday, and a fair annually, at Wyke, near Myton upon the Hull; and in the great Pipe-roll of the ninth year of the same king's reign, 1281, there is a computus of Buonricini Gicidon and others, merchants of Lucca, in respect of the new customs of wool, woolfels and leather, in which the sum of £1,086. 10s. 8d. occurs as being received from Hull, on account of three thousand one hundred and forty-one stones of wool, eighty-eight woolfels, and fifty-nine lasts twelve dicker and seven skins of leather. In the same year the receipts on the same account were, from Newcastle-on-Tyne, £323. 3s. 9d.; from London, £1,602. 16s. 6½d.; and from Boston, £3,599. 1s. 6d. In 1291, Gervas de Clifton, then sheriff of Yorkshire, paid £78. 2s. 10½d. for the carriage by land and water of four hundred and fifteen doles and two pipes of wine from Hull to " Brustwyk, Kowell, Knaresburgh, Hexwra, Alnewyk, Berewyk, and Norham." The preceding early notices of Hull sufficiently prove it to have been a place of trade long before 1296, the year in which, according to most of its historians, it was founded by Edward I.*

In 1293 Edward I. obtained the manor and town of Hull from the abbot of Meaux, in exchange for other possessions; and the king was so pleased with his acquisition, that he ordered the town to be called *Kingston*-upon-Hull. The year 1294 affords the earliest instance of the new name†. Shortly after the town came into the possession of the king, a custos, or warden, was appointed to govern it; and, in 1299, it was constituted a free borough. Among other privileges, the burgesses were allowed to choose a coroner, and to have a market twice a week, on Tuesdays and Fridays, and a fair once a year. In the twenty-eighth of Edward I., 1300, the burgesses of Hull were first summoned to return two members to Parliament; in 1317 Edward II. granted them permission to fortify the town with a wall and a moat; and in 1332, by a charter of Edward III., a mayor and four bailiffs were appointed for the government of the affairs of the

---

* " Notices relative to the Early History of the Town and Port of Hull, by Charles Frost, Esq. F.S.A." 4to. 1827. Prior to the publication of Mr. Frost's researches, all the preceding historians of Hull describe the town as being founded by Edward I. in 1296, and date its origin as a place of trade from that period.

† Kingston, as a prefix to Hull, is now almost obsolete; and though the name was in former times frequently written " Kingston-upon-Hull," yet the place appears to have been more generally known by its old name, Hull.

borough. The first mayor of Hull was William de la Pole, a wealthy merchant, who, previous to his appointment to the office, had entertained Edward III. in a most splendid manner during a visit which he paid to Hull, and had received in return the honour of knighthood.

Shortly after his appointment to the office of mayor, Sir William de la Pole received a grant of the customs of Hull and Boston, in consideration of the sum of £4,000, advanced to Edward III.; and in 1338, when the king was preparing to invade France, he advanced to him a loan of £18,500: an immense sum in those days, when wheat could be bought for 3s. 4d. a quarter, a fat sheep for 6d., and six pigeons for 1d.; and when the daily pay of an earl attending the king in time of war was 6s. 8d.*—in modern times the exact cost of a five minutes' interview with an attorney, and not quite a third of the fee of a physician, who can dispatch a dozen patients in an hour!

Sir William de la Pole, in consideration of his great ability, and the services which he had rendered Edward III., was by that king appointed one of the gentlemen of his bed-chamber, and afterwards promoted to the office of secondary baron of the exchequer. On the death of Sir William de la Pole, in 1366, he was succeeded in his estates by his son Michael, who was summoned to parliament as baron Wingfield, in the 39th year of the reign of Edward III.; and, in the 50th of the same king, he was appointed lord high admiral for the northern coast of England. In the sixth of Richard II., 1383, he was appointed to the office of lord chancellor; and in 1386 he was created earl of Suffolk. From this period his fortune began to decline. He was first charged with peculation, and found guilty; but, after a short confinement in Windsor, he was restored to the favour of his sovereign, Richard II. The ancient nobility, who were displeased at the honours conferred on a merchant's son, and jealous of the influence which he possessed with the king, were wishful to obtain his dismission from the court. In 1389 he was again accused of high crimes and misdemeanors; and being sentenced to perpetual exile, he retired to Paris, where he died in the first year of his banishment. Michael de la Pole †, the first of the name who was earl of

---

* Fleetwood's Chronicon Preciosum, p. 94 ; and a " Collection of Ordinances and Regulations for the Government of the Royal Household made in divers Reigns," p. 9, 4to., printed for the Society of Antiquaries, 1790.

† Michael de la Pole, son of the first earl, was restored to his father's titles and estates, by Henry IV., in 1399. His son, also called Michael, was killed at the battle of Agincourt ; and two of of his brothers also lost their lives in France during the same war. William de la Pole, fourth earl of Suffolk, brother to Michael the third earl, distinguished himself both as a general and a statesman during a seventeen years' service in France, in which long period he never visited his own country. He negociated the marriage between Henry VI. and Margaret of Anjou, in 1445 ; and, in 1448, he was created duke of Suffolk. Like his ancestor Michael, the first earl, he was charged with high crimes by a powerful party of the

Suffolk, was a liberal benefactor to the town of Hull, where he built for himself a large and stately house, known subsequently as Suffolk Palace, which continued in the possession of his descendants till the death of Edmund de la Pole, last earl of Suffolk of that family, on whose execution, in 1513, on a charge of treason, his property was seized by Henry VIII., who regarded him with great jealousy, and tyrannically caused him to be put to death in consequence of his near relation to the crown; his mother having been Elizabeth Plantagenet, sister to Edward IV. Michael de la Pole founded and endowed a priory at Hull for monks of the Carthusian order, which was suppressed in 1538; and the charitable institution, now called the Charter House, also owes its endowment to his liberality. Through his interest the privileges of the burgesses were confirmed and further enlarged by a charter granted by Richard II. in 1382.

In consequence of the decay of the towns of Hedon and Ravenspur* towards the end of the fourteenth century, the trade of Hull was very materially increased. From the accounts of John Liversege and John Tuttebury, from the 16th April to 7th July, 1400, wine appears to have been then one of the principal articles of import. Among other items, we find salt, canvas, Spanish iron, linen cloth, four reams of paper, wax, spices, bow-staves, wainscot, seed-oil, fur, gloves, scoops and wooden dishes, rosin, copper, one thousand "waltill" [perhaps, bricks or flat tiles], paving-stones, patten-clogs, and horns for lanterns. Among the exports are woollen cloths, coals, lead, calf-skins, and worsted.

Leland, speaking of Hull, says that "The first great encreasing of the towne was by passing for fisch into Iceland, from whence they had the whole trade of stock-fisch into England." He also says that, "bycause the burden of stock-fisch was light, the shipes were ballasted with great coble stone, brought out of Iceland, which in continuance paved all the town of Kingston throughout." The merchants of Hull were the first in England who embarked in the whale fishery, in 1598; and, since the revival of that trade in 1765, Hull has sent more ships to Greenland and Davis' Straits than any other port in the kingdom, except London.

The greatest inconveniences to which the town was exposed, in former times,

nobility, and sentenced to be banished for five years. In passing over to France in a small vessel, he was seized by the captain of a ship—a partisan of his enemy, the duke of Exeter—who caused his head to be struck off on the beach near Dover. The circumstances of his death are described by Shakspeare in the Second Part of Henry VI.

* There are no remains existing of the town of Ravenspur or Ravenser, which is supposed to have been destroyed by the overflowing of the Humber towards the latter end of the fourteenth century. Hedon, or, as it is also called, Headon, is a small town about eight miles to the eastward of Hull. It returned two Members to Parliament from the 23d Edward I. to the passing of the Reform Bill in 1832, when it was disfranchised on account of the smallness of its population, which, in 1831, was only 1,080.

N

were a deficient supply of water for the use of the inhabitants, and the occasional overflowing of the Humber and the Hull. In 1376 the mayor and burgesses represented to the king that their town, being built upon a salt soil, afforded them no fresh water; nor could they procure any but such as was brought daily in boats out of Lincolnshire, at great expense and trouble, as the neighbouring villages of Hessle, Anlaby, Cottingham, and others, had combined together, and refused to let them have any water from their streams. Upon this complaint, the king appointed commissioners to inquire into the best mode of providing a supply of water for the town; and, by their authority, a canal was ordered to be cut from Anlaby spring to Hull. In 1392 the inhabitants of the above villages, who seem to have been extremely envious of the people of Hull, assembled in a riotous manner, and, after cutting the banks of the canals, proceeded in a hostile array towards that town, vowing destruction to the inhabitants. The rioters having in a short time dispersed, several of the ringleaders were apprehended, and hung at York. In 1400 a second canal was made for the conveyance of fresh water from Anlaby to Hull, and in 1402 certain inhabitants of the neighbouring villages again attempted to destroy it; and though the principal offenders were punished by imprisonment and fine, still others were not deterred from occasionally throwing carrion and letting salt-water into the canal. In consequence of the continued annoyance, the people of Hull at length appealed to the Pope, who, in 1412, issued an admonitory letter, which proved so effectual that all attempts to destroy the canal or corrupt the water ceased from the time of its publication.

In the annals of Hull, from the reign of Edward I. to that of Elizabeth, frequent mention is made of the Humber and the Hull overflowing their banks, laying the adjacent country under water, destroying property, and drowning both men and cattle. For the purpose of guarding the town against those floods, embankments were from time to time formed; and Taylor, the water-poet, who visited Hull in 1622, says, that in his time it cost five hundred pounds a year,—

"To fence the town from Hull and Humber's tides."

Hull is memorable in English history as being the first town which openly resisted the authority of the king, at the commencement of the civil war between Charles I. and the Parliament. Hull being one of the most important and best fortified towns in the kingdom, besides containing at that time a large magazine of arms and warlike stores, each party was anxious to secure it for themselves. About the beginning of 1642, Sir John Hotham was appointed governor of Hull by the Parliament, which, on the mayor and inhabitants refusing to admit him when he first presented himself, passed an order requiring their obedience under the pain of high treason. Shortly after Sir John had been admitted as governor, the earl of Newcastle came to Hull with a commission from the king appointing him to the same office; but as soon as the object of his visit became known, he was apprehended, and afterwards sent out of the town. On the 23rd of April, the king himself, who had come from York, appeared before the town with about two hundred followers and demanded admission, which being refused by Sir John Hotham, the king ordered a herald to proclaim him a traitor, and retired in great indignation to Beverley. Towards the latter end of June the royalists proceeded to besiege Hull; but a great part of the adjacent country being laid under water, by the governor causing the banks of the Humber and the Hull to be cut, they raised the siege about the end of July, after having lost several men in assaults made on their lines by the garrison. In the next year, 1643, Lord Fairfax then being governor*, Hull was again besieged, from the 2d of September to the 12th of October, by the royal army, under the newly-created marquis of Newcastle. This siege was much more closely pressed than the first, and was also attended with much greater loss on both sides; but through the vigorous resistance of the garrison, the besiegers were again compelled to retire.

In consequence of the trade of the town having increased so much that the vessels frequenting the port could not be sufficiently accommodated in the river Hull, where they usually discharged and received their cargoes, a bill was obtained, in 1774, for the formation of a dock. The work was almost immediately commenced; and in four years a dock, capable of containing a hundred ships, was completed. This dock, which has its entrance from the river Hull, and is now called the Old Dock, being found insufficient for the increasing trade of the port, another, having its entrance directly from the Humber, and called the Humber Dock, was commenced in 1803, and finished in 1809. A third, called the Junction Dock, uniting the Old and the Humber Dock, was commenced in 1827, and finished in 1829. This connected line of docks—which, with the Hull and the Humber, render the old town of Hull completely insular—are capable of containing two hundred and thirty ships. Hull, with respect to the money

* The Parliament having discovered that Sir John Hotham and his son, Captain Hotham, intended to deliver up the town to the King, sent down orders to arrest them. The younger Hotham was seized at Hull early on the morning of 29th June, 1643. His father, having received some intelligence, escaped from his house by a back way, but was apprehended the same day at Beverley by his brother-in-law, Sir Matthew Boynton. They were sent to London by sea; and, being brought to trial on 1st December before a military commission, they were found guilty of having betrayed their trust by corresponding with the Royalists for the surrender of the town. Sentence of death having been pronounced against them, the son was beheaded on Tower-Hill, 1st January, 1644, and the father at the same place on the day following.

received on account of customs, is the fourth port in Great Britain, the three by which it is exceeded being London, Liverpool, and Bristol; and with respect to the number of ships, it is the sixth. In 1835 the sum received at Hull on account of customs was £726,000; and the number of vessels registered at the port was 568, with a tonnage of 70,582 tons. Since Goole—which is situated at the entrance to the Leeds and Wakefield canal, about twenty miles above Hull— was declared to be a port in 1828, the customs and the tonnage of Hull have to a certain extent declined.

Except Trinity church, there is scarcely a building in Hull which is likely to attract the attention of the stranger, either on the score of antiquity or architectural beauty. This noble structure, which stands on the west side of the market-place, is one of the largest parochial churches in England. It is supposed to have been founded between 1285 and 1301; and the transept, which is of brick, is probably one of the earliest specimens of that kind of building in the kingdom, excepting such as are of Roman workmanship. It has generally been supposed that the art of brick-making, which had been neglected in this country since the time of the Romans, was revived in the reign of Richard II.*; but there can be no doubt of its being practised at Hull long before that period; for in 1321 William de la Pole had a *tegularia*, or brick-yard, without the north gate of the town.

By a charter of Henry VI., Hull was appointed to be a county of itself, and was placed under the government of a mayor, twelve aldermen, and a sheriff. By the municipal reform bill of 1835, the mode of electing the mayor and aldermen is altered; and a certain number of town-councillors are directed to be chosen. By the parliamentary reform bill of 1832, the boundary of the borough was enlarged, and the right of suffrage extended to the ten-pound householders. The present members are, Wm. Hutt, Esq., and Col. P. Thompson.

Among the many celebrated men which Hull has produced, the most pre-eminently distinguished are Andrew Marvell and William Wilberforce: their fame is not confined to the local records of a borough, but is written in the annals of their country, where it will live as long as uncorruptible patriotism and active benevolence shall continue to be regarded as virtues.

* Dr. Lyttelton, Bishop of Carlisle, in a paper published in the first volume of the Archæologia, though he expressly notices the antiquity of the old town walls of Hull, which were built of brick, supposes the art might have been revived in the reign of Richard II.

Painted by T. Creswick from a sketch by G. Balmer.

Engraved by W. Finden.

HARTLEPOOL.

HARTLEPOOL.

THE view of Hartlepool, painted by T. Creswick, from a drawing by G. Balmer, is taken from the northward. To the right, between the foreground and the town, are seen the sands of, what is called, the " Slake ; " to the left are the cliffs, at the foot of which are the excavations called " Fairy Coves ; " and, beyond the town, part of the southern coast of Durham is perceived, which extends from Hartlepool southward to the mouth of the Tees. The figures in the foreground are characteristic of the place ; for there is no obtaining a view of Hartlepool from the landside without seeing a group of fishwomen.

The town of Hartlepool stands on a small peninsula on the southern coast of Durham, and is about nine miles north-east of Stockton-upon-Tees. From the " Slake " or pool, which is between the town and the mainland to the west, it probably received the appellation of " *le poole*," to distinguish it from the village of Hart, which is about four miles and a half to the north-west. The word Hart, according to Ducange *, signified in Teutonic a forest ; and, if the name of the parish of Hart be of the same origin, the reason why the place should have been so called is obvious. The old town-seal of Hartlepool contains a rebus of the name—a hart up to his knees in a pool—which assigns to the first part of it a different etymology. Previous to receiving the name of Hartlepool the place was called Heortu, and sometimes Heortness ; the termination *u* is perhaps an abbreviation of *eau*, water ; and the name Heortu synonymous with Hart-le-Pool. The termination *ness* is expressive of the place being built on a point of land which projects into the sea. " At or near this place," says Bishop Tanner, in the *Notitia Monastica*, " was the ancient monastery called Heorthu, founded upon the first conversion of the Northumbrians to Christianity, about A.D. 640, by a religious woman named Hieu, or, as some have it, St. Bega, whereof St. Hilda was some time abbess." This ancient convent was destroyed by the Danes about 800, and its site is now unknown, though it is supposed to have stood on the spot which was subsequently occupied by a Franciscan monastery, founded by one of the Bruce family about 1250, and suppressed by Henry VIII. Of this monastery or its church there is at present no part remaining, though some old houses called the Friary, probably built out of the ruins, still indicate its situation. The church of Hartlepool, which is dedicated

---

* Cited by Sir Cuthbert Sharp in his History of Hartlepool, a curious and interesting book ; 8vo. Durham, 1816.

to St. Hilda, is a large building, and, from the various styles of its architecture, it evidently has been built at different periods. The tower and the nave, which are the oldest parts of the building, appear, from the style of architecture, to have been erected towards the latter end of the thirteenth century. The side-aisles, which have been built at a later period, are of a very mean character and unworthy of the older portion of the structure. The tower is supported, on the north and west, by large buttresses; and, as the church stands on rather an elevated situation, it forms a conspicuous mark for vessels in approaching the harbour.

About the time of the Conquest, the manors of Hart and Hartness belonged to Fulk de Panell; and, upon the marriage of his daughter Agnés with Robert de Brus—one of the Norman followers of William I.—they came, with other rich manors in Yorkshire and in Durham, into the possession of that family. Upon Robert Bruce, a descendant of the above named Robert de Brus, succeeding to the crown of Scotland in 1306, all his English estates were confiscated by Edward I., who granted the manor of Hart and the borough of Hartlepool to Robert de Clifford, " saving the rights of the Bishops of Durham," under whom, since 1189, the property had been held.

In 1201, King John granted a charter to Hartlepool, conferring upon the burgesses the same privileges as those of Newcastle-upon-Tyne; and in 1230, Richard le Poor, Bishop of Durham, granted another charter, appointing a mayor and other officers for the government of the town. In 1593, Queen Elizabeth granted a new charter, under which the affairs of the borough have been since regulated.

From the reign of King John to that of James I., Hartlepool was the most considerable port in the county of Durham; but from the latter period till about seven years ago, its importance as a place of trade appears to have greatly declined; and from 1730 to 1832, its condition was that of a small fishing town, scarcely visited by any ships, except colliers belonging to Sunderland and Newcastle, which occasionally sought refuge in its harbour during a storm. In 1832, a bill was obtained for the purpose of improving the harbour and forming a dock at Hartlepool; and since that period a considerable portion of the projected works have been finished. A railway has since been formed, by which coals are brought to the town; and a considerable quantity are now shipped there for the London and other markets; and from the advantageous situation of the harbour, and the facility with which vessels can be loaded, there seems great probability of Hartlepool becoming, in a few years, one of the principal ports for the shipment of coals in the county of Durham. In 1831, the population was only 1,330; but since the formation of the railway and the improvement of the harbour, it has considerably increased.

Painted by E. W. Cooke.   Engraved by E. Finden.

MEN OF WAR AT SPITHEAD.

London, Published 1837, by Charles Tilt, 86, Fleet Street.

Painted by E. W. Cooke.

Engraved by E. Finden.

ENTRANCE TO PORTSMOUTH HARBOUR.

PORTSMOUTH.

LEAVING the Ports and Harbours between the Humber and the mouth of the Thames, as well as those between the Nore and the Isle of Wight, to be given in future Parts, we shall proceed at once to Portsmouth; where, instead of the colliers and Humber keels, and five-man boats and fishing cobles, characteristic of the eastern coast, we shall obtain a sight of those floating bulwarks of our island—men-of-war.

Before giving any account of Portsmouth, it seems preferable to notice, in continuous order, the five views illustrative of that important naval station, which are all from paintings by E. W. Cooke, who has represented the character of the place with an effective fidelity which has never been surpassed. The composition and accurate detail of the originals have, indeed, been excellently imitated by the engraver; but it is beyond his art to convey, by any combination of lines, an adequate idea of their beautiful colouring.

MEN-OF-WAR AT SPITHEAD.—In this engraving (a vignette), a stern-view is presented of a seventy-four, with her guess-warp booms * out, moored at Spithead. To the right is a victualling hoy, dropping alongside of the seventy-four; and in the distance is seen a first-rate. The time is evening, which invests the whole scene with its calm. We may conclude that the day has been fine, as both ships seem to have availed themselves of the opportunity thus afforded of " drying hammocks," which are seen suspended from their yards and between their masts.

ENTRANCE TO PORTSMOUTH HARBOUR.—In the front of this view, and towards the right, a man-of-war cutter is seen running out of the harbour; and, from her heel to leeward, and the agitated state of the water, we may perceive that it is blowing a stiff breeze. Vessels of her class are chiefly employed in the coast-guard service and as admirals' tenders, or as packets on short voyages, or in communicating between one naval dépôt and another. In the distance, to leeward of her, the Dock-yard Semaphore is perceived; and more to the right, but nearer to the eye of the spectator, is seen the round tower; from which, in former times, an immense chain used to extend to the block-house at Gosport, on the opposite side of the channel, for the purpose of protecting the entrance to the harbour, in the event of its being assailed by the ships of an enemy. Towards the centre of the engraving a broad-side view is presented of the Port-Admiral's flag-ship, a

---

* The guess-warp booms are the spars which are suspended at right angles from a ship's side, and to which the boats are made fast when she is moored.

first-rate ; which, from the flags at her mast-head, appears to be making a signal, a-head of her, in the distance, the hulls are perceived of two ships of war, laid up in ordinary ; and further to the left is seen part of the block-house fort, at Gosport, with a beacon, to direct vessels in making the harbour.

VIEW FROM THE SALUTING PLATFORM.—The correctness of this view will be immediately recognised by every person in the least acquainted with Portsmouth. The platform, from which it is taken, forms the grand promenade of the inhabitants, and is usually the first place visited by strangers, on account of the prospect which is thence obtained. Immediately in front of the engraving is seen the northern extremity of the platform, on which are two soldiers, who seem indulging themselves with a leisurely inhalation of the fresh breeze from the water, after having liberally expended a portion of their own breath in sounding their bugles at parade. Beyond the platform, the most conspicuous object is the Government Semaphore, with three flags displayed as a signal; and to the left, the landing-place called the King's Stairs. Beyond the old round tower is seen the flag-ship of the Port-Admiral; and, between her and the gun-brig which is running in, a distant view is obtained of the Town-hall of Gosport.

RIGGING HULK, WITH A NEW FRIGATE ALONGSIDE.—In this engraving we have a view of a new frigate with only her lower masts in, lying alongside of the Topaze rigging hulk. The latter vessel—which now presents so clumsy an appearance, from her bows and sides being sheathed with a stout doubling of timber, and from a wooden house being built over her stem—was formerly a French frigate; and, when she first came into our possession, she was much admired by nautical men for the beauty of her build. Further in the distance, to the right, is seen a first-rate lying off the dock-yard quay, partly rigged; and, beyond her, are perceived the immense wooden roofs which cover the building slips. The line of buildings to the right is the rigging-house, and the tower erected above it is the dock-yard Semaphore. On the extreme right, towards the front, is seen the fore-part of a mooring lighter, with one of the numerous spar-booms lying afloat near the Common Hard. The original picture is at the present time (14th March) in the Gallery of the British Institution, where it has excited general admiration.

GOSPORT—THE FLAG-SHIP SALUTING.—In this view a portrait is given of the Victory, Lord Nelson's ship at the battle of Trafalgar, and she is represented as firing a salute in honour of the Port-Admiral, who is seen going on board in his barge, accompanied by the Commandant-General of the garrison. A mooring lighter and a government steamer are perceived to the right; and, on the left, is seen the town-hall of Gosport.

Painted by E. W. Cooke.

Engraved by E. Finden.

VIEW FROM THE SALUTING PLATFORM, PORTSMOUTH.

London, Published 1837, by Charles Tilt, 86, Fleet Street.

Painted by E. W. Cooke.

Engraved by W. Finden.

RIGGING HULK AND FRIGATE, PORTSMOUTH.

Portsmouth, one of our greatest naval depôts, is situated near the south-western extremity of the island of Portsea, in the county of Hampshire, and is about 70 miles S. S.W. of London. Adjoining to it, on the northward, is the town of Portsea; and to the south-east, without the walls, lies the suburb of Southsea. The three places may be considered as forming one large town, under the general name of Portsmouth, the aggregate population of which is about 50,000. The population of Gosport, which lies to the westward of Portsmouth, on the opposite side of the Harbour, is, with that of the adjacent hamlet of Stoke, about 12,000. The docks and naval storehouses are within the precinct of Portsea; the hospitals and the victualling establishment are at Gosport; and the offices of the Port-Admiral and the residence of the Lieutenant-Governor are at Portsmouth, within the lines of which are also the barracks for the accommodation of the garrison. Portsmouth is strongly fortified by a circuit of bastions and a moat, which enclose the town on the land side, and which are connected with a similar line, extending in a semicircular form round the land-side of Portsea. In the event of a siege, it would require 14,000 men to form an efficient garrison for the united towns. The situation of Portsmouth is low and marshy: and the peculiar smell which arises from the mud at low water, and from the moat, may be perceived at the distance of two or three miles, in approaching the town from the northward.

Portsmouth harbour is one of the most secure and commodious in the kingdom; and from the depth of water, both within it and at its mouth, ships of the line can enter or depart at all times of the tide. From the narrowness of its entrance,—which, between the old Round Tower at Portsmouth and the Blockhouse Fort at Gosport, is not wider than the Thames at London Bridge,—it is protected from the swell of the sea; and it is sheltered from the violence of winds blowing off the land by the range of hills to the northward. Immediately above its entrance the harbour begins to expand, and about a mile and a half above the old Round Tower it is nearly two miles in breadth. It then branches off into three principal creeks, or *leats* as they are frequently called; one of which runs up to Fareham, another to Porchester Castle, and the third to Portsbridge. In these creeks most of the men-of-war in ordinary are moored. As those ships, when laid up, are each covered over with a large wooden roof, to protect them from the effects of the weather, they appear, when seen from Portsdown Hill, which commands an excellent view of the harbour, not so much like floating castles as like immense floating barns—ample garners, which would contain more corn than the swords and cutlasses of their former gallant crews, beat into reaping-hooks, will ever cut down!

At Portsmouth the tide flows about seven hours and ebbs about five; and the

o

velocity with which the ebb-tide runs out effectually scours the channel at the mouth of the harbour, and prevents the accumulation of sand. It is high water in the harbour at 36 minutes past 11 o'clock at the full and change of the moon; and the rise of spring tides is about eighteen feet, and of neaps about twelve. In the months of March and April the specific gravity of the water in Portsmouth harbour becomes so much increased, that ships lying there are observed to float about two inches lighter than at other times of the year. The latitude of the Observatory in the Dock-yard is 50° 48′ 3″ north; longitude 1° 5′ 59″ west.

The roadstead of Spithead, which is sufficiently large to afford convenient anchorage for nearly all the ships of the British navy, lies between Portsmouth and the Isle of Wight; and the usual place in which ships of war ride is about three miles distant from Portsmouth harbour. It derives its name from the *Spit*, or end of a sand-bank, which extends from the western shore of the estuary towards Southsea Castle, about a mile below Portsmouth. The channel for the harbour, from Spithead, is comparatively narrow, and is commanded by the batteries at Southsea Castle. To the westward of Spithead is the sand called the Motherbank, on the edge of which merchantmen generally anchor; and to the north-eastward are St. Helen's roads, a frequent rendezvous as well for ships of war as for vessels in the merchant service. All these roadsteads are protected from southerly winds by the high land of the Isle of Wight.

Though Portsmouth does not appear to have been a place of much consideration as a naval station previous to the reign of Henry VIII., who may be regarded as the first English King that established a permanent royal navy, it was yet undoubtedly a town of some consequence long before that time. In 1194, Richard I. granted a charter to the inhabitants, wherein, after declaring that he retains the town of " Portsmue " in his own hands, he establishes an annual fair to be held therein for fifteen days, to which all persons of England, Normandy, Poictou, Wales, Scotland, and all others, either foreigners or his own people, might freely resort, and enjoy the same privileges as at the fairs of Winchester, Hoiland, or elsewhere in his dominions. The burgesses of " Portsmue," as the place was then called, were also allowed to have a weekly market, with the same privileges and immunities as those of Winchester and Oxford; with freedom from all tolls of portage, passage, and stallage, and exemption from suit and service at hundred and county courts *. This charter was confirmed in 1201 by King John, and in 1230 by Henry II.; and in 1256 the latter monarch granted another charter, establishing a guild of merchants at Portsmouth. The privileges of the burgesses were at

---

* Anderson's History of Commerce, vol. i., p. 180., edit. 1787.

Painted by E. W. Cooke.

Engraved by W. Finden.

GOSPORT, FLAG SHIP SALUTING.

London. Published 1837. by Charles Tilt. 86 Fleet Street.

several differerent times confirmed by succeeding kings; and, in 1627, Charles I. granted them a charter, whereby a mayor and twelve aldermen were appointed for the civil government of the town. This charter, which was renewed by Charles II., has since been modified by the Municipal Reform Bill of 1835, which directs that the borough shall be divided into six wards, which shall elect a town council of forty-two members. In 1298 the borough was summoned to send two members to parliament, a privilege which it continues to enjoy.

If the number of ships and mariners supplied by the different maritime towns of England for the great fleet of Edward III., in 1348, be considered as affording a tolerably correct idea of their shipping and trade, Portsmouth must at that period have ranked but low as a seaport town; its quota being only 5 ships and 96 mariners, while Southampton supplied 21 ships and 476 mariners, Weymouth 15 ships and 263 mariners, and Shoreham 20 ships and 329 mariners.

While Normandy, Guienne, and other provinces of France continued in the possession of the English, Portsmouth was frequently the rendezvous of armies destined for those parts; and Southsea Common was the spot where they used to encamp previous to embarkation. In the first year of the reign of Richard II. the French made an attack on Portsmouth, and burnt part of the town; but, the inhabitants furiously assailing them in the midst of their triumph, they were obliged to retire to their ships. In 1416 a French fleet again appeared before Portsmouth, and for some time blockaded an English fleet which was lying in the harbour. In 1421 a payment appears to have been made out of the Exchequer for the building a new tower at Portsmouth. Leland, who visited the town about 1540, thus speaks of the fortifications: " The town of Portesmouth is muried from the east tour a furlong length withe a mudde waulle armid with tymbre, whereon be great peaces both of yron and brassen ordinaunces; and this peace of waulle having a diche without it, runneth so far flat south-south-east, and is the place moste apte to defende the town there open to the haven. Ther runneth a dich almost flat east for a space, and wythin it is a waulle of mudde like to the other, and so there goeth aboute the toun to the circuite of a myle. There is a gate of tymbre at the northeast of the toun, and bye it is cast up an hille of erth diched, whereon be gunnes to defend the entre into the toun by land. I learned in the toun that the tourres in the haven mouth were begun in King Edward IV. tyme, and set forwarde yn building by Richard III. King Henrie VII. ended them at the procuration of Fox, bishop of Winchester. King Henrie VIII. of late tyme sette in Portesmouth capitaines and certain souldiours in garrison." The towers, which he mentions as being begun in the haven-mouth by Edward IV., are the old Round Tower on the Portsmouth side, and another which stood opposite to it, near the site of the present

Block-house Fort at Gosport. For the protection of the entrance of the harbour, he says that there was " a myghty chaine of yron to draw from tour to tour."

In July, 1544, a numerous French fleet, having on board an army intended for the invasion of England, appeared in St. Helen's roads. Henry VIII. having been informed of the enemy's intentions, ordered a general rendezvous of his army at Portsmouth; and at the same time his navy, under the command of the high admiral of England, Viscount Lisle, was anchored off Spithead. Henry himself, on hearing that the French fleet had anchored in St. Helen's roads, proceeded directly to Portsmouth. In the third volume of the Archæologia is an account, by Sir Jos. Ayloffe, of some curious old paintings, which were in the great dining parlour at Cowdry House, Sussex, before it was burnt down. In one of those paintings a view was presented of the town and harbour of Portsmouth, Southsea Castle, part of the English camp, and the French and English fleets. In this painting the portrait of Henry himself was introduced. He appeared mounted on horseback, and just about to enter Southsea Castle; and behind him were seen, also mounted, Charles Brandon, Duke of Suffolk, the king's lieutenant, and Sir Anthony Brown, his master of the horse. Between Spithead and Portsmouth harbour, the masts of a large vessel, that was sunk, appeared above the water; and near to them were seen two boats, full of men in great distress, rowing towards the English fleet. This incident probably alluded to the fate of the Mary Rose, one of the largest of the English ships, which sank at the commencement of a partial engagement between the two fleets. The loss of this ship was not owing to any damage that she received from the enemy, but is supposed to have been occasioned by the too great weight of her guns; for she appears to have gone down almost immediately after discharging her first broadside.

The principal church at Portsmouth stands in St. Thomas's Street, and nearly in the centre of the town. It is dedicated to St. Thomas à Becket, and was erected between 1210 and 1220 by Peter de Rupibus, Bishop of Winchester. The transepts and the chancel are the only parts which remain of the original structure, the nave and side-aisles having been rebuilt in 1692. At the same time the old tower, which formerly stood above the intersection of the transepts and the nave, was taken down, and the present one erected at the western entrance. It is surmounted with a cupola, and its height is about 120 feet. The parish register in the vestry contains the following record of the marriage of Charles II. with the Infanta of Portugal:—" Our most gracious sovereign Lord, Charles the Second, by the grace of God King of Great Britain and Ireland, Defender of the Faith, &c., and the most illustrious Princess Donna

Catherina, Infanta of Portugal, daughter to the deceased Don Juan, King of Portugal, and sister to the present Don Alphonso, King of Portugal, were married at Portsmouth upon Thursday, the two-and-twentieth day of May, in the year of our Lord God 1662, being in the fourteenth year of his Majesty's reign, by the Right Rev. Father in God, Gilbert, Lord Bishop of London, Dean of his Majesty's Chapel Royal, in the presence of several of the nobility of his Majesty's dominions and of Portugal." This attestation is written in letters of gold on vellum. The marriage was not, however, solemnised in the church; and, from a passage cited in Harris's Life of Charles II., it would appear that the ceremony was not in reality performed by the Bishop of London *. There is also in the church a monument, with a long Latin epitaph, erected by Susanne, Countess of Denbigh, to the memory of her brother, George Villiers, Duke of Buckingham, who was assassinated at Portsmouth, by Felton, on the 23rd August, 1628.

The house in which the Duke of Buckingham was assassinated by Felton was at that time a large inn called the Spotted Dog, and its site is now occupied by the house, No. 10, in the High-street. Felton, who was strongly tinctured with fanaticism, and of a gloomy temperament, had been a lieutenant in a regiment of foot, and conceiving that his services had been neglected by the duke, and that another had been unfairly promoted over him to the command of a company, he determined on revenge. He was in London when he resolved on the deed, and having purchased a knife for ten-pence at a cutler's shop on Tower-hill, he set out for Portsmouth, where the Duke of Buckingham was then preparing for a second expedition to Rochelle. In order that he might readily draw the knife at any time, he had the sheath sewed to the lining of his pocket. Having reached Portsmouth, partly by walking and partly by an occasional ride on horseback, for his circumstances were very low, Felton contrived to get admission into the hall of the inn where the duke was residing; and as he was passing from an inner room to his coach, the wretched fanatic, who had persuaded himself that the deliberate murder of a fellow creature was an act of duty towards God, reached over the duke's shoulder and stabbed him in the side, with the knife which he had purchased in London. The duke feeling the blow, turned round in the direction from whence it came, and uttering the word " villain !" he plucked the knife from the wound, and staggered towards a table, where he was caught by some of his

* " The King and Queen, being both Catholics, were privately married by a Papist Priest; and the only ceremony which took place on 22nd May, 1662, which was done in the presence-chamber (not in the chapel), was the reading in English and Portuguese the marriage-contract, as it had been previously agreed on by the two governments; which being done, the Bishop stood forth and declared them man and wife."—Dr. White Kennet, on the authority of the Earl of Sandwich, who brought the Queen to England, and was present at the declaration of the marriage.

attendants. As the knife had penetrated the lungs, he died almost immediately. So sudden and unobserved was the blow, that when the officers and others near the duke first perceived him to stagger, they thought that he was seized with a giddiness, and it was not till he drew the knife from his breast that they were aware of the real cause. After striking the blow, Felton had retired unnoticed from the throng of attendants and officers in the immediate neighbourhood of his victim, and might have escaped, at least for a time, had he been so inclined. For a while the attendants of the duke were at a loss to imagine who had struck the blow; but, on Felton's hat, which had fallen off, being picked up, and a paper in the inside read *, he came forward and acknowledged himself to be the person. The officers and soldiers in the room would have immediately put him to death had they not been prevented by Sir Thomas Morton, Sir Dudley Carleton, and others, who caused him to be conveyed to the Governor's house, where he underwent an examination. Subsequently he was sent to London, where he was confined in the Tower, and several times examined, with a view to the discovery of any persons who might have instigated him to the deed, as the duke was much disliked, and the expedition in which he was about to engage was not popular. No discovery was, however, made on this point; for the prisoner never varied from his first declaration, wherein he averred that he was the sole contriver of the deed. He was convicted at London, and executed at Tyburn, from whence his body was sent down to Portsmouth, where it was hung in chains on Southsea Common.

With the exception of the older parts of St. Thomas's Church, which afford one or two good specimens of the Gothic style, Portsmouth contains but little in the shape of architectural antiquities that is likely to attract the notice of the stranger. The building, above which the semaphore is erected, near the northern extremity of the saluting platform, was, in former times, the residence of the governor of the town. Previous to the suppression of the monasteries and religious houses, it belonged to a Domus Dei, or hospital, which was founded in 1238. A part of the church of this hospital is yet standing at a short distance to the southeast of the semaphore, and near to the grand parade. It is now the garrison

---

* In the opinion that he would be killed on the spot by the duke's attendants, Felton had sewed a paper containing the following declaration within his hat :—" If I bee slaine, let no man condemn himselfe ; it is for our sinns that our harts are hardned and become senselesse, or else he had not gone soe long unpunished. He is unworthy of the name of a gentleman or soldier, in my opinion, that is afrayd to sacrifice his life for the honour of God, his king, and his country. John Felton."—The original paper is at present in the possession of Mr. Wm. Upcott, formerly of the London Institution, to whom it was presented by Lady Evelyn, a descendant of Sir Edward Nicholas, one of the magistrates before whom Felton was examined at Portsmouth.

chapel; and against its walls are placed numerous monuments erected to the memory of officers, both naval and military, who have died in the service of their country.

"A tomb is theirs on every page,
An epitaph on every tongue;
The present hour, the future age,
For them bewail, to them belong.

For them the voice of festal mirth
Grows hushed,—their name the only sound;
While deep remembrance pours to worth
The goblet's tributary round.

A theme to crowds who knew them not,
Lamented by admiring foes;
Who would not share their glorious lot?
Who would not die the death they chose * ?"

Though mention is made of a "great ships' dock" at Portsmouth in the reign of Henry VIII., yet this is supposed to have been only a wet-dock; for the first dry-dock at Portsmouth is said to have been formed during the protectorate of Cromwell. Charles II., and his brother James II., who were both partial to the navy, made great additions to the dock-yard and the adjacent storehouses; and in each succeeding reign they have been either improved or enlarged. Persons desirous of visiting the dock-yard ought to apply at the lodge at the entrance by ten in the morning; and permission is never refused, except to foreigners, who are only admitted by a written order from the commissioner. Each person on entering the gate is required to write his name and place of abode in a book kept at the lodge for that purpose; and with each party of visiters a police officer is sent for the purpose of conducting them through the yard, and pointing out the principal objects of curiosity. To the left on entering the yard is the mast-house, where the masts, yards, and bowsprits are made; and to the right, a little further on, is the mast-pond, a large excavation, in which mast and other timber is deposited for the purpose of seasoning. After passing the mast-pond, the visiter will perceive a great number of anchors of various sizes, arranged with great regularity, and painted to preserve them from rust. To the left, on each side of a "camber" or short canal, are the buildings called the rigging-house and the sea store-houses; and opposite to the latter on the right, in proceeding northward, is the end of the rope-house. This building is three stories high, fifty-four feet wide, and one

* Lines by Lord Byron on the death of Sir Peter Parker.

thousand and ninety-four feet long *; and it is floored with cast-iron and tin, in order to guard against accidents by fire. At midnight, on the 3rd of July, 1760, a fire, supposed to have been occasioned by lightning, broke out in the rope-house, and destroyed two of the principal storehouses, containing hemp, tar, and other materials, to the value of £40,000; on 27th July, 1770, another fire broke out which did damage to the amount of nearly £150,000; and on 7th December, 1776, it was set on fire and burnt to the ground by a person called John Atkins, but more generally known by the name of Jack the Painter. At the time that this fire occurred, it was supposed to have been accidental; but a box of combustibles with a tube and a match having been found under some hemp in the following January, the incendiary was by this means discovered. He was tried and convicted at the following Winchester assizes, and was executed in front of the dock gates, on 10th March, 1777. His body was afterwards hung in chains on Block-house Beach.

The hemp is prepared and spun into what are technically called " yarns" in the upper stories of the rope-house, and they are manufactured into cables and other thick ropes on the ground-floor. Some of the largest cables contain nearly seven tons of hemp, and the united strength of eighty men is required to join the strands and twist them closely together. This operation is attended with great labour; and unless the workmen be circumspect, they are liable to meet with dangerous accidents by getting entangled in the strands. In 1819, when the Archduke Maximilian of Austria visited the rope-house, a serious accident of this kind nearly happened to Count Hardigg, one of his suite. The workmen at the time were employed in making a cable, and the Count, whose curiosity was excited by the manner in which the " rogue's yarn" † was twisted in, laid his hand upon one of the strands. Happening to look in another direction, his fingers and hand were drawn in between the strands as they were twisted round by the machinery, and had it not been promptly stopped, he would in all probability have lost his arm. On the strand being untwisted, his hand was released; it was torn on the back, and the fingers were crushed: his shoulder was also much strained.

The principal object of curiosity to all persons visiting the dock-yard is the machinery for manufacturing blocks invented by Mr. Brunel, the celebrated engineer, who has not succeeded quite so well in his plan for excavating a tunnel

---

* The length of each yarn for a cable of 120 fathoms is 1080 feet. It loses about a third of its length in the subsequent operations of twisting the strands and uniting them so as to form a cable.

† This name is given to a rope-yarn which is twisted in a contrary manner to the rest, and is placed in the middle of each strand in all cables or cordage made for the King's service, in order to distinguish them should they be stolen.

under the Thames as in his contrivance for boring a block. Mr. Brunel, who is a native of France, resided in America for some time previous to his coming to this country, where he first took out a patent for his invention in 1802. About 1804 the machinery was first established at Portsmouth, and there completed under the superintendence of the inventor in 1808. During the late war, when not less than a thousand ships were in commission, the number of blocks which the machinery was capable of supplying was found to be more than adequate to the annual demand, not only of the whole navy but also of the ordnance department *.

After the wood, generally elm, for the shell of the block is cut into proper sizes by circular saws, its complete formation, including the pin and the sheave, is effected by means of several different machines, all contrived with the greatest mechanical skill, and put in motion by a steam-engine. There are fourteen principal machines, five of which are employed in finishing the shell, and nine in making the pin and sheave. The first process is that of the boring-machine, which, by means of a centre-bit, pierces a hole to receive the pin, and at the same time, according as the block is intended to be single or double, forms one or two similar holes, at right angles to the former, to receive the first stroke of the chisel which cuts out the space for the sheave. By the second, called the morticing machine, this space is cut out by a chisel acting vertically, and making about a hundred and twenty strokes a minute, and under which the block is caused to move gradually, so that at each stroke a thin piece of the wood is cut away. After this the block is taken to a circular saw, which cuts off the corners and reduces it to the form of an octagon. The shaping machine, to which it is next taken, is perhaps one of the most ingeniously contrived of the whole number, and its peculiar action never fails to excite the admiration of visitors. It consists of two equal and parallel wheels moving on the same axis, to which one of them is permanently fixed, while the other is moveable in the line of the axis, so that, by sliding it nearer to the former or more apart as may be required, the shells of blocks of all sizes may be fixed between their two parallel rims. Ten shells of the same size being firmly fixed at regular intervals between those rims, the wheels are put into motion with extreme velocity, and the shells are rounded by striking against a cutting instrument, which at the same time moves in such a manner as to give to each block its proper shape and curvature. When one half of the side has thus been finished, the motion of the wheels is reversed, and the other half finished in the same manner. When one side has been rounded, the shells are reversed, and the other side completed as above.

* A line-of-battle ship requires nearly fifteen hundred blocks of different sizes. By means of Mr. Brunel's invention, four men can, in the same time, complete as many shells as required fifty by the old method; and six can now supply as many sheaves as before required sixty.—*Quart. Rev.*, No. 43, p. 50.

The last process which the shell undergoes consists in scooping out the groove for the strap, or "strop," as the rope is called, which goes round the block. The shell is now completed, and the visitor is next shown the different processes in forming the sheave and the pin.

The sheaves are generally made of lignum vitæ; and the first operation is performed by a circular saw, which cuts the wood into pieces of a proper thickness. By a second machine the hole for the pin is bored, and they are formed into perfect circles by means of a crown-saw. The third, called the coaking machine, is an admirable specimen of mechanical ingenuity. By its operation a small cutter drills out round the pin-hole, to a certain depth from the flat surface of the sheave, three semicircular grooves for the reception of the metal coak or bush which sustains the friction of the pin. So truly are those grooves formed, that the slight tap of a hammer is sufficient to fix the coak in its place. The fourth operation consists in casting the coaks. By a fifth, after being fitted in the grooves, holes are drilled in the coaks for the reception of the pins which fasten them to the sheave; and by a sixth the pins are riveted. By the seventh operation, the central hole in the coak for the pin, on which the sheave turns, is drilled out. By the eighth the groove for the rope is turned round the circumference of the sheave, and its sides polished. In the ninth, the iron pins, on which the sheave revolve, are cast, turned, and polished; and on their being inserted, the block is complete and ready for use.

Within the dock-yard are also many other workships and magazines, besides those previously noticed, in which a variety of articles required for the equipment of a ship of war are prepared or stored away ready for use. In the anchor-smiths' shop are formed the immense anchors required by ships of the line, the largest of which weigh from ninety to ninety-five hundred weight. At the copper foundry and metal mills all the old copper from ships of war is re-cast, and either rolled into sheets, or manufactured into bolts, gudgeons, and various other articles used in the navy. It requires about 4000 sheets of copper to cover the bottom of a ship of the line, and about a ton weight of nails to fasten them on. The number of sheets rolled in one year, in the time of the late war, amounted to 300,000, weighing 1200 tons; and the saving thus effected by re-manufacturing the old copper, instead of selling it and purchasing new, amounted to upwards of £20,000.

About the middle of the wharf, facing the harbour, is the entrance to the great basin, which is 380 feet long by 260 feet wide, and rather more than two acres in area. Four large dry docks open into this basin; and there are also two others, one on each side of it, which open directly to the harbour. They are covered over with immense roofs of wood and slate, in which are numerous windows to admit the light; and, from the shelter thus afforded, the workmen can pursue their labours in all states of the weather. They are without cross-beams, and are built on the principle of diagonal trussing, introduced by Sir Robert Seppings. The building-slips, which are situated near the water's edge, a little beyond the docks, are also covered over in the same manner; and though each roof costs between six and seven thousand pounds, the advantage that a ship derives, in being protected from the weather while building, more than counterbalances the expense. The docks are in general about twenty-two feet deep, and the communication between them and the external water is formed by means of large swinging gates, on the top of which are foot-bridges of communication for the convenience of the workmen, and other persons connected with the yard. The upper part of one of those dock-gates—the dock at the time being empty—gave way on 14th September, 1825, in consequence of the immense pressure of the water outside. The accident happened at the time of high water, a few minutes before the launch of the Princess Charlotte, a first rate, of 110 guns. Several persons were on the foot-bridge, at the top of the gates, when they broke, and in a moment they were all, with the exception of a few at the sides, precipitated into the dock below. The water rushed in with the violence of a cataract; and, after striking against the opposite extremity of the dock, it recoiled like an immense wave, dashing the unfortunate sufferers gainst the broken parts of the gates and other pieces of timber, and, for a few minutes, the commotion of the water in the dock was like that of a whirlpool. Sixteen persons lost their lives in consequence of this accident, and most of them had evidently been killed by the bruises which they had received from the floating timber, or from being dashed against the bottom and sides of the dock. The tide, on the day of this melancholy occurrence, rose very rapidly, and was more than usually high; and, on examination, it was discovered that the structure of the gates had been weakened in consequence of the number and size of the tree-nails use to fasten the planks to the upright pieces of timber.

Besides the workships and storehouses, there are also several large buildings within the boundary of the dock-yard, for the accommodation of officers and others connected with the establishment. Among the principal are the Royal Naval College*, the official residences ot the Port-Admiral and the Admiral-Superintendant, and a large guard-house for the accommodation of a body of soldiers. There is also a chapel within the yard, more especially designed for the officers and others residing within its precinct, but which is open to the public generally on Sundays during the hours of divine service.

The gun-wharf lies between the camber, or inner haven of Portsmouth, and the

* This institution has recently been discontinued by order of Government

P 2

Common-Hard at Portsea.   Here an immense number of great guns and bombs, belonging to ships of war out of commission, are deposited in rows, and having the name of the ship to which they respectively belong painted on them.   At the present time their number is about six thousand, the greater part of which have been cast at the Carron Foundry in Scotland, and bored at Woolwich.   The 24 and 32-pounders weigh about three tons each; and there are some large bombs, each of which weighs about five tons.   Within the inclosure of the gun-wharf are several large buildings for containing warlike stores, with workships for smiths, carpenters, and armourers, and houses for the residence of the officers.   There is also an armoury, containing about 15,000 stand of small arms, with a vast number of swords, cutlasses, pikes, and other weapons, fancifully arranged against the walls.   The roof of this building is covered with sheet-copper, and, when seen at a short distance, it appears as if it were painted green, in consequence of the action of the atmosphere on the surface of the metal.

The Port-Admiral is the officer who has the chief command of all the ships of war in the harbour, and who forwards to the Admiralty the intelligence he receives from ships arriving at the station; and by means of the semaphore he can transmit intelligence to London, and receive an answer within ten minutes.   His flag-ship, generally a first rate, lies moored off the Common-Hard; and any person who wishes to inspect her may obtain permission by applying on board to the officer who has the command of the watch; and, on writing his name and address in a book, one of the crew will conduct him over every part of the ship.   Sir P. Durham is at present the admiral commanding at Portsmouth, and his flag-ship is the Britannia, of 120 guns.   The Victory, Lord Nelson's ship at the battle of Trafalgar, was for several years the flag-ship at this station.   Being very much out of repair, she was replaced, in 1836, by the Britannia.   She has since been repaired, and is at the present time (April, 1837,) " Commodore of the Ordinary." All persons who have an opportunity, and who feel an interest in the naval glory of their country, ought to visit the Victory.   The place on the quarter-deck where Nelson fell is marked by a brass plate; and on the facia of the poop is painted the signal which he displayed on bearing down to encounter the enemy—" ENGLAND EXPECTS EVERY MAN TO DO HIS DUTY:"—a memorable admonition! which will continue to animate the British seaman, on entering into action, as long as the fame of Nelson shall survive.

Within the last two or three years considerable interest has been excited by the attempts which have been made by a Mr. Dean to raise the guns, and various other articles, belonging to the Royal George, which sank at Spithead on 29th August, 1782.   Several guns have been raised by means of Mr. Dean's apparatus, and a few other things, of comparatively trifling value, have also been recovered.

This ship, which carried 108 guns, and was considered one of the finest in the navy, had just returned from sea, and, as she had made more water than usual for some time before, it was at first intended that she should go into dock. The surveying officers, however, having discovered that the leak was not very far below the water-line, it was resolved to repair the defect, with a view to saving time, by giving the ship a heel as she lay at her moorings at Spithead. On subsequent examination, it was found that a pipe which supplied the water for washing the decks required to be replaced, and, as it lay considerably below the water-line, it became necessary to give her a greater heel than had been at first contemplated. For the purpose of effecting this, some of her guns and part of her ballast were removed to the opposite side. As the ship lay thus considerably inclined on her side, she, from some cause which has not been clearly ascertained, gave an additional heel, and the water rushing in through her lower-deck ports, which had been carelessly left open, she almost instantly filled and sank, carrying down with her a victualling hoy which was lying alongside. At the time of the accident there were nearly twelve hundred persons on board, of which number about nine hundred, including two hundred and fifty women, were drowned. Among the sufferers were Admiral Kempenfelt and several of the officers. About three hundred persons, chiefly belonging to the ship's crew, were saved. The present Admiral Sir P. Durham, at that time one of the lieutenants of the Royal George, was on board when the accident happened, and saved himself by swimming to the shore.

Mr. Kingstone, of the Portsmouth dock-yard, who went down to the wreck in a diving-bell in 1817, gives the following account of its appearance at that time :— " The quarter-deck, forecastle, and roundhead, with the larboard top-side as low down as the range of the upper deck, are entirely gone. The oak-strakes and midships of the flat of the upper deck are much decayed by worms in several places, so as to show the beams and framing beneath. The whole of the fir appears as sound as when first laid. The deck is much twisted, from the ship's falling so much fore and aft. The wreck has a beautiful appearance when viewed about a fathom above the deck, being covered with small weeds, interspersed with shells, star-fish, and a species of polypus, lying on a thin, greasy, grey sediment. All below the deck is a perfect solid of fine black mud; and, when suspended over the larboard side, she appears a rude mass of timber lying in all directions."

As a commercial town, Portsmouth does not rank very high. The number of mercantile vessels registered at the port, in 1831, was only 184, with a tonnage of 8485 tons. The present members of Parliament for the borough are, J. B. Carter, Esq., and F. T. Baring, Esq. The latter gentleman is at present one of the Secretaries of the Treasury.

TINTAGEL CASTLE.

TINTAGEL CASTLE is situated on the northern coast of Cornwall, about a mile to the west of Bossiney, formerly a borough, returning two Members to Parliament, but which, from its want of a sufficient population, was disfranchised by the Reform Bill. The ruins of the castle stand partly on the extremity of a bold cliff and partly on an insular rock, which, in former times, was connected with the mainland by a draw-bridge. It is a place of great antiquity, and the period when it was first built is unknown. There is a tradition that King Arthur was born at Tintagel Castle, but this fact, as well as many others in the history of this hero, " requires confirmation." Of all the early Kings of Britain, whether real or fabulous, no one has so general a reputation. In almost every county there is some hill, or cairn, or castle, with which his name is associated; and you hear of him in Cumberland as frequently as in Cornwall.

From a survey made in the 11th year of Edward III., 1337, it appears that the castle was then out of repair, and that it was in the custody of the priest who officiated at the chapel. In the reign of Richard II. it was made a state prison. In 1285, John Northampton, Lord Mayor of London, was sentenced to be imprisoned there for his unruly mayoralty; and Thomas, Earl of Warwick, was for a short time confined there in 1397.

The situation of the castle is thus described in the Survey of Cornwall by Richard Carew, whose work was first published in 1602 :—" Halfe the buildings were raised on the continent, and the other halfe on an island continued together (within man's remembrance) by a drawe-bridge, but now divorced by the downefaln steepe cliff on the farther side, which, though it shut out the sea from his wonted recourse, hath yet more strengthened the island; for in passing thither you must first descend with a dangerous declyning, and then make a worse ascent by a path, through his stickleness and his steepnesse, threatening the ruin of your life with the falling of your foot. At the top, two or three terrifying steps give you entrance to the hill, which supplieth pasture for sheepe and coneys. Upon the same I saw a decayed chapell. Under the island runs a cave, through which you may rowe at full sea."

Drawn by J. D. Harding from a sketch by ~ Jendle.

Engraved by W. Finden.

TINTAGEL CASTLE.

London. Published 1837, by Charles Tilt. 86 Fleet Street.

Drawn by E. Duncan.

Engraved by E. Finden.

BRIXHAM.

BRIXHAM.

In the engraving of Brixham Quay, from a painting by Edward Duncan, the view is taken from the eastward. To the right, from the end of the pier, several of the larger class of fishing vessels belonging to the place are perceived lying aground; while, further in the harbour, a merchant brig is seen discharging her cargo. In the fore-ground, to the left, the attention of a group appears to be engaged by a small ship which a young fisherman holds in his hands.

Brixham lies about a mile and a half to the westward of Berry Head, the southern extremity of Tor-bay, in the county of Devon, and is about 28 miles south of Exeter, and 198 west-south-west of London. As a fishing town, Brixham is one of the most considerable in the kingdom. The total number of fishing vessels belonging to the place is nearly 200, of which about 110 are from 30 to 40 tons burthen, and the rest from 6 to 18 tons. Besides these, there are several yawls and smaller boats which are employed in the fishery near the shore. For several years past about 70 of the larger class of fishing vessels have been accustomed to proceed to Ramsgate for the purpose of catching fish in the North Sea for the supply of the London market. They usually leave Brixham in November and December, and return again towards the latter end of June. The Brixham fishermen send a great quantity of fish to the Exeter, Bath, Plymouth, and Bristol markets. The principal fish which they take are cod, ling, conger-eels, turbot, whitings, hake, soles, skate, and plaice, with herring and mackerel in the season. A quantity of whitings are generally salted and dried at Brixham. On the coast of Devonshire dried whitings are called " buckhorn," a name sufficiently expressive of their hardness and insipidity. Besides the vessels employed in the fishery, there are ships belonging to Brixham which are chiefly engaged in the West India, Mediterranean, and coasting trades. The population of the place is about 5000. One of the most memorable events in its history is the landing there of William Prince of Orange, afterwards William III., on the 5th of November, 1688. The view of Tor-bay from the cliffs above the town is in the highest degree interesting.

" Here busy boats are seen : some overhaul
  Their loaded nets ; some shoot the lightened trawl ;
  And, while their drags the slimy bottom sweep,
  Stealthily o'er the face o' the waters creep ;
  While some make sail, and singly or together
  Furrow the sea with merry wind and weather."—W. STEWART ROSE.

VIEW FROM THE BEACH AT SIDMOUTH, LOOKING TOWARDS THE SOUTH-WEST.

In this view, from a painting by J. D. Harding, the characteristic features of the coast of Devon are most happily expressed; and the manner in which the subject is treated at once displays the feeling of the artist to appreciate, and his ability to depict, the most beautiful scenery of the English coast. The simplicity of truth is not here outraged for the sake of pictorial effect, but the whole composition is at the same time appropriate, natural, and pleasing.

Sidmouth is situated on the southern coast of Devonshire, about 15 miles south-east of Exeter, and 158 south-west of London. It derives its name from the little stream called the Sid, which there discharges itself into the sea. It is situated at the lower end of a beautiful vale, and is sheltered on the east, west, and north by ranges of hills, which are cultivated to their very summits. On the south it commands an extensive view of the sea. It has a bold and open shore, and many of its newest houses are built near the beach, which is protected from the incroachments of the sea by a natural rampart of shingly pebbles, which rises in four or five successive stages from near low-water mark. The beauty of its situation, the mildness and salubrity of the air, and the conveniences afforded for sea-bathing, have caused Sidmouth to be much frequented within the last forty years as a watering-place.

Sidmouth is a place of great antiquity; and in 1348 it supplied three ships and sixty-two mariners to the great fleet of Edward III. It has been said that there was formerly a good harbour at Sidmouth, but that it became so choked up with sand, that no ships could enter. This account, however, is considered by the Rev. Edmund Butcher to be inaccurate. He says that no sand has destroyed its harbour; and he is of opinion that there never was one of any magnitude at the place. He, however, thinks that there might have been a kind of natural basin, in which the small vessels of former times might have rode, or even discharged their cargoes, with less risk than is at present incurred by vessels which unload on the beach.*

In consequence of the reputation of Sidmouth as a watering-place, the number of its houses has considerably increased since the commencement of the present century. In 1831, the population of the town was 3,126. In 1805, the Right Hon. Henry Addington was elevated to the peerage by the title of Viscount Sidmouth.

* Excursion from Sidmouth to Chester, page 459.

by J. D. Harding, from a sketch by Jenkle.

Engraved by E. Finden.

VIEW FROM THE BEACH AT SIDMOUTH.

LOOKING TOWARDS THE SOUTH-WEST.

London, Published 1837, by Charles Tilt, 86, Fleet Street.

Drawn by J. D. Harding, from a sketch by Jendle.

Engraved by W. Finden.

EXMOUTH.

EXMOUTH.

The town of Exmouth, as its name imports, is situated at the mouth of the Ex, one of the largest rivers in Devonshire, which rising in Exmoor, in Somersetshire, flows past Tiverton, Exeter, and Topsham; and after a course of about seventy miles, discharges itself into the sea. The name given to this river by the Romans was Isca, which appears to have been only the latinized form of the British word *Wysg*—in Irish *Easc* or *Uisg*—signifying water, a stream, a river; and from the same source the word Esk, the name of several rivers in England and Scotland, is probably derived. The primitive meaning of the word, as signifying water or a liquid generally, is still retained in the name of the Irish nectar, *usquebaugh*—whiskey : Anglicè, the " water of life."

In the reign of King John, Exmouth appears to have been a port of some consequence ; and in 1347 it furnished ten ships and one hundred and ninety-three mariners to the grand fleet assembled by Edward III. for his expedition against France. In the reign of Henry VIII. Leland calls it " a fisschar tounlet," in which state it appears to have continued till about the middle of the last century, when it began to increase, in consequence of the number of persons visiting it for the sake of sea-bathing. It is said that Exmouth first came into repute as a watering-place from one of the judges of assize going there to bathe and returning with his health very much improved. The following account of the place, and of the manner in which the visiters passed their time about sixty years ago, is from a letter published in Polwhele's History of Devon :—" The village is a very pretty one, and composed, for the most part, of cot houses, neat and clean, and consisting of four or five rooms, which are generally let at a guinea a week. We have from some of the houses, when the tide is in, a beautiful view of the river, which, united with the sea, forms a fine sheet of water before our doors of large extent. Lord Courtenay's and Lord Lisburne's grounds, rising in inequalities on the other shore, complete the perspective. This is the most gay part of the village; but then its brilliancy is only temporary,—for, the tide returned, instead of a fine sheet of water, we are presented with a bed of mud, whose perfumes are not equal to those of a bed of roses. . . . . . . Exmouth boasts no public rooms or assemblies, save one card assembly, in an inconvenient apartment at one of the inns, on Monday evenings

Q

The company meet at half after five, and break up at ten; they play at shilling whist, or two-penny quadrille. We have very few young people here, and no diversions; no *belles dames* amusing to the unmarried, but some *beldames*. unamusing to the married. Walking on a hill which commands a view of the ocean, and bathing, with a visit or two, serve to pass away the morning, and tea-drinking in the evening."

From the preceding account it would appear that Exmouth, " sixty years since," was but a dull place, even at the height of the season, and more likely to induce lowness of spirits than to prove a remedy for care, " the busy man's disease ;" for what temperament, however mercurial, could bear up against the daily round of tea-parties—where silence was only broken by the " beldame's" scandal —diversified once a week with shilling whist or two-penny quadrille? Since the period when the above-quoted letter was written, Exmouth has been greatly improved, and many large houses have been built for the accommodation of visiters. But since the cot-houses have been elevated to handsome three-storied dwellings, it is only fair to add that the rate of lodgings has also been raised in the same proportion,—" five or six rooms, neat and clean," are no longer to be obtained at a guinea a week. There is now a commodious assembly-room in the town, where the young and the fair—who are not so scarce at Exmouth as they appear to have been sixty years ago—occasionally meet to enjoy the amusement of dancing; while the more elderly have still the opportunity of cheating time at " shilling whist or two-penny quadrille." There are also several billiard and reading-rooms, which are pleasant enough places to while away an hour or two in when it rains ; and the monotony of the morning walk on the hill, and the dulness of the evening tea-drinking, are now frequently diversified with excursions by water to Powderham Castle, Dawlish, Topsham, and places adjacent.

The town of Exmouth lies on the left bank of the river Ex, and is about 11 miles to the south-eastward of Exeter, and 168 from London. It is sheltered from the north-east and south-east winds; and the temperature of the air is mild and highly favourable to invalids. As the bathing-machines are placed within the bar, which breaks the violence of the sea, visiters are thus enabled to bathe in safety at all times. There are also excellent warm sea-water baths in the town for such as require them. There is a convenient market-place at Exmouth ; and a new church was erected by Lord Rolle in 1825. Exmouth and Littleham constitute a united parish, the population of which is about 3400. In 1814 the late admiral Sir Edward Pellew was created a peer, with the title of Baron Exmouth ; and in 1816, after his expedition to Algiers, he was further advanced to the rank of Viscount.

Drawn by J. D. Harding from a sketch by J. Endle
Engraved by W. Finden.

BUDLEIGH SALTERTON.

London. Published 1837. by Charles Tilt. 86. Fleet Street.

BUDLEIGH-SALTERTON.

THE village of Budleigh-Salterton lies about half-way between Sidmouth and Exmouth, and at a short distance to the westward of the mouth of the river Otter. It is pleasantly situated by the sea-shore, and the beauty of the country in its vicinity, and the convenience afforded for sea-bathing, have caused it of late years to be much frequented as a watering place.

The village of East Budleigh, which is also the name of one of the hundreds into which Devon is divided, lies about two miles above Budleigh-Salterton, on the banks of the river Otter. Leland, in his Itinerary, thus notices East Budleigh. " On the west side of the haven is Budelegh, right almost against Oterton, but it is somewhat more from the shore than Oterton. Lesse then an hunderith yeres sins, ships usid this harbour, but it is now clene barrid. Some call this Budeley Haven, of Budeley town." It has been supposed by Polwhele, that the name Budleigh, or Budely, is derived from the British *budelle*, a stream, and that it had originated from the number of springs or small brooks which run through every valley in the parish; for scarcely a house can be found that is more than a furlong distant from a rivulet.

Hayes, near East Budleigh, is celebrated as the birth-place of Sir Walter Raleigh. His father having only a lease of the property, it subsequently came into the possession of a person named Duke, to whom Sir Walter addressed a letter, dated " From the Court, 26th July, 1584," wherein he expresses a wish to purchase the farm and house of Hayes, and says that from " the natural disposition he has to that place, being born in that house, he would rather seat himself there than any where else." The proprietor, not wishing to have so great a man for a neighbour, did not comply with Sir Walter's request. The letter, about fifty years ago, was to be seen at Otterton House, pasted on a piece of board for its better preservation *.

At St. Mary Ottery, about six miles above East Budleigh, on the opposite side of the river, the poet Coleridge was born, in 1772. When young he went to London, where he was educated at Christ's Hospital, and few reminiscences of the place of his birth are to be found in his poems, though he has dedicated one sonnet to his " Dear native brook, wild streamlet of the west,"—the river Otter.

* Polwhele's History of Devon, vol. ii. p. 219.

RAMSGATE. ENTRANCE TO THE HARBOUR.

THE view of the entrance to Ramsgate harbour, engraved from a painting by E. W. Cooke, is taken from the southward, and its fidelity will immediately be recognised by every one who has seen the place. It is blowing a stiff breeze, which causes a swell; and the fishing smack, seen entering, is lowering her sails, that she may not have too much *way* when she gets within the harbour. To the left is the light-house, which stands near the end of the western pier; and the extremity of the eastern pier is perceived to the right.

Ramsgate is situated in the Isle of Thanet, in the county of Kent, about four miles to the westward of the promontory called the North Foreland, and seventy-two miles E. S. E. from London. In the eighth year of the reign of Queen Elizabeth, 1566, it appears to have consisted of only twenty-five inhabited houses. There were then fourteen boats and vessels belonging to the place, which were navigated by seventy men, and chiefly employed in fishing and carrying grain.

Camden, in his Britannia, gives the people of the Isle of Thanet, and more particularly the inhabitants of Ramsgate, Margate, and Broadstairs, the following character: " They are, as it were, amphibious, seeking their living both by sea and land, and turning to account both elements. They are fishermen and ploughmen, farmers and sailors; and the same man that holds the shafts of a plough, turning up a furrow on land, can also take the helm at sea. According to the season, they make nets, catch cod, herring, mackerel, and other fish; go to sea, and export their own commodities—and those very men also dung the ground, plough, sow, harrow, reap, and house the corn." The inhabitants of Ramsgate, and of the Isle of Thanet generally, no longer retain this amphibious character; the " division of labour," the advantages of which are so strikingly pointed out by political economists in the manufacture of pins, has abridged their multifarious pursuits; the same man does not now till the earth and plough the sea; and few indeed are to be found who can handle an oar as well as a flail: the consequence is, that we have better boatmen and better agriculturists.

The frequent loss of vessels between Deal and the North Foreland, in consequence of their being driven from their anchorage in the Downs, by gales of wind from S. S. E. to S. S. W., appears forcibly to have excited the attention of the merchants and ship-owners of London, to the propriety of con-

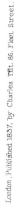

Drawn by E. W. Cooke.

Engraved by W. Finden.

R A M S G A T E.

London, Published 1837, by Charles Tilt. 86. Fleet Street.

structing a harbour at Ramsgate, where vessels might find refuge when driven by bad weather from the Downs. On the 8th of February, 1749, a petition was presented by several merchants of London, owners and masters of ships, to the House of Commons, setting forth the advantages of such a harbour. A committee having examined witnesses on the allegations of the petitioners, and made a favourable report, an act was passed in the same session authorising the construction of a harbour " at the Town of Ramsgate, proper and convenient for the reception of ships of and under 300 tons' burthen, and from whence larger ships in distress in the Downs may be supplied with pilots, anchors, cables, and other assistance and necessaries." By the same act provision was made for the means of defraying the expense, and trustees appointed for carrying the work into execution.

The Committee of Trustees, after having advertised for plans and estimates, and consulted several engineers, determined to erect an east pier of stone, according to the plan of William Ockenden, Esq., one of their members; and a west pier of wood, according to the plan of Captain Robert Brooke. The work was accordingly commenced without delay; and on the 25th July, 1751, a committee of the Trustees reported, " That the stone pier extended 390 feet, of which 104 feet was completely ready for the parapet, and the rest above the reach of a spring tide, and that, while the committee was there, the foundation was continued 83 feet further, in the whole 473 feet; also, that the west head was carried out about 460 from the cliff, and that 540 thereof was proposed to be completed that year." *

At a general meeting of the Trustees, held the 14th December, 1753, it was resolved that the harbour should be contracted, according to a plan submitted by Mr. Ockenden. The contraction of the harbour, was, however, strongly objected to by many owners and masters of ships; and on a petition being presented to Parliament in 1755, it was ordered that Sir Piercy Brett and Captain Desmaretz should examine the works, and give their opinion with respect to the most proper plan for completing the harbour. In 1756 Sir Piercy Brett and his colleague made a report to the Lords of the Admiralty, wherein they say that, " According to the best of their judgment the works already made, and every plan hitherto proposed, seem liable to very material objections; and that the work done upon the contracted plan should be taken up, and the materials made use of in carrying out the west pier." At this time the east pier was carried out 757 feet from the shore, and the west 849;

* Smeaton's Historical Report on Ramsgate Harbour, p. 16.

and the Parliamentary Surveyors estimated that the expense of finishing the harbour, and forming a basin on its east side, according to a plan of their own, would be £195,906. 7s. 6d. The effect of this report was the suspension of the work, which was not resumed till the 20th June, 1761, when the Committee of Trustees gave orders for the walls which were intended to contract the harbour to be taken up.

In the Committee's report of their visitation on the 25th August, 1766, when the work appears to have been carried on with great vigour, they notice " a collection of sand in the harbour, increasing under the east head, near the stairs, and recommend, as the principal work for the next year, that the west head should be finished as soon as possible, in the hope that it would prevent the further accumulation." As the work advanced, however, the sand continued to increase, and there seemed every appearance of the proposed harbour being choked up, even before the piers were completed. On the 31st January, 1773, the Committee stated in their report, that, notwithstanding upwards of 50,000 tons had been taken out since January, 1770, it was feared that the sand rather increased than diminished.

The Committee having requested the advice of Mr. Smeaton as to the best mode of removing the sand, that distinguished engineer visited Ramsgate in 1774; and after having made a survey of the harbour, he transmitted a report to the Trustees on 24th October in the same year.

In this report Mr. Smeaton makes the following remarks on the tendency of all artificial harbours which have no back-water to become filled with mud or sand. " A large mass of silt, consisting partly of mud, but chiefly of fine sand, has been brought into the harbour by the tide flowing into the same. The tide water upon this part of the coast being charged with a considerable quantity of mud and sandy matter, whenever it is agitated by the wind, accompanied with a quick flowing tide, this silty matter, being thus carried into the harbour along with the water that contains it, and there finding a place of repose, settles to the bottom; and as there is nothing to raise the mud upon the reflux, the water quietly ebbs out of the harbour, leaving the silt behind. And as the same causes constantly operate to produce the same effects, a continual increase of silt must be expected to take place till some cause is brought to operate in a contrary way. This is the natural tendency of all harbours; for wherever there is mud or other matter to deposit, an addition to the soil is the natural consequence of a place of repose, and a deposition and an increase must take place unless there are powers, either natural or artificial, to produce a contrary effect. The common natural power is a fresh water river, which, continually tending towards the sea—and often in time of floods with great impetuosity—makes an effort to carry out whatever opposes it; the sand and silt therefore brought in with the tides, are carried out by the torrent of fresh water. Harbours, therefore, that have no land-water or back-water, cannot naturally keep open for a long course of years. These being the effects of the powers of nature, we must by no means wonder that the harbour of Ramsgate, into which and through which not the least rivulet or runner of fresh water takes its course, has obeyed this general tendency; for, in proportion as the work of the piers has advanced, the space been enclosed, and the waters rendered more quiet, and, in that respect, more fit for the purposes of a harbour, in much about the same proportion has the silting of the harbour taken place; and must continue to increase till the area of the harbour becomes dry land, and, instead of a receptacle for ships, a field for corn; that is, unless recourse is had to such artificial means as have the due efficacy."

When this report was made there was not less than 268,700 cubic yards of silt in the harbour; and as the two barges, with ten men each, employed by the trustees, got only about 70 tons a day, each ton being something less than a cubic yard, it would at that rate, and allowing the men to work every day, have required upwards of twelve years to clear the harbour, even supposing that there should be no fresh deposit of silt during that time. Considering all the circumstances, Mr. Smeaton concluded that the most effectual mode of clearing the harbour would be by means of an artificial back-water discharged from a basin or reservoir by means of sluices.

Mr. Smeaton's report was not taken into consideration by the committee until the following August, and the result of their deliberation appears to have been the *nominal* rejection of his plan; though at the same time they adopted his suggestion by giving orders to their master-mason, a Mr. Preston, to commence the formation of a basin for the purpose of scouring the harbour by means of sluices. The only difference between Mr. Smeaton's plan and that called Mr. Preston's was, that the latter proposed to make all the upper part of the harbour into a basin, while Mr. Smeaton proposed to form two connected basins of four acres each, in order that they might be reciprocally employed for clearing each other. Until Mr. Smeaton's report was made, Mr. Preston had conceived no better plan of cleansing the harbour than by harrowing up the sand, so that it might mix with the water, and be carried out with the ebb tide.

The walls necessary for the formation of a basin were accordingly commenced, and having been got up to the level of high water, and four of the sluices completed in 1779, a trial was made of their efficacy about the middle of August in that year. The basin having been filled, and the sluices closed at high water, the committee attended at low water to see them opened ; but from the imperfection of the machinery the workmen were only able to raise the two sluices in the gates. "The force and power," says Mr. Smeaton, "of the stream issuing through these two sluices only was so amazingly great, that in its immediate action it forced up the chalk rock to the depth of six and seven feet, and carried pieces of it, of three to four hundred weight, to the distance of sixty or seventy feet ; and in its course it cleared away the silt and sullage down to the chalk, to low water mark, the stream continuing strong two or three hundred feet without the harbour's mouth." An improvement having been made in the large sluices, which allowed them to work with sufficient ease, and additional ones having been constructed, it was found that the water discharged from them would effectually cleanse the harbour and prevent the future accumulation of sand and mud.

It having been found that the cross wall of the basin had occasioned a much greater swell in the harbour than before, from the sea breaking against it, instead of running in and spending itself against the shore as formerly ; with a view to remedy this inconvenience, a hundred and fifty feet of the western end of the cross wall was taken down, and a returning wall carried from its extremity to the cliff : and an opening to the extent of a hundred feet was made in the western pier, the communication being kept up by means of a wooden bridge. In consequence of these alterations the swell in the harbour abated considerably.

The basin, when finished, not only answered the purpose of a reservoir for a supply of back-water, but also could afford accommodation to not less than sixty vessels of from two to four hundred tons burthen each. With a view to the further improvement of Ramsgate as a harbour, the committee resolved upon forming a dry-dock where ships entering the harbour in distress might be repaired, and on building a large storehouse for the reception of the goods which it might be necessary to land while the vessels were undergoing repair. A dock was accordingly commenced in 1784, according to a plan furnished by Mr. Smeaton, who recommended that the floor should be of wood. The plan of a stone floor was however preferred by the committee on the recommendation of their master-mason ; but, after two unsuccessful experiments, they were obliged to adopt Mr. Smeaton's original plan of a flooring of wood. When the dock-gates were closed, the pressure of the water under the bottom was so great as to force up the stone floor, although it consisted of blocks of Portland stone, each four feet by three, and two feet and a half thick, and weighing about a ton and a half. The joints of the side wall of the dock, on the north side next the basin, were also forced open so as to admit the water, but in much less quantity than what appeared to rise through the floor. The force of the pressure, when the water on the outside was only eight feet above the floor, was estimated by Mr. Smeaton at one thousand tons on the area of the dock. " This power," says he, " acting upwards, would indeed be the same, whatever material the floor was composed of; but from its construction as an arch of stone laid very flat, its *lateral pressure* would in this case be much greater than the *absolute weight* of the wall upon its base, and therefore no wonder that it should shove it out." In consequence of the delay occasioned by taking down and rebuilding the north wall and relaying the floor with wood, the dock was not finished till 1791.

In 1787, as a considerable swell prevailed in the outward harbour in gales of wind from the eastward, a continuation of the east pier in a south-easterly direction was commenced according to a plan of Mr. Smeaton's, for the purpose of breaking the force of the sea and rendering the entrance of the harbour more safe and easy. In laying the foundations of this extended pier, the diving-bell was frequently employed; and, on one occasion, Mr. Smeaton went down in it with Mr. Aubert, the chairman of the committee of trustees, and remained at the bottom of the sea for three-quarters of an hour. This work, which occupied several years, was found, on being finished, to effectually answer the purpose for which it was intended. After the lapse of upwards of forty years from the period of its commencement, Ramsgate harbour might now be considered complete. Its value as a place of refuge was fully demonstrated by the fact of upwards of two thousand vessels having taken shelter there between 1782 and 1790. In January, 1791, there were a hundred and thirty vessels in the harbour that had been driven there by stress of weather; and in December, 1795, it is said that not less than three hundred vessels sought refuge there in a violent gal

Between 1792 and 1802 several additional buildings were erected, among which was a new light-house at the head of the west pier. The basin was also widened ; and, subsequently, the old western pier of wood, extending five hundred and fifty feet from the cliff, was rebuilt with stone, and a more convenient passage formed to it for the embarkation and landing of troops. The cost of the harbour, dock, light-house, and other requisite buildings, is said to have amounted to about £650,000. The form of the harbour is nearly circular, and its area is about forty-six acres. The length of the eastern pier, following its angles, or " cants " as they are technically termed, is about 2000 feet, and that of the western about 1500. Their general width is about 26 feet, including the thickness of the parapets ; and the width of the entrance to the harbour between their heads is 240 feet. The harbour is maintained by a tonnage duty on all ships passing, whether sailing on the east or west of the Goodwin Sands, and by a duty on coals and stones discharged in the harbour

The light displayed from the light-house is stationary, and is only exhibited when there is ten feet water between the pier heads. In the day time a flag is hoisted while there is the same depth of water at the entrance of the harbour. In spring tides, the depth of water increases to sixteen feet in about an hour from the time that the ten-feet signal is displayed; in about two hours to twenty feet; and in three hours, or about high water, to twenty-one feet. In neap-tides the depth of water at those periods respectively is fourteen, seventeen, and eighteen feet between the pier heads. It is high water at Ramsgate at fifty minutes past eleven at the full and change of the moon. In 1830 there were seventy ships belonging to Ramsgate, the aggregate tonnage of which was 4397 tons. In 1831 the population of the town was 7985.

During the summer, Ramsgate is much frequented by visiters from London, who come by the daily steam-packets to enjoy the benefit of sea-bathing, for which the beach to the southward of the pier affords excellent opportunity. Powerful steam-packets ply every day between London and Ramsgate, and the passage up or down is usually made in seven hours; and a steam-packet makes a trip from Ramsgate to Boulogne once a week, going one day and returning the next, thus affording her passengers an opportunity of " spending an evening in France." There are several excellent hotels and many convenient lodging-houses at Ramsgate, and the charges generally are moderate. At the close of the year, when the summer visitants have all retired to their several homes, another description of persons make their appearance at Ramsgate—the Torbay fishermen, who generally establish their rendezvous there from December to June for the sake of fishing in the North Sea. It seems probable that Ramsgate, as a port, will continue to increase very considerably in importance; and in the event of a continental war, when steam vessels are likely to be much employed, its eligibility as a place for the embarkation of troops and as a packet station, will doubtless not be overlooked. It not unfrequently happens in stormy weather that the Dover packets enter Ramsgate with safety when they cannot approach their own harbour.

George IV., on his departure to visit his Hanoverian dominions in 1821, embarked at Ramsgate; and to commemorate the event an obelisk was erected by subscription of the inhabitants. Within the last two or three years the visits of the Princess Victoria, now our gracious Queen, and her mother the Duchess of Kent, have increased the popularity of Ramsgate as a watering-place, and not a few of the more sanguine of its inhabitants confidently anticipate that Ramsgate will in a few years have its Pavilion as well as Brighton,—

" Sed non ego credulus illis."

CHATHAM.

Drawn by - Warren.

Engraved by E. Finden.

London, Published 1837, by Charles Tilt, 86, Fleet Street.

CHATHAM DOCK-YARD.

THE view of the Dock-yard at Chatham is taken from the opposite side of the Medway, a little above Upnor Castle, which was built by Queen Elizabeth to defend the passage of the river. To the left is seen a sheer hulk, so called from her "sheers,"—two strong pieces of timber of great height, inclining towards each other and joined together at the top, which are used for the purpose of raising and placing in their proper situations the lower masts of ships of war. Further to the right are perceived the large roofs of the building slips and dry docks; nearly abreast of which are two ships of war laid up in ordinary. A-head of those vessels are two others of the same class; and further up the river, directly in front, a view is obtained of part of the town of Chatham.

The Dock-yard of Chatham lies at a short distance to the northward of the town of that name, and on the right bank of the river Medway. The first dock-yard at Chatham for the service of the navy was established by Queen Elizabeth. It was situated higher up the river than the present yard, on a narrow slip of land, and had only one dock. In 1622 a new dock-yard was formed by James I., and the site of the old one, which was too circumscribed for the service of the increasing navy, was assigned to the Board of Ordnance. In the reign of Charles I., additional dry docks and building slips were formed and several store-houses erected.

In 1667, the Dutch Admiral De Ruyter, being anchored off the Nore with a powerful fleet, detached a squadron of seventeen ships of war and eight fire-ships, under Vice-Admiral Van Ghent, for the purpose of capturing such English vessels as were in the Medway, and destroying the arsenal at Chatham. They took Sheerness, which was then merely a small fort, after a stout resistance by Admiral Sir Edward Spragge; and on the 10th of June they sailed up the Medway. The wind and tide being in their favour, they succeeded in breaking the strong chain which was stretched across the river, and also sank several ships that attempted to hinder their advance. The Dutch Vice-Admiral proceeded up the river, with six ships of war and five fire-ships, as far as Upnor Castle; but meeting there with a warm reception, and considering it hazardous to advance higher up, as the country was by this time aroused, he returned down the river and rejoined Admiral De Ruyter. In this attack the Dutch burnt three ships which had been captured from them, the Matthias, the Unity, and the Charles the Fifth; and three English-built ships—the Royal Oak, the Loyal London, and the Great James. The only English ship which they succeeded in carrying off was the Royal Charles, which they captured near Upnor Castle. The Dutch in this expedition lost two of their ships, which ran aground, and were burnt by order of the Vice-Admiral Van Ghent, to prevent their falling into the hands of the English. The celebrated General Monk, then Duke of Albemarle, went down to Chatham, on intelligence being received of the Dutch having appeared in the Medway, and on his return to London he accused Mr. Phineas Pett*, the Commissioner of Chatham Dock-yard, with wilful neglect of duty in not sufficiently providing for the defence of the river. On this charge the Commissioner was impeached by the House of Commons, but the accusation was not substantiated.

This attack of the Dutch called the attention of the government to the necessity of strengthening the entrance of the Medway, and providing more efficient means of protection for the dock-yard and arsenal at Chatham. The fort at Sheerness was accordingly rebuilt upon a more extensive scale; another was erected at Gillingham, a little below the dock-yard; and Upnor Castle was put into a better state of defence. In the reign of Queen Anne, considerable additions were made to the dock-yard; and a large store-house was built in the reign of George I., but no regular fortifications appear to have been erected there previous to 1758. In that year, when the kingdom was threatened with a French invasion, an Act of Parliament was passed authorising the purchase of certain lands in the vicinity of the yard, and shortly afterwards the fortifications now called "the Lines" were commenced. They extend about a mile in length, from the river, a little below the northern side of the yard, to the river again, a little above the old dock; inclosing within their boundaries not only the dock-yard and the marine and artillery barracks, but also nearly the whole of the village of Brompton. Those lines were further strengthened and enlarged during the American war; and in 1803 a strong redoubt, named Fort Pitt, was erected, flanking their western extremity and overlooking the town. Since the peace, Fort Pitt has been chiefly occupied as a military hospital.

In forming the Lines a number of Roman antiquities were discovered, and not less than a hundred graves were opened by Mr. Douglas, then a captain in the corps of engineers, but who afterwards abandoned " the spurtle blade and dog-

---

* Phineas Pett was one of the most able English shipwrights of his day, and contributed much towards the improvement of the navy. Subsequently, when certain charges were brought against him respecting his conduct as Commissioner of Deptford-yard, James II. proceeded there with several learned men for the purpose of investigating them. When the whole of the charges had been gone through and refuted, except the last. which was that of his having cut the wood cross-grained, the king became impatient, and, turning to Pett's accusers, observed that " the *cross-grain* was in the shipwrights, and not in the wood."

skin wallet," for the surplice; and, as the Rev. James Douglas, gave some account of those sepulchral remains in his work intitled Nenia Britannica, published in parts, between 1786 and 1793. Many of the graves were discovered near the south-eastern extremity of the Lines, in the neighbourhood of Upberry Farm; where also were found the remains of swords, spear-heads, beads of various colours, the umbo or boss of a shield, several pieces of armour, a bottle containing a kind of red earth, an urn filled with ashes, a number of Roman coins, and a variety of other articles. On breaking up the ground in another part of the Lines, the workmen met with the foundation of a building, and on removing the earth, it was found to be the outer wall of a range of small apartments. The largest did not exceed ten feet square, and their inner walls were painted in fresco with red, blue, and green spots. On the south-west side of those small apartments the foundation of a larger building was discovered, which, being traced within the redoubt as far as the bank of earth thrown out of the ditch would permit, was found to measure thirty feet by twenty-one. Pieces of Roman tiles, spear-heads, pateræ, lachrymatories, and many other ancient remains, were dug up in the same neighbourhood. The purpose for which the buildings had been erected has not been ascertained.

Chatham dock-yard is enclosed on the land side by a high wall, and the principal entrance is through a lofty gateway to the south-west, above which are the royal arms, and on each side an embattled tower. Strangers wishing to see the yard are furnished with a ticket by the superintendant of the dock-police on entering their names in a book kept at the lodge within the gate. There are four docks and seven building slips at Chatham, most of which are covered with immense roofs. To the south-westward of the docks there is a long range of store-houses facing the river, and having in front a spacious quay, part of which is occupied as an anchor wharf. Behind this line of buildings, which is upwards of a thousand feet in length, is the ropery, where cables and all other kinds of ropes are manufactured for the use of ships of war. Beyond the docks, to the northward, are the mast-ponds and sheds for storing timber, on the right; and on the left is the boat-house. At the smiths' shop anchors and other articles of iron work are made for the use of the navy; and towards the north-eastern extremity of the yard is the saw-mill, erected by Mr. Brunel, the inventor of the block-machinery at Portsmouth. The mill is situated on an eminence, and the timber intended to be cut is floated through a tunnel from the Medway into an elliptic basin, from which it is raised by machinery to the level of the mill. The saws are put in motion by a steam engine; and the timber, after having been cut, is conveyed away by trucks running on rail-ways to different parts of the yard. When M. Charles Dupin—the celebrated French author of several works on the dock-yards, roads, bridges, and harbours of Great Britain—visited Chatham in 1817, he objected to this saw-mill being erected on an eminence; but he seems to have overlooked the consequent advantage of the timber being thence conveyed by a gentle slope, with very little labour, to the different docks and slips, without interfering with any of the other works *.   The commissioner has a handsome residence within the walls of the yard, and there are also many excellent houses which are occupied by the officers and principal artificers.   A neat chapel, of brick, for the convenience of the officers and workmen, was erected within the yard in 1811.   At one period during the late war, the number of men employed was 3000.

The Ordnance wharf is situated to the south-westward of the dock-yard, on the site of the old yard established by Queen Elizabeth, and it is still frequently called the Old Dock.   The guns are placed in rows, and have painted on them the name of the ship to which they belong, and their weight of metal; the carriages are also placed separately, but under sheds.   Large piles of shot are seen in various parts of the wharf; and there is also within its boundary an armoury, where various kinds of weapons—chiefly muskets, pistols, pikes, and cutlasses—are arranged in admirable order.

A fund—commonly called the Chest of Chatham—for the relief of disabled seamen, was established there by Queen Elizabeth on the recommendation of Sir Francis Drake and Sir John Hawkins, in 1588;—the seamen of the royal navy, after the defeat of the Spanish Armada, having agreed to give up a portion of their pay for the relief of their wounded and disabled brethren.   In 1802, the " Chest" was removed to Greenwich, and the management of its funds is now committed to the First Lord of the Admiralty, the Comptroller of the Navy, and the Governor of Greenwich Hospital.

In the time of Edward the Confessor, the manor of Chatham was in the possession of Godwin, Earl of Kent, on whose death it descended to his eldest son Harold, afterwards king of England.   After the death of Harold, who was killed at the battle of Hastings, his possessions were seized by William the Conqueror, who gave the manor of Chatham to his half-brother, Odo, Bishop of Bayeux. The town of Chatham adjoins the city of Rochester on the eastward.   It returns one member to Parliament, by the Reform Bill; and in 1831 the population was 17,936.

* Quarterly Review—Dupin on the Marine Establishments of France and England—No. XLIII., p. 41

Drawn by G. H. Wse.

HASTINGS.

Engraved by E. Finden.

London. Published 1837, by Charles Tilt, 86, Fleet Street.

HASTINGS.

THE town of Hastings is situated on the coast of Sussex, about sixty-four miles S. S. E. of London. It has been supposed that the place was so called from Hastings, a Danish pirate, " who, where he landed for booty, built sometimes little fortresses; as we read, in Asserius Menevensis, of Beamflote Castle built by him in Essex, and of others at Appledore and Middleton in Kent"*. This conjecture, however, does not appear to be well-founded; for there can be little doubt of the place having been called Hastings about the year 780, in the reign of king Offa, whereas Hastings, the pirate, did not invade England till about 880, in the reign of Alfred the Great. " Some there are," says Camden, " who ridiculously derive the name from the English word *haste;* because, as Matthew Paris writes, ' apud Hastings ligneum *agiliter* castrum statuit Gulielmus Conquestor '—at Hastings William the Conqueror. *hastily* set up a fortress of timber." Truly, as old Fuller might have said, there has been more *haste* than speed in the endeavour to provide this place with a godfather.

It is said that the old Saxon town of Hastings stood considerably to the southward of the present one, and that it was destroyed by the incursions of the sea previous to the Conquest. The town, however, would appear to have been in a short time rebuilt; for William the Conqueror, soon after landing at Pevensey, marched to Hastings, from whence he advanced about eight miles into the country, where he encountered the English army under Harold, at the place since called Battle in commemoration of the event.

Hastings, though not the oldest, is considered to hold the first rank among the ancient maritime boroughs called the Cinque Ports, which were originally instituted for the defence of the coast, and endowed with special privileges on condition of supplying a certain number of ships and mariners for that purpose. Dover, Sandwich, and Romney are considered the oldest of the Cinque Ports, as they are the only ones which are mentioned in Domesday as privileged ports. Hastings and Hythe are supposed to have been added by William the Conqueror; and the number being thus increased to *five,* occasioned the community to be called the *Cinque* Ports. Although Winchelsea and Rye, which had previously been

* Camden's Britannia, Bishop Gibson's Translation.

members of Hastings, were constituted principal ports at some period between the Conquest and the reign of King John, the name of *Cinque* Ports still continued to be given to the community. The Cinque Ports are governed by a lord warden, who is also governor of Dover Castle. A certain number of persons (called Barons) deputed from the Cinque Ports, have the privilege of supporting the canopies above the king and queen at coronations.

There was formerly a pier at Hastings, at which vessels could unload; but it was destroyed in a violent storm about the commencement of the reign of Queen Elizabeth, and never rebuilt. From the remains of this pier, which are still to be seen at low water, it appears to have run out in a south-eastern direction from the centre of the Marine Parade, below where the fort now stands. The fort in a great measure answers the purpose of a breakwater in resisting the waves, which in high tides, accompanied with a strong wind from the seaward, would otherwise be likely to do serious damage to the lower part of the town.

The trade of Hastings is very inconsiderable; its imports being chiefly coals for the consumption of the town, and its exports principally oak timber and plank for the purposes of ship-building. The great supports of the town are the numerous visiters who take lodgings there during the bathing season, and the fishery, which gives employment to about 500 persons. What may now be considered the old town of Hastings is situated in a hollow between two hills, the East and the Castle Hill, and consists chiefly of two streets which run nearly parallel to each other, and are called High Street and All-Saints Street. The new town of Hastings, which has been almost wholly erected within the last thirty years, lies to the south and westward of the Castle Hill, so called from the ruins of the old castle on its top. There are two old churches at Hastings, St. Clement's and All-Saints', and a modern chapel, St. Mary's, in Pelham Crescent, immediately under the Castle Hill. From the accommodation which it affords to visiters, and the beauty and interest of the walks and rides in its vicinity, Hastings is one of the most agreeable watering places on the southern coast of England. The town returns two members to Parliament, and the number of inhabitants, according to the population returns of 1831, was 10,097.

FOLKSTONE.

KENT.

London, Published 1837, by Charles Tilt, 86, Fleet Street.

FOLKSTONE.

FOLKSTONE is in the county of Kent, and lies about seventy-two miles south east of London, and seven west-south-west of Dover. In the beautiful vignette, from a drawing by T. Boyes, the view is taken from the eastward. Whether the Romans had a station there or not is uncertain; there are, however, unquestionable evidences of Folkstone having been a place of some consequence in the Saxon period. Eadbald, son of Ethelbert, sixth king of Kent, built a castle at Folkstone, and also founded a nunnery there at the request of his daughter, Eanswith, who became the first abbess. This lady seems to have enjoyed as great a reputation in Kent as her contemporary St. Hilda did in Yorkshire. Like the latter, she had the power of working miracles; one of the most remarkable of which was her causing a beam of wood, which had been cut three feet too short, from the carpenters' missing their measure, to be extended to the length required. After her death the holy abbess was canonized by the pope, and her festival appointed to be held on the 12th September. The nunnery built by Eadbald having been destroyed by the Danes, Nigel de Mundeville, lord of Folkstone, about the year 1095, re-founded it as a priory for Benedictine monks, dependent on the abbey of Lallege, in Normandy. Though this priory originally was built more than a quarter of a mile from the shore, yet in less than half a century it was rendered unsafe by the encroachments of the sea; and a new church and priory were erected in 1136, by William de Albrincis, or Avranches, then lord of Folkstone. At the time of the Domesday survey, there were no less than five churches in Folkstone. "The town there," says Leland, "by al lykeliod is mevelously sore wasted with the violence of the se, yn so much that they say one paroche chyrche of our Lady, and another of St. Paule, is clene destroyed and etin by the sea."

In 1378 the greater part of the town was burnt by the French, assisted by a body of Scots; and in the eighth year of the reign of Elizabeth, it contained only a hundred and twenty houses, with the same number of able men, of whom seventy were employed in the fishery. The number of fishing-boats then belonging to the town was twenty-five. In 1831 the population of Folkstone was 3638. Folkstone is a member of the Cinque Port of Dover. The harbour is formed by piers, for there is no creek or river at the place, and is very imperfect. A considerable number of persons visit Folkstone in the summer for the sake of sea-bathing, but the principal support of the place is the fishery.

S

WEYMOUTH.

WEYMOUTH and Melcombe-Regis lie on opposite sides of the same river, the latter on the east, and the former on the west. They are connected by a bridge, the central part of which can be swung open, to allow of the passing and repassing of ships. The name of Weymouth is generally given to the united towns, which are both in the county of Dorset, and about 130 miles to the south-westward of London.

Weymouth derives its name from the Wey, or Way, a small river which there discharges itself into the sea. It is a place of great antiquity; it is mentioned in a charter granted by Ethelred, about the year 880, giving certain lands there to his faithful minister, Altsere. In the Domesday Survey there are no less than eight places in the county with the name of *Wai* or *Waia*; that however which is described as having twelve *salterns*, or salt ponds, was undoubtedly the Weymouth of the present time. In the reign of Edward II. Weymouth returned two members to Parliament; and in 1347, probably in conjunction with Melcombe, it supplied 15 ships and 263 mariners to the grand fleet of Edward III.

Melcombe owes its adjunct, " Regis "—King's—to its having been a part of the demesne lands of the crown in the time of Edward I. It is not mentioned in the Domesday survey; but it appears to have been summoned to return two members to Parliament several years earlier than Weymouth, though the latter in all charters has precedence as the more ancient town. The inhabitants of the two places had frequent quarrels respecting their rights to the harbour and the profits thence accruing; and in consequence of those dissensions, the towns were deprived of the privileges of a staple port by Henry VI. In the thirteenth year of the reign of Elizabeth the two towns were united into one borough, having their privileges in common, and jointly returning four members to Parliament. By the Reform Bill the number of members returned by the united towns has been limited to two.

The following is Leland's account of the two places at the time of his visiting them, in the reign of Henry VIII. : " Ther is a townlet on the hither side of the haven of Waymouth caullid Miltoun [or Melcombe], beyng privilegid and having a mair. This town, as it is evidently seene, hathe beene far bigger then it is now. The cause of this is layid on to the Frenchmen, that in tymes of war rasid this towne for lak of defence. For so many houses as be yn the town, they be welle and strongly buildid of stone. There is a chapelle of ease in Milton. The paroch church is a mile of: a manifest token that Milton is no very old town. . . .

Drawn by H. Warren.

Engraved by E. Finden.

W E Y M O U T H .

London, Published 1837, by Charles Tilt, 86. Fleet Street.

Milton standith as a peninsula, by reason of the water of the haven that a little above the toun spreedith abrode and makith a bay, and by the bay of the mayne sea that gulfith it in on the other side. The tounlet of Waymouth lyith strait agaynst Milton on the other side of the haven, and at this place the water of the haven is but of a small brede; and the *trajectus* is by a bote and a rope bent over the haven, so that in the fery bote they use no oars. Waymouth hath certein liberties and privileges, but ther is no mair yn it. Ther is a key and warf for shippes *."

During the civil war between Charles I. and the Parliament, the united towns suffered severely. In 1649 the mayor, bailiffs, and aldermen, presented a petition to Parliament in which they set forth that the fair and large chapel at Weymouth, which was sufficient to contain all the people of both towns, was destroyed; that the bridge, which had cost them £1500, was in decay; and that the harbour was filled with rubbish. In order that they might be enabled to enlarge Melcombe church, rebuild the bridge, and cleanse the harbour, they prayed that the sum of £3000 might be granted to them out of the excise or the customs. Their request, however, was not complied with.

In the same manner as at many other towns on the southern coast, the trade of Weymouth appears to have declined considerably from the time that the English ceased to have any possessions in France; and the comparatively small depth of water in the harbour has tended to prevent the increase of its shipping in modern times. The harbour at Weymouth is what is called a tide-harbour. The channel is about fourteen feet deep at high water; and at the quays on each side the ships lie aground at low water. The large lake at the westward of Melcombe-Regis receives at spring tides a vast body of water, which on its return scours the harbour and prevents the accumulation of sand. The number of ships belonging to the port of Weymouth is about eighty-five, the aggregate tonnage of which is 7175 tons. In 1831 the population of the united towns was 7655.

The increase of Weymouth within the last forty or fifty years is chiefly owing to the number of persons who take up a temporary residence there to enjoy the benefit of sea-bathing, for which the excellent beach affords the greatest convenience. It is said that the place first began to obtain celebrity on this account about 1763, in consequence of Ralph Allen, Esq., of Prior Park, near Bath, having derived great benefit while residing there, and recommending it to his friends. Weymouth was visited, in 1789, by George III., who resided there for about ten weeks, and was so much pleased with the place that in several succeeding years it was honoured with a royal visit.

* Leland's Itinerary, vol. iii., p. 79. Edition 1769.

CAVES AT LADRAM BAY.

LADRAM BAY is on the southern coast of Devonshire, and lies between Sidmouth and the mouth of the river Otter. It is of small extent; and is neither noticed by any of the historians of the country, nor described in any guide book. The Lade rock forms its eastern extremity; and to the westward it is bounded by a similar promontory, near to which are the caves represented in the engraving. The bay is only accessible to pedestrians proceeding from Sidmouth at low water through a cave at its eastern point; and its approach from the westward is also through a perforated rock. This small and secluded bay is extremely romantic, and the cliffs between its extreme points are lofty and nearly perpendicular. It is frequently visited in summer by pic-nic parties from Sidmouth, Otterton, and Budleigh Salterton; and it is said that smugglers, availing themselves of its retired situation, occasionally manage to land a cargo there, notwithstanding the vigilance of the preventive men, who have a look-out near the bay, but not a regular station. The only house in its immediate vicinity is a fisherman's cottage, near the end of the road leading to it from Otterton.

There are several curious caverns and perforated rocks on the southern coast of Devon. Just within the promontory called the Bolt-head, at the western end of Salcomb-bar, is a cavern called the Bull-hole, which is believed by many persons of the neighbourhood to extend for about three miles to a similar cavern, in a creek near Sewer-mill. The tradition is that a bull entered at one cavern and came out at the other, and hence the name of the Bull-hole. Nearly at the top of the cliff of Bolberry down, about a mile to the eastward of the Bolt-tail, is a cavern called Ralph's-hole, which is about twenty feet long, seven feet wide, and eight feet high. It is nearly four hundred feet above the sea; and the rock by which it is approached is within three feet of the precipice, and only admits of one person passing at a time. It is said that a man named Ralph made this cave his abode for many years in order to avoid being arrested, and that with a hay-fork as a weapon to defend the entrance he set the bailiffs at defiance. A few miles further westward, directly off Thurlston sands, in Bigberry bay, is a perforated rock, about thirty feet high, called Thurlston rock. At very low ebb-tides it is left dry, but as the flood increases the sea washes over it, making a noise in stormy weather that is heard at a great distance.

CAVES AT LADRAM BAY.

DEVONSHIRE.

London, Published 1837, by Charles Tilt, 86, Fleet Street.

Drawn by J.D.Harding from a sketch by - Jendle

Engraved by W. Finden.

PLYMOUTH.

DEVON.

London. Published 1837, by Charles Tilt, 86, Fleet Street.

PLYMOUTH.

THE view of Plymouth is taken from the grounds of Mount Edgecumbe, looking across the lower part of the Sound. About the middle distance is St. Nicholas' Island; beyond which are perceived the ramparts of the citadel. Between the citadel and the point of land to the right, where several small vessels are seen, is the entrance of the creek called the Catwater.

The towns of Plymouth and Devonport—the latter until 1824 having usually been called Plymouth Dock, or, briefly, Dock—stand nearly in the same relation to each other as Portsmouth and Portsea, except that they are not contiguous, the distance between them being about a mile and a half. Plymouth is the old borough, and Devonport is the modern town; the latter, indeed, has been entirely built within the last hundred and fifty years, since the establishment of the royal dockyard by William III. in 1691. Each town returns two members to Parliament, this privilege having been conferred on Devonport by the Reform Bill; and the municipal government of each is vested in separate authorities. Plymouth and Devonport, with Stonehouse, which lies between them, may be considered as forming one large town, which occupies a parallelogram about two miles and a half in length by one in breadth, and contains, with the suburbs of Morice-town and Stoke, about a hundred thousand inhabitants.

The name of Plymouth indicates the situation of the town at the mouth of the river Plym; which, considering the Catwater as a continuation of it, enters the lower part of Plymouth Sound at the strait formed by Mount Batten and the Citadel Point. The Catwater, however, is more properly a creek, or branch, of the Sound, into which the Plym discharges itself, after expanding into an estuary called the Lary.

The Catwater is on the eastern side of the Sound; and on the western side, between Cremill Point and the old Blockhouse at Mount Edgecumbe, is the entrance of the river Tamar, which expands immediately above this strait, and forms, opposite to Devonport, the noble harbour called the Hamoaze, where the largest ships of the line can lie afloat at all times of the tide. From the Hamoaze upwards, the Tamar separates the counties of Devon and Cornwall: Mount Edge-cumbe and a considerable part of Maker parish, in which it is situated, though within what may be considered the natural boundary of Cornwall, are yet held politically to be in the county of Devon.

"The town of Plymouth," says Leland, in his Itinerary, "is very large, and at this tyme is devided into four wards; and ther is a capitaine yn eche of these wards, and under eche capitaine three constables. This town, about Henry II. time, was a meane thing as an inhabitation for fischars, and after increased by litle and litle. The oldest part of the town stood by north and west sumwhat, and this part is sore decayed, and now cum to the lest of the four [wards]. The name of Plymmouth toun, and the privilege to have a mair, was in King Henry VI. dayes, the xvi yer of his reign, first grauntid by act of Parlament. The toun was caulled afore by the old name of Sutton, and was divided into Valetort, that was on the north part of the town, now the lest part of it. This was longing to one Valetorte. The midle and herte of the town was caulled Sutton Prior. The est part was caulled Sutton [Ralph]*." The harbour at Plymouth, where merchant-vessels load and deliver their cargoes, is still called Sutton Pool.

In the reign of Edward III., the town was certainly known by its present name; for in the twenty-first year of that king's reign, 1347, we find *Plymouth* furnishing ships and mariners for the expedition against France. If we are to judge of the importance of the place from the number of ships and mariners which it supplied, Plymouth must at that period have been one of the principal ports in the southern part of England. In 26th and 33rd of Edward I., Plymouth sent two members to Parliament, and also in the 4th and 7th of Edward II. No representatives seem to have been returned by the town from the latter year till the time of its incorporation by Henry VI., since which it has regularly sent two members to Parliament.

Before 1253, Plymouth had increased from "a meane thing, inhabited by fischars," to a considerable market-town. In the subsidy roll of 1377, which was compiled shortly after a pestilence had ravaged the country, 4837 persons, of fourteen years of age and upwards, were rated in Plymouth as liable to the poll-tax, from which only mendicants and the clergy were exempt. It seems, therefore, highly probable that the whole population of the town, about that time, could not be much less than 10,000. In 1547 the town appears not to have been so populous; for, in the Chantry-roll of that year, it is stated, that there were only 2,000 "*houselyng*" inhabitants; that is, such as were capable of communicating. According to the canons of the church, the age at which persons were admitted to receive that sacrament was fourteen years †.

* Leland's Itinerary, vol. iii., p. 42.   Edition 1769.
† Lysons' Magna Britannia, vol. vi. Devonshire.

In 1338 the French attacked Plymouth, and attempted to burn the town; but Hugh Courtenay, Earl of Devon, coming to its assistance with a considerable force, attacked the assailants, and compelled them to retire to their ships with great loss.   In 1350 the French, after having burnt Teignmouth, again made an attempt on Plymouth; but finding it well defended, they proceeded to ravage and burn "the farm houses and fair places" in the neighbourhood.   In 1411 the inhabitants petitioned Parliament, praying that the town might be fortified.   In this petition Plymouth is described as a great port, affording harbour for many vessels, and trading with foreign places for wines, cloth, salt, and iron.   It is further stated that the place was totally defenceless, and had frequently been attacked in time of war.   This petition was, however, disregarded at the time; and it was not till 1439 that the inhabitants obtained their request.   In that year they had a grant of a toll on all merchandise shipped or landed at the place, to enable them to build walls and towers for the defence of the town.   Leland, who visited Plymouth about a century afterwards, thus speaks of the fortifications then existing : " The mouth of the gulph wherin the shippes of Plymmouth lyith is waullid on eche side, and chainid over in tyme of necessitie.   On the south-west side of this mouth is a blok-house ; and, on a rokky hill hard by it, is a strong castel, quadrate, having at eche corner a great round tower.   It seemith to be no very old peace of worke."   The only part remaining of the old walls of Plymouth is the Hoe-gate, on the south side of the town, at a short distance from the entrance to the citadel.

Though Plymouth was the last place, except Pembroke, at which a royal dock-yard was established, it was from an early period the frequent rendezvous of the naval armaments of the country.   In 1355 Edward the Black Prince, after having been detained forty days at " Sutton," by contrary winds, sailed from this port for France; and on his return, in 1357, after the battle of Poictiers, he landed there with his royal prisoners, the King of France, and the Dauphin his son.   In 1470 the Earl of Warwick, called the King-maker, with the Earls of Pembroke and Oxford, landed at Plymouth in their expedition—which was attended with temporary success—to restore Henry VI.; and at Plymouth were fitted out the vessels with which the Earl of Cumberland, Sir Francis Drake, Gilbert, Hawkins, Carlisle, Grenville, and Cavendish proceeded on their voyages of discovery. When the Spanish armada passed the Sound, on the 20th July, 1588, a part of the English fleet, under the command of Lord Charles Howard and Sir Francis Drake, were at anchor near Plymouth; and it is said that Sir Francis was playing at bowls on the Hoe when he received intelligence of the enemy being in sight.   Some of the Spanish ships entered a short distance within the Sound;

and their admiral, the Duke of Medina Sidonia, is said to have been so much pleased with the situation of Mount Edgecumbe, that he determined to make it his residence, when the forces under his command should have conquered England. As soon as the armada had passed, the English fleet proceeded to sea, and on the following day overtook the enemy, when Lord Howard encountered the Spanish vice-admiral. A running-fight was kept up until the 24th, when the Plymouth squadron being joined by another division off the Isle of Wight, the engagement became more general. It was continued at intervals till the 28th July, when the English assailed the enemy with fire-ships, as they lay at anchor off Calais, and on the two following days succeeded in totally dispersing the grand armada, which had been blessed and pronounced invincible by the pope. Plymouth on this occasion supplied seven ships and one fly-boat to the English fleet; a greater number than was sent by any other port, except London. In 1596, Plymouth was the rendezvous for the expedition against Cadiz, or Cales, as the town was then called, under the Earl of Essex and the Earl of Nottingham. The English having succeeded in taking Cadiz, the Earl of Essex knighted so many persons of "weake and small meanes," that a "Knight of Cales" became a proverbial expression for a poor gentleman *.

As great inconvenience had been felt by the inhabitants of Plymouth from the want of a plentiful supply of fresh water, an act of Parliament was obtained, in 1584, by Sir Francis Drake, empowering the corporation to bring water, by means of a *leat*, from Dartmoor, and to charge a certain sum for each house to which it should be supplied. The leat, after a course of twenty-four miles, discharges itself into a large reservoir, to the north of Plymouth; from which it is conveyed in pipes to the different parts of the town. On the increase of Devonport, or "Dock," as it was formerly called, the inhabitants, like those of Plymouth at an earlier period, suffered great inconvenience from the difficulty of procuring a plentiful supply of fresh water. They applied to the corporation of Plymouth for leave to obtain a supply from their leat, but were refused. The reason which the Plymouth people assigned for the refusal was, that the stream was insufficient for the supply of both places; but it has been supposed that a feeling of jealousy towards the new town materially influenced the decision. In 1793 a water-company was established at Devonport, and a leat formed similar to that of Plymouth, by which a plentiful supply of water is conveyed to the town. The water is obtained from Dartmoor; and the length of the leat, following its various windings, is about

---

* Queen Elizabeth was greatly displeased at Essex for this exercise of authority without her express permission. "My Lord Essex," said the Queen, when she was informed of it, "might have done well to have built his alms-houses before he made his knights."

thirty-seven miles. When Dr. Johnson visited Plymouth, in 1762, the propriety of supplying the inhabitants of Dock from the old town leat was the subject of general discussion. Dr. Johnson, affecting to enter into the party-spirit of the Plymouth people, was opposed to the concession, and, half laughing at himself for his pretended zeal, exclaimed, " No, no! I am against the *Dockers;* I am a Plymouth man. Rogues, let them die of thirst; they shall not have a drop!"

At the commencement of the civil war, in 1642, the parliamentary party obtained possession of Plymouth, and kept it till the end of the contest, notwithstanding the frequent and vigorous attempts made by the royalists to take it. Soon after the commencement of hostilities, the Earl of Ruthen was appointed governor of the town, and the command of the fort and of the island of St. Nicholas was entrusted to Sir Alexander Carew. A body of royalists, commanded by Sir Ralph Hopton, appeared before the town in 1642, but were in a short time compelled to retire by the Earl of Stamford. In the following September, it having been discovered that Sir Alexander Carew had been holding communication with the king's party with the intention of betraying to them the forts under his command, he was sent to London, where he was brought to trial. Having been found guilty, he was beheaded on Tower-hill; where the two Hothams, father and son, were shortly afterwards executed, for having conspired to surrender Hull to the King. About the beginning of September, 1643, General Digby was sent with a considerable force to blockade Plymouth. He fixed his head-quarters at Plymstock, and his army erected batteries at Oreston and Mount Batten, and a guard was stationed at Hooe, the three latter places being all in the parish of Plymstock and on the south side of the Catwater. About the same time several small vessels were, with great labour, brought over land from the river Yealm, and moored in Pomphlett creek, a little above Oreston. After having made one or two unsuccessful attacks upon the outworks of the town, the royalists, about the 10th October, were reinforced by the army under Prince Maurice, who, having succeeded in taking Dartmouth, marched forward to lay siege to Plymouth. The prince's head-quarters were at Widey-house, and his army, which occupied a line of posts between Plympton and Tamerton, cut off all communication with the town from the northward. The siege was now closely pressed; and on 5th November the royalists took Mount Stamford. On 18th December they attempted to storm the town; but being repulsed with great loss by the garrison, they raised the siege, and retired on the 25th. At the commencement of this siege, Colonel James Wardlaw, who was then governor of the town, took possession of the fort and the island of St. Nicholas, which at that time were under the charge of the mayor, and entrusted them to the command of approved parliamentary officers. About

T

the same time all the inhabitants were required to make a protestation to defend Plymouth and Stonehouse, with the fort and the island, to the uttermost.

About the middle of April, 1644, Sir Richard Grenville, advancing with a royalist army towards Plymouth, was encountered by the governor, Colonel Martin, and defeated near St. Budeaux. About three days afterwards, Sir Richard made a second attempt to approach the town, but with no better success. In July, the royalists, having been reinforced by Prince Maurice, made an attack upon Plymouth, but were repulsed by the garrison ; and the prince shortly afterwards withdrew, leaving Sir Richard Grenville to blockade the town. About the end of July, on the parliamentary army under the Earl of Essex approaching Plymouth, Sir Richard Grenville abandoned the blockade ; and Mount Stamford, which had continued in the possession of the royalists since the preceding November, fell into the hands of the Earl of Essex. After the surrender of the earl's army in Cornwall, the king came in person before Plymouth. He took up his quarters at Widey-house on the 9th September; and on the 11th, the town was summoned to surrender. On the determined refusal of Lord Roberts, who was then governor, the royalists thought it most prudent not to venture on an assault, and the king with his army retired on 14th September, Sir Richard Grenville being again left to blockade the town. On the 10th January, 1645, the royalist army, which then amounted to about 6,000 men, assaulted the town with so much vigour that they succeeded in taking four of the principal outworks; but the garrison having rallied, the outworks were retaken and the besiegers compelled to retire with great loss. Other attempts on the part of the royalists met with no better success. In June, the command of the blockading army was entrusted to Sir John Berkeley, who in September was superseded by General Digby. All the efforts of the royalists to take the town having proved unavailing, the blockade was finally abandoned on the 10th of January, 1646.

Plymouth harbour, or, as it is generally called, Sutton Pool, is on the land side nearly surrounded by houses, and the entrance to it from the Catwater is protected by two stone piers, about ninety feet apart. Plymouth has a considerable coasting trade with London, Bristol, Hull, Newcastle, and other parts of England, and also carries on a direct trade with the Baltic, the Mediterranean, America, and the West Indies. The principal exports are copper, tin, and lead-ore, manganese, granite, and pilchards. There are about fifty decked fishing-boats belonging to Plymouth, which not only supply its market and that of Devonport with plenty of excellent fish, but also furnish a considerable quantity for Bath, London, and other places. The fish most common in Plymouth market are hake, basse, gurnards, pipers, tub-fish, whiting-pouts, soles, mullets red and grey, and

John-Dories. Quin, that he might enjoy the latter fish in perfection, took an express journey from Bath to Plymouth. The export of granite, and other kinds of stone for the purposes of building, is greatly facilitated by a railway, which extends from about the middle of Dartmoor to the quays at Sutton Pool and Catwater. The larger class of merchant-vessels generally anchor in the Catwater; and in time of war it is the usual rendezvous for transports. It is sheltered from south-westerly gales by Mount Batten, and is sufficiently spacious to afford anchorage for six or eight hundred sail of such ships as are usually employed in the merchant service. There are about 320 ships belonging to Plymouth, the tonnage of which, according to the old admeasurement, is about 26,000 tons. It is high water at Plymouth at half-past five o'clock at the full and change of the moon, and the rise of the spring tides is about eighteen feet. The latitude of Plymouth New Church is 50° 22' 20" north; longitude, 4° 7' 16" west.

Though the neighbourhood of Plymouth affords so many beautiful and interest-ing views, the town itself presents but little to excite the admiration of the stranger. It is very irregularly built; and most of the old houses have a very mean appear-ance, more especially when contrasted with some of recent erection. Several large buildings, within the last twenty or thirty years, have been erected at Plymouth and Devonport, in the *pure Grecian style;* and the two towns afford ample evidence of the imitative genius of the architects. At the corner of almost every principal street, the stranger is presented with reminiscences of Stuart and Revett's Athens.

By the Municipal Corporation Act of 1835, an alteration was made in the old mode of electing the officers of the borough. Plymouth is now governed by a mayor, recorder, town-clerk, and twelve aldermen, with thirty-six councillors, elected by the six wards into which the borough is now divided. Plymouth is 215 miles west-south-west of London, and 44 miles south-west of Exeter.

Plymouth citadel is situated to the southward of the town, and at the eastern extremity of the rocky elevation called the Hoe. It commands the passage to the Hamoaze, between St. Nicholas' island and the main-land, as well as the entrance of the Catwater. It was erected on the site of the old fort, in the reign of Charles II., and consists of five bastions, which are further strengthened with ravelins and hornworks. The ramparts are nearly three-quarters of a mile in circuit; and there are platforms for a hundred and twenty cannon. The entrance to the citadel is on the north, through an outer and an inner gate. Within the walls are the residence of the lieutenant-governor, officers' houses and barracks for the garrison, with a magazine, chapel, and hospital. In the centre of the green is a bronze statue of George II., the work of an artist named Robert Pitt, and erected, in 1728, at the expense of Louis Dufour, Esq., an officer of the garrison.

An excellent panoramic view of Plymouth, Saltram, the Catwater, the Sound, Mount Edgecumbe, and other places, is to be obtained from the ramparts, round which visitors are permitted to walk.

The heights called the Hoe lie between the citadel and the creek named Mill-bay, their rocky cliffs fronting the southward, and forming the northern boundary of the Sound. The view from the Hoe is one of the finest that can be imagined. Directly in front is the Sound, in which are frequently to be seen men-of-war,—some lying at anchor within the Breakwater, and others under sail, cleaving the blue sea with easy and life-like motion. In the distance, to the left, is perceived the Mewstone, and opposite to it, on the right, is Penlee-point, which forms the south-western extremity of the Sound. About a mile within the Sound the ridge of the Breakwater is seen, with Bovisand-bay on the left, and Cawsand-bay on the right. Nearer to the spectator, on the right, are the woody slopes of Mount Edgecumbe, which are contrasted, on the opposite side, with the bleak-looking heights of Mount Staddon. Still nearer, and almost directly in front, is St. Nicholas' Island; and to the left, are Mount Batten and the Catwater. In a clear day, the Eddystone Lighthouse, which is about fourteen miles distant, may be perceived from the Hoe with the naked eye. Previous to the formation of the Breakwater, to restrain the violence of the inward swell from sea-ward in south-west gales, many vessels used to be wrecked on the rocks at the foot of the Hoe; but of late years such melancholy occurrences have been much less frequent.

The insecurity of Plymouth Sound, in consequence of the heavy sea rolling in during the prevalence of south-westerly gales, became strikingly apparent during the late war, when the English fleet employed in blockading Brest, or cruising in the channel, were frequently obliged, in stormy weather, to seek for shelter on their own coast. In 1806, the subject having excited the attention of the government, the late Mr. Rennie, the celebrated civil-engineer, and Mr. Whidbey, master-attendant of Woolwich dock-yard, were directed to make a survey, and report their opinions as to the best mode of opposing a barrier to the violence of the sea. After several plans had been proposed, it was finally resolved, on the report of Messrs. Rennie and Whidbey, to form an immense breakwater, extending about 1700 yards, across the middle of the Sound. It was calculated that by the shelter thus afforded a fleet of fifty sail might anchor in safety within the breakwater, in all weathers, and have ample room for working in or out through the channels on each side. Various objections, however, were made to this plan, and the order for carrying it into execution was not signed till 22nd June, 1811. In consequence of this authority, a piece of ground, situated at Oreston on the western shore of the Catwater, of twenty-five acres extent, and covering a rock of indurated lime-stone, or grey marble, was purchased of the Duke of Bedford, for £10,000. Quarries were immediately opened * at this spot, and huge blocks of stone, weighing from one to four tons each, prepared. The first stone of the Breakwater was sunk on 12th August, 1812, and by the conclusion of the year 1816 upwards of a million tons had been deposited. A great portion of the work was now visible above the sea at low water, and its efficacy ceased to be doubtful; the swell in the inner part of the Sound being so much diminished by its resistance that the fishermen were no longer able, as heretofore, to judge from it of the state of the sea without. The total length of the Breakwater, at the base, is about a mile, or 1,760 yards; the middle portion, directly opposed to the swell, is about 1,000 yards long; and the *cants*, or portions inclining inwards, at angles of about 120 degrees with the middle, are each about 380 yards long. The base is from 80 to 120 yards broad, according to the depth of water, diminishing upwards in the proportion of three feet horizontal to one perpendicular, on the side exposed to the swell, and in the proportion of one and a half horizontal to one perpendicular, on the land side. The average perpendicular height of the Breakwater is about fourteen yards, and its breadth at the top is sixteen yards. By the end of August, 1824, the quantity of stone deposited was upwards of two millions of tons; and since that time at least two hundred and fifty thousand tons more have been sunk. The vessels employed in conveying the stone from the quarries are of a peculiar construction. They are about seventy tons burthen, and sloop-rigged. They have two large stern-ports, from each of which a kind of railway extends the whole length of the hold. The stones, with the trucks on which they are conveyed from the quarries, are run in through those ports; and, on the vessel arriving at the place where they are to be sunk, a strong frame is suspended from the stern, the trucks are run out from the hold on to it, and, their inner ends being elevated, the stones are thrown into the sea. The trucks, as they are emptied, are drawn up over the stern on to the deck of the vessel.

In a violent storm on the 9th January, 1817, the Breakwater received considerable damage. The upper stratum, to the length of two hundred, and of the width of thirty yards, was displaced by the violence of the sea, the immense blocks of stone of which it consisted, weighing from two to five tons each, having been forced up and rolled over on to the inner slope. In consequence of the damage

---

* In working these quarries, numerous fossil remains have been discovered, consisting of bones of the rhinoceros, wolf, deer, cow, horse, and other animals. The cavity in which the greater part were found, was seventy feet below the surface, and every side of it was of solid rock, without any appearance of an opening from above which might have been closed by infiltration.

sustained by the breakwater, it was resolved to case the sea-front with immense blocks of stone, which, presenting a smooth surface to the action of the sea, would be less liable to be torn up than a mass of stones irregularly placed. On the 23rd November, 1824, in one of the most tremendous storms ever remembered at Plymouth, and in which the water rose upwards of six feet above its usual level, the upper part of the breakwater again sustained considerable injury. The centre and the western end suffered most, and the landing-place was destroyed. It was, however, considered that the advantage gained from the settlement of the stones, and the consequent consolidation of the work, more than compensated for the damage done to the surface. The summit of the breakwater is paved with large blocks of stone, forming a walk forty-eight feet wide; and near the centre, on the land side, is a spacious landing-place. A visit to the breakwater, which is about two miles and a half from the Hoe Cliffs, forms a pleasant excursion from Plymouth or Devonport in fine weather.

Stonehouse, which lies about midway between Plymouth and Devonport, has within the last forty years increased from a village to a considerable town, the population of which is about 17,000. On the westward it is bounded by an inlet called Stonehouse-creek, which is much frequented by merchant-vessels and steam-packets. At Stonehouse are the marine barracks; and at the southern part of the town, near the entrance of the creek, a large victualling-office for the supply of the navy has recently been erected. The Royal Naval Hospital is situated in the north-eastern part of the town; and opposite to it, on the Devonport side of the creek, is the Military Hospital. At each establishment there is a landing place from the creek, for the convenience of receiving patients sent in boats from transports or men-of-war. The whole of the parish of Stonehouse is the property of the Earl of Mount Edgecumbe; and the moderate terms on which his lordship has granted building sites, have materially contributed to the increase of the place. The principal road between Plymouth and Devonport crosses a bridge at Stonehouse, which is the joint property of the Earl of Mount Edgecumbe and Sir John St. Aubyn, the owners of the ground on the opposite shores. A profit of about two thousand pounds per annum is derived from this bridge, which arises chiefly from a toll of a halfpenny exacted from each foot-passenger for once passing and repassing. This toll is much complained of by the inhabitants of Plymouth and Devonport, and it is to be hoped that the representatives of these boroughs will bring the subject before Parliament.

After passing Stonehouse Bridge, a rather steep road, about a quarter of a mile long, leads to a gate forming the south entrance into Devonport, which on the land side is enclosed by a line of fortifications which were commenced in the reign of

George II., and have since at different periods been further strengthened and extended. The town is built on an eminence, declining towards the Hamoaze, and from many points excellent views may be obtained of Stonehouse, Plymouth, Mount Edgecumbe, and the surrounding country. The streets are mostly regular and spacious, and the houses well built. "The pedestrians of Devonport," says a writer, in describing the town, "as well as those of Plymouth and Stonehouse, literally walk on marble, the pavements being composed of that material, which speedily becomes so much polished as to have a beautiful appearance when washed by heavy rains." Nearly the whole of the ground on which Devonport is built, is the property of Sir John St. Aubyn, of Clowance, Cornwall, of whom almost every house is held under a renewable lease.

The residence of the lieutenant-governor, commanding the garrison, is at the Government-house on Mount Wise, a strongly fortified eminence at the south of the town, commanding the entrance to the harbour. Near to the Government-house is the official residence of the port-admiral, and in its immediate vicinity is the semaphore by which intelligence is transmitted to his flag-ship, usually a ship of the line stationed in the Hamoaze, or to the Admiralty in London. Near the centre of the town is a column, erected in 1824, to commemorate the year in which the name of the place was changed from Plymouth-Dock to Devonport. In 1823 the inhabitants presented a petition to George IV., praying that the former name might be altered, and suggesting that of Devonport, which his majesty was pleased to approve. By the Reform Bill the privilege of returning two members to Parliament was conferred on the town. The first members chosen by the new borough were Admiral Sir Edward Codrington and Sir George Grey, who still represent the place, having been re-elected by their constituents on each subsequent dissolution of Parliament.

The dock-yard, which was first established in 1691, is on the west side of the town, and is separated from it by a lofty wall. Its extent is about seventy-five acres, of which only about ten acres are the freehold property of the crown, the remainder being held of Sir John St. Aubyn, on a lease renewable every seven years. Permission to visit the dock-yard is to be obtained by applying to the captain-superintendant, and is never refused except to foreigners, who are only admitted by an express order from the Admiralty. On entering the yard, the first buildings that present themselves are the chapel on the right, and the residence of the director of the dock-police, adjoining it. In front of the latter building is a large bell, which announces the time for the men employed in the dock to begin and leave off work; it formerly belonging to the Tonnant, a French man-of-war taken at the battle of the Nile. The bell-post on which it is hung is a single p·ece of teak, sixty-four feet high, which, previous to being applied to its present use, had been the main-mast of an Indiaman. On the right of the main road, further in the yard, is the military guard-house, over which is the navy pay-office; and on the left is the surgery, where such workmen as happen to receive any hurt in the course of their labours are immediately attended to. Not far from the surgery is a handsome range of buildings consisting of the residences of the captain-superintendant, the surgeon, master-shipwright, storekeeper, and other officers of the yard. There are five docks at Devonport yard, all of which, except one, are covered with immense roofs; and all the building-slips, of which there are five, are covered in the same manner. There is also what is called a *graving-slip*, which is in all respects like a dock, except that it has no gates. It is employed for the purpose of making such repairs in the bottoms of vessels as can be completed in one tide. To the southward is the camber, or canal, 60 feet wide and extending to the length of 820 feet into the yard. On one side of the camber is the blacksmiths' shop, where anchors and other articles of iron-work are manufactured for the use of the navy; and near its mouth is the anchor-wharf, where anchors of all sizes, painted to preserve them from rust, are arranged in regular rows. In its neighbourhood are immense warehouses for the reception of various kinds of naval stores. There are within the yard a mast-pond, a ropery, a rigging-house, boat-builders' sheds, with workshops for various classes of artificers. The different buildings are the most complete of their kind of any dock-yard in the kingdom. The gun-wharf is on the margin of the Hamoaze, north of the dock-yard, from which it is separated by a street. The area of the ground contained within the walls is about five acres. An immense quantity of guns, belonging to the ships laid up in ordinary in the Hamoaze, are deposited on this wharf; and in the armoury are many thousands of muskets, pistols, and cutlasses, placed in racks, or arranged ornamentally against the walls.

That part of the Tamar which is called the Hamoaze is about four miles long, and from ten to fifteen fathoms deep at low-water. There are moorings in the Hamoaze for about a hundred ships of war; and at the present time there are between sixty and seventy laid up there in ordinary

Drawn by J.D. Harding, from a sketch by Jeddie.

Engraved by E. Finden.

MOUNT EDGCUMBE.

DEVON.

MOUNT EDGECUMBE.

THE view of Mount Edgecumbe is taken from Cremili point, a little to the south-east of the entrance of Stonehouse Creek. About the centre of the view is perceived a battery, near to the old blockhouse which was erected in the reign of Queen Elizabeth; between the masts of the brig, which is sailing in towards the Hamoaze, the house is seen; and to the left, in the distance, is Cawsand Bay.

For upwards of two hundred years the situation of Mount Edgecumbe, whether looking towards it or from it, and the beauty of the grounds in its vicinity, have been the subject of general admiration. In visiting Mount Edgecumbe from Plymouth or Devonport, the most usual way is to cross at the ferry from Cremill point. The gardens generally first claim the visitor's attention. Near the lodge, on the left, is a garden laid out in the Italian style, and surrounded by a bank planted with evergreens. In this garden is the orangery, and opposite to it is a beautiful terrace, on which, and in the grounds below, are several statues. The visitor is next shown the French flower garden, which is planted with the most beautiful shrubs and flowers, and was the favourite retreat of Sophia, Countess of Mount Edgecumbe, who died in 1806, and to whose memory a cenotaph, consisting of an urn and a tablet, is erected within its bounds. The English garden and the shrubbery display less art, but are no less beautiful than the imitative gardens of Italy and France. The walks round the grounds are extremely pleasing, and from many points excellent views are obtained of Plymouth Sound, the Hamoaze, Devonport, and the surrounding country. It seems, however, doubtful if the circumstance of a nobleman's seat commanding a view of a large town, at the distance of less than a mile, be an advantage to it. It is perhaps not altogether pleasant to have a *country* seat overlooked by, and overlooking, a large town. Dr. Johnson, alluding to the view from Mount Edgecumbe, has observed, that " though there is the grandeur of a fleet, there is also the impression of there being a dock-yard, the circumstances of which are not agreeable."

The house at Mount Edgecumbe was erected about the year 1550, in the castellated style, with circular towers at the corners. About seventy years ago those towers were pulled down, and rebuilt in their present octangular form.

U

COWES.

East and West Cowes, in the Isle of Wight, lie on opposite sides, and near the mouth, of the river Medina, which rises on the southern side of the island, and after passing Newport, discharges itself into the strait—usually called the Solent Sea—that separates the Isle of Wight from the main land. The view of the harbour in the engraving is taken from West Cowes.

In the reign of Henry VIII. two castles were built at the mouth of the river Medina to defend the passage to Newport. The old castle at West Cowes is still standing, but that of East Cowes has long been demolished. The castellated building seen in the engraving is a gentleman's seat, and is of modern erection.

Cowes harbour is spacious and commodious; and the roads off the mouth of the river, which afford excellent anchorage, used frequently to be crowded in time of war with merchant-vessels waiting for convoy; and the towns derived great advantage from supplying ships, while thus detained, with provisions and small stores. The loss of a great part of this trade, on the termination of the war, has perhaps been more than compensated by Cowes having become the rendezvous of the Royal Yacht Squadron, which was first established under the name of the Yacht Club, in 1815. The number of vessels belonging to the squadron is about a hundred, and their aggregate tonnage is about 9,000 tons. The members have a club-house at Cowes: and at the annual regatta, which generally takes place about the last week in August, there are usually upwards of two hundred vessels assembled in the roads, to witness the sailing for the different prizes.

The town of West Cowes is situated on the declivity and at the base of a hill, on the summit of which stands the church. The streets are mostly narrow, and irregularly built; but since the peace the town and its vicinity have been much improved by the erection of several large houses and beautiful villas. There is a regular communication between Cowes and Southampton, by steam-boats, which, in summer, leave each place twice a day. East Cowes is a much smaller place than West Cowes; but, like the latter, it has been much improved within the last twenty years. The population of the two towns is about 4,000; and the number of vessels belonging to the port in 1833 was 151, with an aggregate tonnage of 6,015 tons. It is high water at Cowes at forty-five minutes past ten, at the full and change of the moon, and the average rise of the water at spring-tides is fifteen feet.

Drawn by T. Creswick.

Engraved by W. Finden.

COWES.

HAMPSHIRE.

London. Published 1837, by Charles Tilt, 86, Fleet Street.

Drawn by T. Nash.

Engraved by E. Finden.

SOUTHAMPTON.

HANTS.

London, Published 1837, by Charles Tilt, 86, Fleet Street.

SOUTHAMPTON.

THE town of Southampton is situated in the county of the same name, or, as it is more frequently called, Hampshire. It is built on a point of land, at the confluence of the river Itchin with the estuary called the Anton *, but which is much more generally known as Southampton Water. The origin of the name of the town—which has unquestionably given its name to the county—does not appear to have been satisfactorily ascertained; some writers supposing it to be composed of the Saxon words, *ham* and *tun* or *ton*—which are nearly synonymous, and each equivalent to the modern English, town—with the prefix *South* to distinguish it more emphatically from Northampton. Others, however, consider that the name has been derived from the river Anton, on the banks of which the town is situated. "The town of *An*dover," says Sir Henry Englefield, " the village of Abbot's-*An*, the farm of North*anton*, and the hamlet of South*anton*, both near Overton, and not far from the eastern source of the river *Anton* or rather *Ant*, are abundant proofs of the probability of this etymology†." Sir Henry is also of opinion that the name of the Roman station of Clausentum, which was most certainly at Bittern, about a mile and a half to the northward of Southampton, was formed from the An or Ant, which he conceives to have been the British name of the river and the estuary. Camden says, " That this place was called Hanton and Henton, no one need question; because, in Domesday-book, the whole county is expressly called Hantscyre, and in another place Hentscyre." Bishop Gibson, the translator of Camden, after noticing that Florence of Worcester calls the county Hantunscyre, says that it is " a mistake of the librarian for Hamtunscyre; since the Saxon annals call it so, and he transcribed from them." On a question of etymology depending in the least on the manner of spelling a name, the Domesday-book is but of small authority, for it is evident that the compilers of that work paid but little attention to the correct spelling of the names of places ‡.

* The estuary is also called Trisanton Bay; and the modern name of the river, which Sir Henry Englefield supposes to have been called the Anton, is the Test.

† A Walk through Southampton, page 2.

‡ " In Domesday, Cudlington (now Kidlington) in Oxfordshire, the Norman inquisitors and their scribes pronounced and wrote *Chedelintone*. They softened all the old Saxon appellations; as, in Oxfordshire, *Rovesham* for Rousham, *Misseberie* for Mixbury, *Blicestone* for Blechingdon, *Hansitone* for Hensington, *Esefelde* for Ellsfield, &c. Other places they totally misrepresented, with the carelessness or affectation of a modern Frenchman; as *Chenefelde* for Clanfield, *Chenetone* for Kencot, *Geresdune* for Garsington,

The fact of the county being still frequently called *Hants*, seems to be much more decisive in favour of Sir Henry Englefield's opinion than the circumstance of the name being spelled Hantscyre in the Domesday Survey. With respect to the prefix *South*, Sir Henry's opinion is as follows:—"Although the consequence of Clausentum evidently declined as the new Hantun increased, yet it was by no means deserted; for there are large remains yet existing of a magnificent Saxon or Norman fortress or castellated mansion, built on the ancient Roman wall of Bittern; and as the new town is situated directly south of the old one, it was natural that it should be distinguished from it by the prefix of *South*."

In 980 the town was ravaged by the Danes; and it was there, according to Camden, who quotes the account from Henry of Huntingdon, that Canute gave a reproof to a flattering courtier, who pretended that all things would obey his royal will. In 1086, the probable date of the Domesday-book, Southampton, or, as it is called in that record, Hantone, was undoubtedly a place of some consequence, though no correct idea of its extent or of the number of the inhabitants can be formed from the mere mention of the number of persons residing there who held lands or houses of the king. At that period it is probable that the greater part of the inhabitants of all towns were a kind of bondage-tenants almost entirely dependent on their more powerful neighbours. From the Domesday-book it appears that there were then seventy-six persons in the town who held lands of the king, and for which they paid yearly seven pounds, as in the time of Edward the Confessor. Besides those tenants of the king, there were sixty-five aliens and thirty-one English inhabitants, who paid jointly the sum of four pounds and sixpence, in lieu of all customary rents. By the especial favour of the king, the payment of all customary dues is remitted to a certain number of persons, who have houses in the town.

Southampton, as a chartered borough, may rank with the oldest in tne kingdom. Madox, in his Firma Burgi, says that Henry II. "confirmed to his men, or burgesses of Southampton, their guild and their liberties and customs by sea and land: he having regard to the great charges which the inhabitants thereof have been at in defending the sea-coasts." From a grant by the same king to the priory of St. Dionysius, it appears that there were then four churches in Southampton. While the English were in possession of Guienne, the merchants of Southampton carried on a considerable trade with Bayonne, Bordeaux, and other towns in the south of France. In the fourth volume of the Fœdera are two

&c. Hence it has happened that we cannot always appeal with certainty to this ancient and venerable record, which would otherwise have possessed the highest authority, and would have afforded information now never to be obtained."—Warton's History and Antiquities of Kiddington, p. 35. Edition, 1815.

remonstrances of Edward III. addressed to Alphonso, king of Castile, on the subject of piracies committed by the people of St. Andero, Castro, St. Sebastian, and other places in Spain, on English vessels, and more especially on those belonging to the merchants of Southampton. In 1338 the town was assaulted and burnt, by a party of French or Genoese; and in the next year an act was passed for its better fortification. Leland evidently considers that the town which was burnt in 1338 did not stand on the same site as the present town. "The town of *Old-Hampton*," saith the Itinerant, "a celebrate thing for fischar men and sum merchaunts, stoode a quarter of a mile or thereabout above from *New Hampton*, by north-est, and stretched to the haven-syde. The plotte wherein it stoode berith now good corn and grasse, and is namyd *S. Maryfeld*, by the chirch of *S. Mary* standing hard by it.——The old town of Hampton was brent in tyme of warre, spoyled and raysed by French pyrates. This was the cause that the inhabitants there translated themselves to a more commodious place, and began, with the kinges licens and help, to build New-Hampton, and to waull it yn defence of the enemies." This account is, however, incorrect; for Sir Henry Englefield has clearly shown that the town of Southampton, when it was assailed in 1338, stood upon its present site, and that a castle had been built there before 1153. Whatever injury the town might have sustained from the attack of the French or Genoese, it would seem that its trade as a port was not diminished by it; for, nine years afterwards, Southampton supplied 21 ships and 476 mariners to the great fleet of Edward III. In consequence of another attack by the French, in the reign of Richard II., the fortifications were further strengthened. In 1415 the army of Henry V., destined for the invasion of France, assembled at Southampton, where previous to their embarkation the Earl of Cambridge, Lord Scrope, and Sir Thomas Grey, were executed for high treason. The result of this memorable expedition was the victory of Agincourt. While the English continued to hold possession of part of France, the trade of Southampton appears to have been very flourishing, and the port was one of the principal in the south of England for the import of wine. Camden, writing about 1586, describes it as a town famous for the number and neatness of its buildings, the wealth of its inhabitants, and the resort of merchants; "but now," adds Camden's translator, writing about a hundred years afterwards, "it is not in the same flourishing condition as formerly it was; for having lost a great part of its trade, it has lost most of its inhabitants too; and the great houses of merchants are now dropping to the ground, and only show its ancient magnificence *."

For the last forty years the trade of Southampton as a port has been gradually reviving; and at present there seems great reason to believe, that in a few

* Camden's Britannia, translated by Bishop Gibson, vol. i. p. 213.

years it will be very materially increased, when the London and Southampton railway, now in course of formation, shall have been finished. As Southampton is only about sixteen miles from Cowes, and as steam-boats can make the passage in less than two hours, it is highly probable that most persons proceeding to the Isle of Wight from London will go by way of Southampton. Looking at the advantages which the town will then enjoy, as an *entrepôt* for London, more especially as regards Portuguese, Spanish, and Mediterranean produce, it is likely that the traffic between the two places will be very materially increased. Looking at the saving of time and the diminution of risk in a voyage from Southampton to any port in Spain, Portugal, the south of France, or the Mediterranean, compared with a voyage from London to the same port, there seems every reason to believe that, if the rate of carriage by the railway be not too high, a considerable quantity of goods, now imported into London direct from those countries, will in future years be first landed at Southampton, and thence forwarded to London by the railroad. Instead of going down to St. Catherine's or the London Docks, to taste wine in the wood, we shall perhaps hear of gentlemen taking a trip for that purpose to the Docks at Southampton; and west-end fruiterers and Italian-warehouse keepers, instead of dealing as heretofore with a merchant in Botolph-lane or Tower-street, may transfer their favours to a wholesale orange-merchant or importer of olives and maccaroni, residing in Southampton. With a view of affording every facility to the anticipated increase of the trade of the port, a dock-company has been established at Southampton, and a large plot of ground purchased, sufficient for the site of four large docks, with requisite warehouses. The proposed docks will be bounded on the east by the river Itchin, and on the south and west by Southampton-Water; and at their entrance, on the land side, will be the terminus of the London and Southampton railway. The depth of water at ebb-tide, on the Itchin side is sixteen feet, and on the side of the Southampton-Water ten feet.

Southampton is a corporate town, governed by a mayor, recorder, and other officers. By the Municipal Reform Bill it is now divided into five wards, which return altogether thirty town-councillors. Southampton is also a parliamentary borough of ancient date, having been first summoned to send two representatives to the national council in 23rd of Edward I. The present members are Viscount Duncan and A. R. Dottin, Esq. In 1831 the population of the town was 19,324; and in 1833 the number of ships belonging to the port was 178, with a tonnage of 8,120 tons. It is high water at Southampton at forty minutes past eleven o'clock, at the full and change of the moon; and the rise of the water at spring tides is eighteen feet.

BRIGHTON.

BRIGHTON is in the county of Sussex, and lies about fifty-two miles south of London. The old name of the town was Brighthelmstone, which some antiquaries suppose to have been derived from Brighthelm, a Saxon bishop ; while others, premising sundry "ifs," suppose that it may be derived from the Saxon *beorht, briht, berht,* and *byrt,* signifying *bright; heal,* a light-house or watch-tower, a corner oi point of a wedge, a hall; and the word *tun,* or *ton,* signifying a town. The advantage of this etymology; or rather, bunch of *roots,* is that the reader has plenty to choose from ; " Suave est ex magno tollere acervo." Dr. Relhan, who appears to have carefully studied Dean Swift's Etymological Essay, says that the name " perhaps may be deduced from the ships of this town having their *helms better ornamented* than those of their neighbours." This is about as good as the Dean's derivation of the name of the son of Hector, Astyanax—a sty, an ax !

The name, spelled Bristelmstune, occurs in Domesday-book. Three manors are described under this name, and they all appear to have been formerly in the possession of Earl Godwin, the father of King Harold. Brighton, or Brighthelmstone, until it began to be frequented as a watering-place, about the middle of the last century, is seldom noticed by historians ; and until that period it never appears to have risen above the condition of a small fishing-town. In 1313, John de Warren, then lord of the manor, obtained a charter to have a market at Brightelmstone every Thursday ; and in 1513 the place was pillaged by the French. In the reign of Henry VIII. a block-house was erected at Brighton ; and this defence appears to have been either rebuilt or further strengthened in 1558. In 1579 there were eighty fishing-boats belonging to the place, and the number of fishermen and mariners was four hundred. It is a fact worth noticing, that in the seventeenth century almost every place on the southern and eastern coast of England, which depended on the fishery, was in a declining state. The decline of the fishery appears to have commenced in the reign of Elizabeth on the re-establishment of the Protestant form of worship, when the non-observance of the fasts enjoined by the church of Rome considerably diminished the demand for fish. Elizabeth endeavoured to prevent the decline of the fishery, by enjoining her subjects to eat fish once a week, not as a religious duty, but as conducive to health and the benefit of the state. The many projects for improving the English sea-fishery, in the reigns of James I., Charles I.

and Charles II., afford abundant proofs that it was not flourishing at that time. During the period of the civil war between Charles I. and Parliament, and in the time of the Commonwealth, the English fishery appears to have been at its lowest ebb. The Puritans of that age, who considered the eating of mince-pies at Christmas as the observance of a popish rite, appear to have had an aversion to fish, which most likely originated in the scruples of an exceedingly tender conscience: to have eaten fish on a Friday would have been rank popery. To avoid therefore the very semblance of sanctioning such a custom, they appear to have resolved to eat very little fish on any other days.

About 1750, Brighton, which was then recovering from the depressed state in which it had been for upwards of a century*, began to be visited during the summer as a bathing place. In 1782, the Duke of Cumberland, brother to George III., when residing at Brighton, received a visit from the Prince of Wales, afterwards George IV., and his royal highness was so much pleased with the place, that he determined to build for himself a marine residence there. The Pavilion was accordingly commenced in 1784; but from the alterations and additions which the royal owner was almost constantly making, it would be difficult to say when it was finished. On the decease of George IV., the Pavilion became the property of his successor, William IV., from whom it has descended to her present Majesty. The inhabitants of Brighton are remarkable for the ardent expressions of loyalty with which they welcome the heirs of the " royal property."

> "———————————— A fashionable host,
> That slightly shakes his parting guest by the hand;
> And with his arms out-stretch'd, as he would fly,
> Grasps in the comer: Welcome ever smiles,
> And Farewell goes out sighing.
> *   *   *   *   *   *
> One touch of nature makes the whole world kin,—
> That all, with one consent, praise new-born gauds,
> Though they are made and moulded of things past,
> And give to dust that is a little gilt
> More laud than gilt o'erdusted."

By the Reform bill the privilege of returning two members to Parliament was conferred on Brighton. The present representatives, November 1837, are Sir A. J. Dalrymple and Captain Pechell. In 1780 the population of Brighton was only 3,600; in 1811 it was 12,012; and in 1831 it had increased to 40,634.

* In addition to its depression from the decline of the fishery, 130 houses were swept away at Brighton in 1699 by an inundation of the sea.

Drawn by J.D. Harding

Engraved by W. Finden.

DOVER.

KENT.

London, Published 1837, by Charles Tilt, 86. Fleet Street.

DOVER.

DOVER is in the county of Kent, and lies about seventy-two miles south-south-east of London. The town is situated in a valley, having on one side the cliffs on which Dover Castle is built, and on the other the eminence called the *Heights*, which are strongly fortified and form the principal defence of the town and harbour. The greater part of the town lies on the western side of a small stream, called the Dour, which there discharges itself into the sea. The view in the engraving is taken from the beach on the eastern side of the harbour, looking towards the north-east. The row of houses seen extending in a line nearly parallel with the beach, is called the Marine Parade: and crowning the cliff, is perceived what of old was termed " the Key and Bar of England *,"—Dover Castle. Its importance as a place of defence against the attacks of an invading enemy has, however, been seldom proved; and for the last three centuries the best defence of England against the invasion of her foes has been her wooden-walls:

> " Britannia needs no bulwark,
>   No towers along the steep;
>   Her march is o'er the mountain waves,
>   Her home is on the deep.
>   With thunders from her native oak,
>   She quells the floods below,
>   As they roar on the shore,
>   When the stormy tempests blow;
>   When the battle rages loud and long,
>   And the stormy tempests blow."

Dover is a place of great antiquity, and it has retained its name with but little alteration from the period of the Roman domination in Britain to the present time. In the Itinerary of Antoninus it is mentioned under the name of *Ad Portum Dubris;* and in Richard of Cirencester's description of Britain, which is

---

* " *Clavem et repagulum Angliæ* vocat Matthæus Parisiensis," says Camden.—" It is reported that Philip, surnamed Augustus, King of France (when his son Lewis made his attempts upon England, and had taken some cities), should say, ' My son has not yet got so much as footing in England, if he have not got into his hands the castle of Dover;' looking upon it to be the strongest place in England, and to lie most convenient for France."—*Camden's Britannia, Bishop Gibson's translation.*——Dover Castle was besieged by the Dauphin in his invasion of England, to aid the insurgent barons, in the reign of King John; but the place being bravely defended by the governor, Hubert de Burgh, the French raised the siege and proceeded straight to London.

generally supposed to have been chiefly compiled from materials afforded by writers of an earlier age, it is called both *Dubræ* and *Dubris* *. By the Saxons it was called *Dorfa* and *Dofris;* and in the Domesday-book it is spelled *Dovere.* The name is doubtless of British origin; some antiquaries suppose it to be derived from *Dufyrra*, signifying in that language a steep place; while others consider it to have been derived from *Dufir,* which in the same language signifies water or a stream. From the stream which discharges itself into the sea at Dover being called *Dubris* by Richard of Cirencester, and from its still retaining the name of the Dour, the latter opinion appears to be the most probable; and it is further strengthened by the fact, that the name given to the place in the Itinerary of Antoninus may be literally translated, " the Port of the Dubris, or the Dour."

The height of the cliff, on which Dover Castle stands, is about three hundred and twenty feet above the level of the sea; and the area of the ground inclosed by the outward walls is about thirty-four acres. It has been supposed that the Romans, in one of Julius Cæsar's expeditions, first built a castle and established a military station at Dover; but this opinion is founded on mere conjecture, and is extremely improbable. That the Romans, at some subsequent period, had a station not far from the present keep, is certain; for the remains of the walls and ditch are still perceptible. It however appears to have been but of small size, and was probably only a *castrum exploratorum*, or look-out station, garrisoned by a small body of soldiers detached from a neighbouring camp. Within the boundary of the exploratory camp the Romans had built a pharos, or watch-tower, the greater part of which is yet standing. The upper part is of more modern date; and as the arms of Sir Thomas Erpingham are to be seen sculptured on a stone in the north front, the additions were probably made when that renowned Norfolk knight was governor of Dover Castle, in the reign of Henry V. The present height of the building is about forty feet; it is of octangular form without, and square within. The walls, which in the lower part are about ten feet thick, are built of a stalactical concretion, mostly cut into small blocks about a foot long and seven inches thick, and of tiles; two layers of tiles being placed above every seven courses of blocks. Immediately adjoining the pharos are the remains of an old church, which is said to have been founded by Lucius, a British king, in the second century. The accounts which we have of King Lucius and of his conversion to Christianity are, however, extremely doubtful; and though a church may have been founded there at a very early period, the church whose ruins are still in

* In the work of Richard of Cirencester, the stream which runs into the sea at Dover is also called *Dubris.*

existence, has evidently been built several centuries subsequent to the pretended date of its foundation by King Lucius. From the pieces of tiles which are to be perceived in the walls, it appears to have been partly erected from the remains of some Roman building, which had probably occupied the same or an adjacent site.

Previous to the Norman conquest, there was undoubtedly a castle or fortress at Dover, probably near the spot where the keep or principal tower of Dover Castle now stands. Previous to the death of Edward the Confessor it appears to have belonged to Harold, afterwards King of England; for William, Duke of Normandy, who was then probably devising measures to secure to himself the English crown, refused to allow Harold to depart from Rouen, till he had taken an oath to deliver up to him "the Castle of Dover and the well of water in it," on the decease of Edward. After the battle of Hastings, the Conqueror marched without delay to Dover, took possession of the castle, and put the governor to death. It appears that he also burnt the town, which perhaps might not have received him with sufficient humility, in order to terrify others into immediate submission to his authority. The foundation of the present keep of Dover Castle was laid by Henry II. in 1153, the year before he succeeded to the English crown on the death of King Stephen. The ground plan is nearly a square, and the building in its general appearance bears a great resemblance to Rochester Castle, which was erected according to the designs of Bishop Gundulph—the architect of the White Tower in the Tower of London — in the early part of the reign of William Rufus. The walls of the keep of Dover Castle are from eighteen to twenty feet thick, and are traversed by galleries communicating with the principal apartments. The summit is embattled; and the top of the northern turret is 93 feet high from the ground, and about 465 feet above the level of the sea, at low water. The view from the top is extremely grand and interesting, including the North Foreland, Reculver Church, Ramsgate Pier, Sandwich, and a great part of the intermediate country, with the straits of Dover, the town of Calais, and the line of the French coast from Gravelines to Boulogne. In 1800 a bomb-proof arched roof was constructed, and several large cannon mounted on it. During the late war the fortifications were greatly strengthened, the old towers on the walls repaired, and additional quarters for soldiers constructed, in order that the garrison, in the event of invasion, might be able to withstand a regular siege. Most of the towers on the outer walls appear to have been built subsequent to the erection of the keep. At a short distance from the entrance to the castle is mounted the long brass gun, usually called Queen Elizabeth's pocket-pistol, which was presented to her Majesty by the United Provinces. It is twenty-four feet long; but is so much "honey-combed," that, were it fired, it would be certain to burst. Popular tradition says that it contains an inscription to this effect :—

> " Sponge me well, and keep me clean,
> And I'll throw a ball to Calais green."

There is, indeed, an inscription on it in the Dutch language, but though it commemorates the destructive power of this long piece of ordnance, it says nothing which implies that its range was so extraordinary. The distance from Dover castle to the church of Notre-Dame, at Calais, is rather more than twenty-six miles. This gun was cast at Utrecht in 1544, by James Tolkys, and the verses inscribed on its breech have been translated as follows :—

> " O'er hill and dale I throw my ball ;
> Breaker, my name, of mound and wall."

The constable of Dover castle is usually a nobleman of high rank, or some eminent statesman, who is also Lord Warden of the Cinque Ports. The office is at present held by the Duke of Wellington.

At the period of the Conquest, Dover was unquestionably a place of considerable note. It is mentioned, with Sandwich and Romney, in the Domesday-book, as a privileged port; and is said to have enjoyed, from an earlier period, sundry privileges and immunities in common with those two towns, on consideration of supplying a certain number of ships and mariners for the defence of the adjacent coast. In the reign of King John, Dover received charter as one of the Cinque Ports; and in several succeeding reigns, its shipping and mariners were frequently employed in the fleets assembled to convey English armies to France. As it was considered the key of England, it was surrounded with walls and strongly fortified; and as it was the principal port in the kingdom for persons taking shipping in proceeding to France, acts were passed in the reign of Edward III. and Richard II., appointing the rate of passage. Henry VIII. expended large sums in the improvement of the harbour, the entrance of which had been much choked up by shingle washed in by the sea. A pier was commenced, and carried on at a great expense, but he died before it was completed ; and in the reign of his successor, the work appears to have been almost wholly suspended. In the reign of Elizabeth further attempts were made to improve the harbour ; and in 1606 an act was passed appointing eleven commissioners, who were empowered to receive certain rates, and employ the money in repairing the pier and improving the harbour. In succeeding times various plans have been tried to prevent the increase of the bar, which, after a gale of wind from the seaward, is sometimes increased so much, as to prevent all vessels, except such as are of very light draught of water, from entering or leaving the port.   At present a large reservoir is in course of formation, under the superintendence of Mr. Walker, which, it is expected, will effectually scour the entrance of the harbour, and prevent the formation of the bar which has been for so many years an obstacle to the increase of Dover as a port.   It is high water at Dover pier at sixteen minutes past eleven on the full and change of the moon; and the rise of the water at spring tides is about twenty feet.   In 1833 there were 120 ships belonging to Dover, with a tonnage of 5525 tons; and in 1831 the population of the town was 11,924.   It sends two representatives to Parliament; and the present members, returned at the last election in 1837, are Sir J. R. Reid, and E. R. Rice, Esq.   The latter gentleman resides in the neighbourhood, and is no relation of the Right Hon. T. S. Rice, at present Chancellor of the Exchequer.   Dover is much frequented in summer as a watering place; and for the convenience which it affords, and the beautiful and interesting scenery in its neighbourhood, it is surpassed by no other town on the southern coast.

About a mile to the southward of the town is the celebrated cliff which is supposed to have been described by Shakspeare in King Lear.

" *Gloster.*—Dost thou know Dover ?
 Edgar.—Ay, master.
 Gloster.—There is a cliff, whose high and bending head
            Looks fearfully in the confined deep:
            Bring me to the very brim of it.
                  *   *   *   *   *
 Edgar.—Come on, sir ; here's the place :—stand
            Still.—How fearful
            And dizzy 'tis, to cast one's eyes so low !
            The crows, and choughs, that wing the midway air,
            Show scarce so gross as beetles : halfway down
            Hangs one that gathers samphire ; dreadful trade !
            Methinks he seems no bigger than his head :
            The fishermen that walk upon the beach
            Appear like mice ; and yon tall anchoring bark,
            Diminished to her cock ; her cock, a buoy
            Almost too small for sight : the murmuring surge,
            That on the unnumber'd idle pebbles chafes,
            Cannot be heard so high.   I'll look no more,
            Lest my brain turn, and the deficient sight
            Topple down headlong."

Much unnecessary criticism has been wasted on this passage by persons who have not attended to the intention of the speaker, and who have judged of Shakspeare's purposely exaggerated description, as if it were a sober account, in plain prose, in a county history.   Mr. Fenimore Cooper, the American novelist, in his ill-natured work entitled " England, with Sketches of Society in the Metropolis," has made some blundering remarks on this passage, and in the fullness of his nautical knowledge writes to his friend in America as follows: " The great bard makes the gradation in diminutiveness pass from the ship to her boat, and from her boat to the buoy ! This is poetry, and as such is above comment; but one of the craft would have been more correct." A writer in a recent number of the Quarterly Review, however, shows, that " even in this miserable detail, our nautical critic is wrong;" the writer having ascertained that of a sloop of war the jolly-boat is about one-sixth of the length of the hull, and the buoy one-sixth of the jolly-boat. It is said that the late Sir Walter Scott, when at Dover, on his road to Paris, a few years ago, expressed himself thus with respect to Shakspeare's cliff: " Shakspeare was a *low*-land man, and I am a *high*-land man; it is therefore natural that he should make much more of this chalk cliff than I can do, who live among the black mountains of Scotland." There is, however, a distinction to be attended to, in fairly criticising Shakspeare's description, which Sir Walter has overlooked. Edgar is describing a precipice, from the edge of which he pretends to be *looking down ;* while Sir Walter speaks of the description as if it were that of a lofty mountain, at the foot of which the speaker is standing without dread, and *looking up.* Terror is the feeling which Edgar is wishful to inspire; and few persons, I am inclined to think, can stand on the verge of Shakspeare's cliff and look down without dread to the beach below. The passage is, in reality, rather the exaggerated description, from memory, of the *feelings* excited by such a situation, than the true and accurate measurement of the height as seen with the eyes of a land-surveyor looking at it from a point where he runs no risk of toppling down. When viewed from the sea, or from Dover, the height does not seem at all remarkable; it is only about three hundred and fifty feet above the level of the sea, which is certainly no great altitude to *look up* to; but had Sir Walter Scott ever stood on the edge of the cliff and *looked down,* it is likely that he would not have expressed himself as he has done about Shakspeare making so much of a " chalk cliff." It is also scarcely possible to believe that the great dramatist, though a low-land man, knew so little about mountains, as to take the cliffs in the neighbourhood of Dover for " Alps and Apennines." His ideas of " heaven-kissing hills" were probably derived from other originals. Stratford is not more than sixty miles from the borders of Brecknockshire, one of the most mountainous counties in Wales; and it is as likely that Shakspeare had seen Brecknock Beacon as that he had looked down from Dover cliffs.

Drawn by H. Warren.

Engraved by E. Finden.

HARWICH.

ESSEX.

HARWICH.

HARWICH is in the county of Essex, and lies on the south side of the estuary formed by the confluence of the Stour and the Orwell, about sixty-two miles to the north-eastward of London. The view in the engraving is taken from the southward, and comprises three of the most conspicuous objects in the town : the church, which is of modern erection, the upper and the lower light-house. In the distance, to the right, is perceived Landguard Fort, which lies on the Suffolk shore on the opposite side of the channel.

In 1318 Harwich was incorporated by Edward II., at the request of his brother, Thomas de Brotherton, Earl of Norfolk. In 1347 the town supplied 14 ships and 183 mariners to the grand fleet of Edward III.; and in the 17th and 18th years of that king's reign, Harwich returned two members to Parliament; but the exercise of this privilege was discontinued till 1616, when it was restored by James I. The present members, returned at the last election, in 1837, are the Right Hon. J. C. Herries, and Capt. Ellice.

The trade of Harwich never appears to have been very great; and its prosperity seems to have greatly depended on the Post-office packets, which formerly used to sail from the place with passengers and letters for the northern parts of Europe. The introduction of steam-packets has however rendered Harwich a place of no further importance as a packet-station, and for several years past the town has been in a declining state. The fishery, which formerly contributed to the prosperity of the place, has greatly declined since the commencement of the present century. In 1778 there were seventy-eight fishing-vessels, averaging about forty tons each, belonging to the port; in 1833 there were not more than ten. Harwich is the only harbour between Yarmouth Roads and the mouth of the Thames that is capable of affording refuge, in gales of wind from the eastward, to vessels navigating the eastern coast. During the prevalence of strong north-east winds, sometimes from two to three hundred light colliers, and other vessels proceeding northward, are to be seen anchored in the harbour. It is high water at Harwich at thirty minutes past eleven at the full and change of the moon; and the rise of the water at spring-tides is fourteen feet. In 1831 the population of the town was 4,297; and in 1833 the number of vessels belonging to the port was 96, with a tonnage of 5,513 tons.

YARMOUTH.

YARMOUTH, in the county of Norfolk, sometimes called Great Yarmouth, to distinguish it from Yarmouth in the Isle of Wight, lies about 123 miles north-east of London, and about twenty-four to the eastward of Norwich. In the vignette engraving, from a beautiful painting by E. W. Cooke, the view is taken from the shore a little to the northward of the Jetty, which is seen extending into the sea. Nearly in the centre of the engraving is seen the column erected by the county of Norfolk to the memory of Nelson : and to the right are perceived several *look-outs*, like so many elevated scaffolds, from which, as the shore is very low, the pilots are enabled to take a wider survey when looking out for ships which may require their assistance.

The name of Yarmouth obviously alludes to the situation of the town near the mouth of the river Yare ; the word Yare, according to Druery, in his Historical Notices of Great Yarmouth, is derived from the Celtic, *Iar*, dark, supposed to have been given to this river from the dark colour of its waters. According to Sir Henry Spelman, the ground on which Yarmouth stands became firm and habitable in the year 1008, from the recession of the sea, and the accumulation of the sands. If this account be correct, it would appear that the town began to be built almost immediately afterwards ; for in the Domesday-book, which was compiled between 1080 and 1086, the place is mentioned, with the usual carelessness of the Norman scribes, by the name of Cernemude ; and the entry further records that the place had been held by King Edward [the Confessor], and that it " always had seventy burgesses."

In 1208 Yarmouth received a charter of incorporation from King John ; and the privileges of the town were confirmed and enlarged by several succeeding kings. In 1228, in the reign of Henry III., Yarmouth had become a considerable port, both for the importation and exportation of merchandize ; and in a charter of Edward I., granted in 1306, it is especially mentioned as a place where fishing-vessels, from an early period, had been accustomed to land the herrings which they caught during the season of the fishery. In 1347 Yarmouth supplied 43 ships and 1095 mariners to the grand fleet of Edward III.; and in 1349 the town was visited by a dreadful plague, which carried off seven thousand of the inhabitants. In the 31st of Edward III., an act was passed regulating the annual herring fair at Yarmouth, and appointing it to be governed by the barons of the

YARMOUTH.

NORFOLK.

London. Published 1837, by Charles Tilt, 86, Fleet Street.

Cinque Ports, according to the composition made between them and the inhabitants of the town in the reign of Edward I., the king's grandfather. One William Beukelem, of Biervliet, in Flanders, who died in 1397, according to Anderson, in his History of Commerce, is said to have been the inventor of the method of pickling herrings; but this cannot be correct; for though he may have introduced some improvements in the mode of cleaning and barrelling the fish, the inhabitants of Yarmouth and other places on the eastern coast were accustomed both to pickle and smoke herrings, long previous to the time when the practice is said to have been introduced by Beukelem *. Yarmouth is still the principal place of resort on the eastern coast of England for vessels engaged in the herring fishery, which there commences about the 21st September, and concludes about 14th December. Most of the Yorkshire five-man boats come to Yarmouth in the herring season, and make their fishery from that place, disposing of all the herrings which they catch to curers who live in the town.

The quay at Yarmouth is one of the longest and most spacious of any in the kingdom; but from the shallowness of the entrance of the harbour, there only being fourteen feet of water on the bar at spring tides, the trade of the place is chiefly carried on in small vessels. It is high water in Yarmouth Roads at forty minutes past eight; and at Yarmouth Sands at thirty minutes past ten on the full and change of the moon. In 1833 there were 585 vessels belonging to the port, out of which number 426 were each less than one hundred tons burthen; the tonnage of the whole was 44,134 tons. In 1831 the population of the town was 21,115. Yarmouth has enjoyed the privilege of sending representatives to Parliament since 26th Edward I., 1297. The present members, returned at the last election, in 1837, are C. E. Rumbold, Esq., and W. G. Wilshere, Esq.

The column erected to the memory of Nelson, stands on the low sandy flat, called the Denes, to the south of the town. Its total height, including the basement and the figure of Britannia at the top, is 144 feet, and it is ascended by a staircase consisting of 217 steps. It forms a conspicuous object when seen from the sea; and to the crews of vessels passing through Yarmouth Roads it is a proud memento of Nelson's fame and the Naval glory of their country.

" O England!—dearer far than life is dear,
If I forget thy prowess, never more
Be thy ungrateful son allowed to hear
Thy green leaves rustle, or thy torrents roar!"

* Marchantius, in his Flandria Descripta, calls him Gulielmus Bouclensis, and places his death in 1347. Lib. i. p. 50. Antwerpiæ, 1596.

Y

CROMER.

CROMER is a fishing village, situated near the north-eastern extremity of the county of Norfolk; it lies about 129 miles north-north-east of London, and about twenty-two miles nearly due north of Norwich. The view in the engraving is taken from the sands, looking to the westward. About a year and a half ago, part of the cliff, with two or three houses beyond those which are now seen standing on its extremity, fell down in consequence of the encroachments of the sea. At that time a subscription was entered into by the inhabitants of the place, and by several of the neighbouring gentry, for the purpose of forming a break-water; for without some such protection it is apprehended that at no very distant period many more houses, with the fine old church, will fall a prey to the violence of the sea.

It is supposed that Cromer was formerly a place of much greater importance than it is at present; and that at the time of the Domesday survey it was included in the town of Shipden, which, with its church, is supposed to have been destroyed by the sea in the reign of Henry IV. At low water many large portions of wall are to be seen, which have evidently formed part of the houses of the old town of Shipden. "The set of the great tidal current of the German ocean," says Mr. R. C. Taylor, in his Geology of East Norfolk, "is from the north-west, along the eastern shores of this island.—In their progress southward, the tides meet with an extensive obstruction in the projecting county of Norfolk. About twenty miles of its coast has been subjected from time immemorial to the abrasive action of ocean currents. The ancient villages of Shipden, Wimpwell, and Eccles, have disappeared; several manors, and large portions of neighbouring parishes, have, piece after piece, been swallowed up by the encroaching waves; and their site, some fathoms deep, now forms a part of the bed of the German ocean."

Cromer is much frequented in summer by visitors for the sake of sea-bathing, for which the fine sandy beach to the eastward affords great convenience. Cromer is a place of very little trade, and is chiefly dependant on the fishery. The population in 1831 was 1232. Cromer light-house stands on an eminence, about three quarters of a mile to the eastward of the village. It is a revolving light, and is visible, in clear weather, at a distance of five or six leagues. It appears in its brightest state once in every minute, and then gradually becomes eclipsed.

LONDON:
BRADBURY AND EVANS, PRINTERS, WHITEFRIARS.

Painted by T. Creswick.

Engraved by E. Finden.

C R O M E R .

London. Published 1837, by Charles Tilt, 86, Fleet Street.